REINTERPRETING THE
SPANISH AMERICAN ESSAY

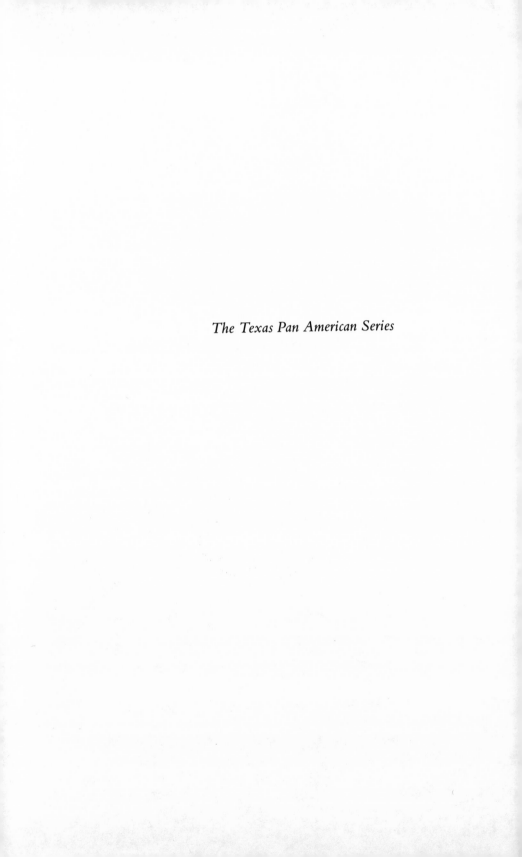

The Texas Pan American Series

Reinterpreting the Spanish American Essay

WOMEN WRITERS OF THE 19TH AND 20TH CENTURIES

Edited by Doris Meyer

UNIVERSITY OF TEXAS PRESS

AUSTIN

First edition, 1995

Requests for permission to reproduce material from this
work should be sent to Permissions, University of Texas
Press, Box 7819, Austin, TX 78713-7819.

∞ The paper used in this publication meets the minimum
requirements of American National Standard for
Information Sciences—Permanence of Paper for Printed
Library Materials, ANSI Z39.48-1984.

ISBN 0-292-75167-2   1001 272563

Library of Congress Cataloging-in-Publication Data

Reinterpreting the Spanish American essay : women writers
    of the 19th and 20th centuries / edited by Doris Meyer. —
    1st ed.
        p.   cm. — (The Texas Pan American series)
    Includes bibliographical references.
    ISBN 0-292-75167-2 (alk. paper)
    1. Spanish American essays—Women authors.
    2. Spanish American essays—19th century.   3. Spanish
    American essays—20th century.   I. Meyer,
    Doris.   II. Series.
    PQ7082.E8R38   1995
    864.009'9287'098—dc20   94-17119

Contents

The essay's innermost formal law is heresy. Through violation of the orthodoxy of thought, something in the object becomes visible which is orthodoxy's secret and objective aim to keep invisible.

THEODOR W. ADORNO
"THE ESSAY AS FORM"
NOTES TO LITERATURE

REINTERPRETING THE
SPANISH AMERICAN ESSAY

Doris Meyer

INTRODUCTION
THE SPANISH
AMERICAN ESSAY:
A FEMALE
PERSPECTIVE

The literary terrain of the essay in Spanish America is vast and remarkably varied. From the liberation of the new republics in the nineteenth century through the turbulent years of the twentieth, it has been a ubiquitous form of expression among major and minor writers of all persuasions. Indeed, one cannot appreciate the literary and intellectual history of this region without reading its essayists.

Despite its importance, the geography of the essay has not been as well mapped or explored as that of other genres—and not only in Spanish America. It has traditionally been considered a marginal genre, lacking the rigor of academic discourse as well as the allure of creative fiction. Compared with its more popular prose counterparts, the essay does not beckon readers looking for an authentic literary experience in an unfamiliar culture. A recent study of the essay as a literary form calls it the "'invisible' genre in literature, commonly used but rarely analyzed in itself" (Good ix).

Its modern European origins are ascribed to Michel de Montaigne's *Essais* (1580). In the Spanish language, its antecedents can be traced back to the fifteenth-century writings of Jewish "converso" writers, most notably Fernando del Pulgar, and thereafter to the great humanists of the Golden Age, such as Antonio de Guevara, Juan Luis Vives, and Francisco de Quevedo. As Juan Marichal points out, the essay as we know it could only evolve to the degree to which its earliest authors managed to cast off old rhetorical models and find the linguistic freedom to express their own personal styles; one of the first to do so in Spanish was Santa Teresa de Jesús, a sixteenth-century Carmelite nun who rejected the stylistic norms of her time and wrote with "an urge toward expressive freedom, personal openness and sincerity" (60). Now recognized as an important precursor, Santa Teresa stands apart and virtually alone in the androcentric history of the early Spanish essay. Writers of the subsequent Enlightenment period, such as Feijóo, Cadalso, and Jovellanos, are generally credited with being the fathers of the genre.

On the other side of the Atlantic, the letters, chronicles, and ethnographic reports assiduously forwarded to Spain by the early colonizers of the conquered lands served to nourish an indigenous essay tradition. Amid native oral cultures the written word took hold with a vengeance, changing the cultures of the Americas to suit Spain's preoccupation with documenting and controlling every aspect of colonial life. With the rise of journalism in the eighteenth century, essayistic discourse reached a wider readership and flourished in the increasingly discontented criollo relationship of self to society. The Napoleonic Wars in Spain in the early 1800s helped precipitate the independence of most of its colonies, forcing essayists on both sides of the Atlantic to consider local problems of reconstruction and reform. It was in this period, around the mid-nineteenth century, that the term *ensayo* was first used in its current literary sense and the modern Hispanic essay took shape.

The evolution of the Spanish American essay since the days of Andrés Bello and Simón Bolívar has been customarily associated with an obsessive search for cultural or national identity. While looking inward, however, the essayists in these new Spanish American republics did not write in an intellectual vacuum. Their work responded to the historical circumstances they perceived and reflected the unique cosmovision of Latin American nation-builders cognizant of an old order undergoing rapid change. Spain's decline as a world power after 1898, the increasing geopolitical influence of the United States, disenchantment with scientific positivism and Yankee materialism, World War I, and the Russian Revolution were all factors affecting their vision of Latin America's potential. Their work was influenced by what was written in Europe as well as in the Americas, and they published with other educated readers in mind; the essays of Spain's José Ortega y Gasset were read in Argentina just as those of Mexico's Alfonso Reyes were in Spain. The awareness of failures in the Old World rekindled interest in a New World humanism, often linked to a mystical notion of the land and its native peoples. A common metaphor for the mestizo cultural dilemma was the dual heritage of the maternal Amerindian and the paternal Spanish—*eros* and *logos*, the mother's passion and the father's intellect. The mythologies of Eurocentric Spanish American culture, like the foundations of its modern society, were based on unquestioned gender stereotypes.

In their search for an Americanist equation of cultural authenticity, male essayists—even self-declared liberals—were virtually oblivious to the one-sided nature of their discourse. The female presence in their midst was depersonalized, mythologized, and trivialized in accordance with a long history of gender discrimination in Hispano-Catholic society. As essayists who dominated the literary landscapes of their time, men of the generations of Rodó, Vasconcelos, or Arciniegas essentially disenfranchised women writers by denying them the intellectual space in which to formulate and articulate their visions of culture and society.

Given this situation, it should not surprise us that, with only a very few exceptions, anthologies of Spanish American essays have excluded the work of women authors. The essay canon is decidedly male although it has been touted as the genre most closely related to historical circumstance. Perhaps this merely confirms the gender blindness of both authors and critics. Some of the most respected interpreters of the Spanish American essay tradition have conveyed the impression that female essayists either did not exist or were not worthy of note. Take, for example, Martin S. Stabb's introductory words to *In Quest of Identity: Patterns in the Spanish American Essay of Ideas, 1890–1960*: "My basic criterion for one essayist's inclusion and another's exclusion is the degree to which each man's ideas are germane to the theme under consideration" (11). Gender implications are never addressed when Stabb examines the theme of identity in Spanish America. Peter G. Earle observes the problem but also succumbs to its metaphoric mind-set: "Most essays of the past two centuries, like the domino games played in casinos and cantinas throughout the Hispanic world, are a masculine activity. Seldom forgotten, but often displaced, woman waits in the shadows until the game is done and it's time to go home or for the poetry to begin" (79). If the essay itself is an invisible genre in Western literature, then we can safely and sadly say that essays by women—and, more specifically, those by Spanish American women—have been victims of invisibility in the third degree, which is akin to being literarily "disappeared."

On their own, nonetheless, in the shadows cast by men of imposing literary and public proportions, women all over Latin America have been steadfastly, often privately, writing essays. Contrary to the impression created by standard anthologies and critical assessments, the "intellectual consciousness" of Spanish America *does* include the work of women writers, foremost among them being another nun, Sor Juana Inés de la Cruz, who lived a century after Santa Teresa. Sor Juana's autobiographical essay to "Sor Filotea" is paradigmatic in the strategies she devises for affirming her own intellectual autonomy despite the overbearingly patriarchal, neoscholastic mentality of her religious superiors. The "tricks of the weak" Sor Juana has shown us involve transforming the space to which she is confined into a zone of intellectual subversion and, ultimately, intellectual freedom; according to Josefina Ludmer, "the combination of respect and confrontation can establish another truth, another approach to science, and another subject of knowledge" (93).

This appropriation of intellectual space from within the shadows is characteristic of many Spanish American women's essays in the nineteenth and twentieth centuries. Particularly noteworthy is the fact that, early on, women turned so often to the essay rather than other genres to inscribe their personal truths. The essay has lent itself to the expressive needs of a marginalized gender precisely because it is so adjustable to mood or frame of mind; in E. B. White's inimitable words, "There are as many kinds of essays as there are human attitudes or poses, as many essay flavors as there are Howard Johnson ice creams" (vii). The essay is essentially user-friendly. It seeks not eternal but rather provisional truth; it records the writer's sense of a given time and place, often with immediacy if not urgency. Its logic, according to Theodor Adorno, is more akin to music, demanding a coherence of the whole more than an orderly arrangement of its parts (22). The essay has been called malleable and chameleonic, and perhaps for this reason it has been undervalued by traditional scholars looking for definitive interpretations, as well as by deconstructionist critics for whom the personal is merely another "fabulation" (Good 180–181). But for O. B. Hardison, Jr., "the essay is the enactment of a process by which the soul realizes itself even as it is passing from day to day and from moment to moment. It is the literary response to a world that has become problematic" (20).

We can therefore begin to understand why the essay has appealed to women writers, from Santa Teresa and Sor Juana to the present day, as a means of autonomous expression within the confines of official discourse. For a Spanish American woman whose gender identity was defined by Church and State, the essay offered a chance to demythologize herself, to bear witness to reality from her perspective. For a woman with little formal education and limited access to the literary establishment, the essay was a nonthreatening literary form. Ironically, like the imaginary construct of the feminine, the essay could be molded to suit a woman's purpose: an essay-letter, an essay-confession, an essay-novel, an essay–travel diary, or the more traditional expository essay. Its flexibility as a genre is its inherent resistance to boundaries of containment; in its potential for aesthetic hybridization, it defies definition.

However, personal expression often involved questioning the status quo—the powers behind official discourse—and such transgression carried consequences. A woman's essay could openly or in veiled discourse call for social or political reform, but it might be dangerous or difficult to publish; thus, many essays have been lost to posterity. With some influence or cajoling, an essay might find an audience in selected journals or literary circles, in lecture halls, and even occasionally in books. Many of the publications in which early Spanish American women's essays appeared were owned or edited by women, going as far back as the 1830s. Of course, women who published were generally aware that readers' attitudes might work against them, so what they wrote often underwent, consciously or unconsciously, a degree of self-censorship that today's reader must anticipate. The fact that Sor Juana and other women writers from the seventeenth to the twentieth century found it necessary to encode their testimony in a double-voiced discourse tells a great deal about the persistent social pressure to conform to gender stereotypes. In view of this, the triangular relationship of author, text, and reader can present complicated dynamics where women's essays are concerned.

With the obstacles they faced, it is understandable that Spanish American women essayists were among the first to call for improved education for all segments of society but especially for females. In Argentina in 1852, Rosa Guerra founded the journal *La Educación*, espousing the position that more schooling for women would benefit all of society. Several generations later, Gabriela Mistral would take up the same banner in Chile and around the world, becoming herself the embodiment of the maternal teacher-nurturer. The idealized *persona* Mistral acquired as a Nobel-prize-winning poet—the first woman from Latin America to receive this distinction—obscured the fact that she had to make ends meet by being a journalist and lecturer. Her output in the essay genre far surpasses the quantity of her verse; undeniably, Mistral was one of the continent's most linguistically expressive and insightful essayists, whose vivid prose deserves a wider reading. A similar situation has befallen the writing of Alfonsina Storni. Like Mistral, her essays bear attention for what they can tell us about the author as well as the social history of her time.

Women essayists have often challenged the dominant discourse. They were among the earliest proponents of the abolition of slavery, as in the case of Cuba's Gertrudis Gómez de Avellaneda, whose writing predated Harriet Beecher Stowe's. Avellaneda, like other early women essayists in Spanish America, also spoke out claiming the intellectual equality of the sexes. Her writing in the woman's magazine *Album Cubano de lo Bueno y lo Bello*, which she founded in 1860, echoed much of the feminist spirit of Seneca Falls a decade earlier. Yet Avellaneda could also equivocate and, in other works, appear less of a feminist than biographical evidence would indicate. The Venezuelan author Teresa de la Parra wrote several generations later with similar ambivalence. Her essay-lectures of 1930 show that the mantle of feminist crusader was too heavy for many women intellectuals, even—or maybe especially—for women of means and social standing. A generation after Parra, Mexico's Rosario Castellanos would voice her impatience with gender stereotypes and yet agonize over the burden of her own image in *machista* literary circles. The alienation she felt as a woman undoubtedly helped her identify with the indigenous peoples of her country to whom she devoted many pages of her work.

Women essayists who dared to face the consequences, such as Peru's Clorinda Matto de Turner in the late 1800s, could provoke public outrage; this author was burned in effigy by crowds who resented and feared the radical reforms she advocated. Matto finally went into exile in Argentina, where she continued to publish articles in a journal she founded and directed. Other Spanish American women, such as Elena Poniatowska in Mexico or Julieta Kirkwood in Chile in recent decades, have challenged authoritarian governments by speaking out against the oppression of women and the voiceless underclass. Provoking a different kind of opprobrium, contemporary women essayists such as Puerto Rico's Rosario Ferré and Uruguay's Cristina Peri Rossi have confronted the issue of sexuality and female eroticism. Their uncompromising frankness, often laced with irony and humor, not only defies the patriarchal notion of women as asexual beings but also disputes male control of erotic language.

When one reads women's essays, the mirror of Spanish American identity reflects different kinds of images. For the most part, the female essay tends to be more personal, more stylistically idiosyncratic, and consequently more dramatic as it reveals, at or near the surface, the shape and substance of female concerns. An early example can be found in

Flora Tristan's *Mémoires et pérégrinations d'une paria (Peregrinations of a Pariah)*, originally published in French in 1838. This semiautobiographical account of her return to Peru after having been raised in France brings out another paradigm of the female condition: that of exile in her own country. Tristan's sense of dislocation—of not having a national space with which to identify fully—enables her to sympathize with the plight of prostitutes as victims of society and to take up the cause of defending them against moral repudiation. In the essays of Victoria Ocampo, Gabriela Mistral, Rosario Castellanos, and Rosario Ferré, among others, we find the recuperation of female identity through the portraiture of other respected women—portraits that become reciprocal reflections that "authorize" subject and self. When women write essays they find supportive echoes in other women's lives and words—and sometimes too in the visual images they convey as artists or photographers, as when Elena Poniatowska writes about the eye/I of Graciela Iturbide or Tina Modotti, bringing them out of the shadows of their art.

Time and again, women essayists confront the monolithic authority of "received truth" with iconoclastic responses. The essays of the Countess of Merlin, Eduarda Mansilla, Magda Portal, Yolanda Oreamuno, and Carmen Naranjo contest public policy and examine cultural practices with a critical eye. But the politics of the female essay can also be more personal, as in the way Margo Glantz uses language itself to question the stability of identity and to celebrate diverse interpretations of cultural signs. Ultimately, language is the protean medium through which all these women essayists transcend the limitations of their existence and convey a powerful vitality, intellect, and vision of their own.

The history of the Spanish American essay must be rewritten to include the contributions of women and their historical circumstances. It must be flexible enough to include essays written in French by women such as the Countess of Merlin, Flora Tristan, Eduarda Mansilla, or Victoria Ocampo who were brought up in cultural environments that separated them from their native or ancestral tongue. There must be room for difference in women's approach to the gender norms of their time, despite sharing the collective female experience of oppression. We need all of their testimonies in order to formulate an understanding of the role played by the essay in the construction and deconstruction of cultural discourse in Latin America. In every instance we must consider the ideological and aesthetic relationship of gender to genre, along with other determining factors like race, class, religion, nationality, or ethnicity.

Eventually the canon may cease to exist as we know it and simply embrace the plurality of human experience in Latin America.

In the hope of exploring some uncharted terrain in this generic landscape, I decided to put together this collection of studies. My introductory remarks have been intended to give an idea of the wealth of information it contains. The twenty-one scholars who have contributed to this collection are all experts in the area of Latin American literature, many working on the cutting edge of a critical re-vision of Latin American cultural and intellectual history. I am extremely grateful for their collaboration in this project and for the intelligence and insight they bring to it.

Although it only begins to uncover the female essay tradition in Spanish America, this collection deals with women writers from a variety of countries and historical circumstances, excluding Portuguese-speaking Brazil. In their individual attempts to capture the female perspective in words, these essayists are unique to their place and time, but they also remind us of women who write in other parts of the world. My hope is that such connections will become more evident and that Spanish American women writers will cease being marginalized not only in their own countries but also in the international literary context.

For the English-speaking reader, and in the interest of brevity, all quotes from texts in Spanish have been translated into English; the works cited at the end of each study will lead an interested reader to the Spanish originals. To help make these neglected works better known, my intention is to follow this volume with one of translations of original essays selected to reflect the critical studies in this volume. Together, I hope these two collections will point the way toward a reinterpretation of the Spanish American essay that evaluates and incorporates the difference of women's voices. Only then can we fully comprehend the importance of this genre, alongside others, as dialogic discourse within the authentic range of human intellectual experience.

Connecticut College*
March 1993

*I would like to acknowledge the support of the R. F. Johnson Faculty Development Fund of Connecticut College, which helped me complete this two-volume project.

WORKS CITED

Adorno, Theodor W. "The Essay as Form." In *Notes to Literature*, 1:3–23. Ed. Rolf Tiedemann. Trans. Sherry Weber Nicholsen. New York: Columbia University Press, 1991.

Earle, Peter G. "The Female Persona in the Spanish American Essay: An Overview." In *Woman as Myth and Metaphor in Latin American Literature*, 79–93. Ed. Carmelo Virgillo and Naomi Lindstrom. Columbia: University of Missouri Press, 1985.

Good, Graham. *The Observing Self: Rediscovering the Essay*. London: Routledge, 1988.

Hardison, O. B., Jr. "Binding Proteus: An Essay on the Essay." In *Essays on the Essay: Redefining the Genre*, 11–28. Ed. Alexander J. Butrym. Athens: University of Georgia Press, 1989.

Ludmer, Josefina. "Tricks of the Weak." In *Feminist Perspectives on Sor Juana Inés de la Cruz*, 86–93. Ed. Stephanie Merrim. Detroit: Wayne State University Press, 1991.

Marichal, Juan. *Teoría e historia del ensayismo hispánico*. Madrid: Alianza Editorial, 1984.

Stabb, Martin S. *In Quest of Identity: Patterns in the Spanish American Essay of Ideas, 1890–1960*. Chapel Hill: University of North Carolina Press, 1967.

White, E. B. "Foreword." In *Essays of E. B. White*. New York: Harper and Row, 1977.

Mary Louise Pratt

"DON'T INTERRUPT ME"

THE GENDER ESSAY AS CONVERSATION AND COUNTERCANON

> *Like the Sanyasis-Nirvanis of the Vedas, who taught in a whisper in the crypts of the temples prayers and evocations that were never written down, woman, silent and resigned, crossed the frontiers of centuries repeating, with frightened secrecy, the magic words: freedom, justice.*
>
> CLORINDA MATTO DE TURNER
> "LAS OBRERAS DEL PENSAMIENTO EN LA AMÉRICA DEL SUD"

The two students walked in looking downcast. They had just come, they reported, from yet another literature course whose syllabus included no women writers. This time it was a course on the Latin American essay. There were, the professor had explained, no women essayists of sufficient caliber to merit inclusion in the course. "Who says?" they asked, "and how do we know it's true?"

Most literary scholars and teachers have been affected in some way by the *toma de conciencia* ("taking of consciousness") that has taken place in literary studies regarding processes of canonization. Even the most conservative scholars find they must now defend the proposition they once could take for granted: that canons consist of intrinsically great works that have risen to the top by virtue of their greatness, the cream on the milk. This "naturalized" concept of canons has been thoroughly undermined by literary historians on empirical grounds. Two of their arguments have been particularly forceful: first, they have demonstrated that canons, eternal as they may seem in a given historical moment, are

anything but stable over time, that today's masterpiece was yesterday's
doggerel, and probably tomorrow's too. Second, critical scholars have
explored the ways canons and canonization processes are socially determined, along lines that correspond to lines of social hierarchy. (Even
many traditionalists concede the constructedness of canons. They may
agree that canons *are* built around the interests and ideologies of ruling
classes, genders, and races, and simply argue that these are ideologies to
which they, as traditionalists, subscribe.)

Canon-busters, that is, scholars who seek to open processes of canonization to historical scrutiny, often find it useful to distinguish two
dimensions of their inquiry: the examination of canons as *structures of
exclusion* and as *structures of value*. The first (the easy one) involves finding
works that, one argues, meet the criteria for inclusion in the canon but
that have been excluded for illegitimate reasons. This is the case of, say,
texts denied canonization because their author is a woman. Such an argument could be made for the fiction of Juana Manuela Gorriti, for example, or most of the poetry of Gabriela Mistral. Often, as in the cases
of Gorriti and Mistral, the excluded writings were widely read in the
author's own time, only to be left behind by androcentric literary historians committed, consciously or otherwise, to maintaining male governance over culture and the literary.

The second inquiry, into canons as structures of value, is more difficult. This is the project of showing that the criteria used to determine
literary value are themselves constituted in ways that reflect structures of
hegemony in the society. This involves questioning the process through
which "legitimate" literary inclusions and exclusions are made. Texts by
members of subordinated or marginal social groups, the argument goes,
will always appear to lack "sufficient caliber to merit inclusion" if they
are read through the codes of interpretation and value that produced
the exclusionist canon in the first place. Canons, from this perspective,
are overwhelmingly self-confirming structures, reproducing themselves
through *practices of reading*, in the most basic aspects of literary experience, such as horizon of expectation, genre, subject matter, language, or
point of view. Readers trained only on canonical texts, it follows, are by
definition unequipped to evaluate texts by subordinated or excluded
groups. They will invariably misread such material, dislike it, dismiss it
as illegible or (more likely) trivial in content and form. To evaluate non-
canonical writing, this argument goes, you must first learn to read it. To
judge it on the basis of *established* literary norms is by definition to pre-
judge it and reproduce the structure of exclusion (pre-judice) that mar-

ginalized it in the first place. Canons are not just lists of books, but value machines that generate their own truth.

Just as access to literacy, to institutions of writing, and to the circuits of print culture have been socially restricted, so has access to canonicity and the power to canonize. The latter power has rested above all with the academy, traditionally one of the most exclusionary institutions of all. No one disputes that the wave of critical and relativistic thinking about canonization in the 1970s and 1980s was itself a result of the steady democratization of universities in the industrial countries after World War II. The transnational crisis of 1968 began, as we all recall, in student movements that initially rallied around the critique of canonical structures of knowledge in the academy. No one disputes the pivotal role played by feminism in opening up this inquiry and upholding it against harsh and relentless attack.

Hence the present volume on Latin American women essayists. Here indeed is a challenge! It would be hard to find a literary corpus more androcentrically constituted than the Latin American essay. Its anthologies (those great mirrors of canonicity) are monuments to male intellectuality, their tables of contents populated by a dozen or so familiar, and worthy, names: Bello, Echeverría, Sarmiento, Montalvo, González Prada, Hostos, Martí, Rodó, Henríquez Ureña, Vasconcelos, Mariátegui, Martínez Estrada, Arciniegas, Reyes, Picón-Salas, Zea, Paz, Anderson Imbert. A brief survey of essay anthologies and criticism in my university library (Skirius 1981, Earle and Mead 1973, Vitier 1945, Rey 1985, Ripoll 1966, Urrello 1966, Guillén 1971, Foster 1983) revealed few exceptions to the male monopoly: Chilean Gabriela Mistral, included among twenty-six authors in an anthology of twentieth-century essays (Skirius 1981), and Puerto Rican Concha Meléndez, author of the shortest excerpt in an anthology of contemporary essays (Guillén 1971). A comprehensive history of the Latin American essay (Earle and Mead) included brief mentions of Meléndez, her compatriot Margot Arce, and Argentine Victoria Ocampo. In an innovative and illuminating critical study of the essay that appeared in 1983, North American critic David William Foster raised the question of women's essayistic practice in a brief final chapter on Victoria Ocampo's *Testimonios*, which are most conspicuously characterized, he argues, by the insignificance of their subject matter. While Foster attempts to argue for reading strategies that would recover a serious intent for the *Testimonios*, his analysis remains compatible with the traditional view of women as outside the truly intellectual. Yet Ocampo wrote many pages of what are unambiguously essays. Why, one wonders, have *they* not been candidates for critical studies, course syllabi, or anthologies of the genre? In one of her essays, titled *La mujer y su expresión* (Woman and Her Expression, 1936), Ocampo offers a possible diagnosis for her own exclusion. She writes,

> *I believe that for centuries all conversation between men and women, as soon as they enter on a certain terrain, begins with a "Don't interrupt me" on the part of the man. Until now, the monologue seems to have been his preferred form of expression. (Conversation among men is simply this same monologue in dialogue form.)*
> (12 – 13)

Men, she concludes, "do not feel, or feel only very weakly" the need for dialogue with women ("that other being similar and yet different"): "In the best of cases, he has no taste for interruptions. In the worst case, he forbids them. Hence man is content to talk with himself, and it matters little to him whether anyone listens. As for *him* listening to anyone else, it scarcely occurs to him" (13). Applying Ocampo's terms, one could say that literary history has construed the essay as one of those male monologues that women have been either discouraged or prevented from interrupting. Ocampo offers a grim account of women's response to the centuries of "Don't interrupt me." Women, she says, have "resigned themselves, for the most part, to repeating crumbs (*migajas*) of the masculine monologue, sometimes concealing among them some seeds of her own sowing (*algo de su cosecha*)" (13). In what follows, I propose to offer a few observations about the male monologue that has been canonized as the Latin American essay, followed by some remarks suggesting that women's participation in the genre may have been livelier and more coherent than Ocampo saw it—that she had more foremothers than she perhaps knew.

THE CRIOLLO IDENTITY ESSAY, "THAT CENTAUR OF GENRES"

Let me begin with a generalization readily confirmed by those anthologies and critical studies I mentioned earlier. What has formed the backbone of "the Latin American essay" *as a canon* has been a particular strand of intellectual inquiry, which I will call the *criollo identity essay*. (*Criollo* here is used in its Spanish meaning, denoting the class of Spanish Americans who identify themselves as of European descent, and who since independence have composed the ruling elites of most Spanish American countries.) I propose this label "criollo identity essay" to refer to a series of texts written over the past 180 or so years by criollo (i.e., elite Euro-American) men, whose topic is the nature of criollo identity and culture, particularly in relation to Europe and North America. This fascinating textual series reflects an ideological project. How, the identity essay asks, are criollo identity and culture to be defined and legitimized in the postindependence era? How might criollo hegemony represent itself to itself? What is, or should be, its social and cultural project? Most students of Latin American literature can readily list many members of this canon. It is sometimes seen as beginning with Bolívar's Jamaica letter or the prologue to Bello's *Gramática de la lengua castellana*; its first undeniable monument is Sarmiento's *Facundo*, followed by Martí's *Nuestra América* (*Our America*, 1977), Rodo's *Ariel*, Vasconcelos' *La raza cósmica* (*The Cosmic Race*, 1979), Mariátegui's *Siete ensayos de interpretación de la realidad peruana* (*Seven Interpretive Essays on Peruvian Reality*, 1971), Henríquez Ureña's *Seis ensayos en busca de nuestra expresión* (Six Essays in Search of Our Expression), Paz's *Laberinto de la soledad* (Labyrinth of Solitude), Fernández Retamar's *Calibán*. There are of course many other candidates for inclusion.

Now obviously the texts listed differ a good deal among each other. Some were written as books, some as polemics, some as journalism; some originated as speeches delivered in public (not to mention Bolívar's letters or Bello's prologue). Some pose the identity issue at a national level, others from a continental or hemispheric perspective. Whatever the differences, it seems a matter of empirical observation that the criollo identity essay was (as they say in Hollywood westerns) no place for a woman. Skirius (9 and passim) poetically titles it "that centaur of genres." The explanation is no mystery. By definition, women are one of the populations that the criollo identity essay implicitly aimed to deny the civic powers the elite men claimed for themselves. The speaking subject of that essay canon, in other words, is male (and white) in a directed, exclusionary way. It is the figure of the *pensador*, the thinker, proprietor of *el pensamiento*. As criollo hegemony was mapped and remapped following independence, Euro-American men resolutely privileged themselves as the only full bearers of culture and citizenship. Women were to be denied the power to speak *as* citizens *for* all citizens.

Needless to say, this discursive situation reflected women's legal and judicial status under nineteenth-century republicanism. Historians have described the processes by which women (along with many other sectors of American society) were denied full citizenship in the American republics, denied such powers as property rights, voting rights, reproductive rights, education, access to public office (even to public speech!), and equality under the law. Fortunately, their access to literacy, print culture, and the public sphere was established *before* the republican era. They could not be silenced completely. If they were to speak and be heard, however, they were to speak *as women*. And that, as I shall discuss below, is what they did much though not all of the time.

WOMEN INTELLECTUALS AND THE "GENDER ESSAY"

To the extent that the criollo identity essay *is* the Latin American essay, there will be no women essayists: this is how canons continually reproduce their own truth. It is equally a matter of observation, however, that women intellectuals continually refused to heed the reverberations of what Ocampo called the "Don't interrupt me." From the beginning, within their restricted access to education and to print, criolla (Euro-American women) writers sought to assert themselves as citizens, as social subjects, as agents of history, and as *pensadoras*. In fact, one can readily identify a women's alternative to the criollo identity project. Running parallel to the male-based identity essay, criolla intellectuals generated a tradition that could accurately be called the *gender essay*. As a label, I use this term to denote a series of texts, written over the past 180 years by Latin American women, whose topic is the status and reality of women in modern society. It is a contestatory literature that aims, using Ocampo's terms once again, to interrupt the male monologue, or at least to challenge its claim to a monopoly on culture and history. As with the identity essay, the full corpus of essayistic writing on this subject would comprise hundreds of texts and thousands of pages. A few examples by some better-known women writers (see Marting, 1987, 1990) include Gertrudis Gómez de Avellaneda's "La mujer" (Women, 1860), Juana Manso's "Emancipación moral de la mujer" (Moral Emancipation of Women, 1858), Mercedes Cabello de Carbonera's "Influencia de la mujer en la civilización moderna" (Influence of Women on Modern Civilization, 1874), Clorinda Matto de

Turner's "Las obreras del pensamiento en la América del Sud" (Women Workers of Thought in South America, 1895), Soledad Acosta de Samper's *La mujer en la sociedad moderna* (Woman in Modern Society, 1895), Amanda Labarca Hubertson's *¿A dónde va la mujer?* (Where Are Women Going?, 1934), Alicia Moreau de Justo's *El feminismo y la evolución social* (Feminism and Social Evolution, 1911) and *Socialismo y la mujer* (Socialism and Women, 1946), Teresa de la Parra's "Influencia de la mujer en la formación del alma americana" (The Influence of Women in the Formation of the American Soul, 1930/1961), Victoria Ocampo's *La mujer y su expresión* (Woman and Her Expression, 1936), Magda Portal's *Hacia la mujer nueva* (Toward the New Woman, 1933), and Rosario Castellanos' *Sobre cultura femenina* (On Women's Culture, 1950) and *Mujer que sabe latín . . .* (Woman Who Knows Latin, 1973). The above catalogue is emphatically *not* proposed as a potential canon, but only as an index of the large, continuous, and unexamined body of essayistic production around the question of gender.

Though it does not always say so outright, the gender essay contests the disenfranchisement of women implied by the criollo identity essay, and indeed by all the official institutions of politics and culture. Historically, it can be read as the women's side of an ongoing negotiation as to what women's social and political entitlements are and ought to be in the postindependence era. Ideologically, its discussions of womanhood are eclectic, operating both within and against patriarchal gender ideologies. Like the criollo identity essay, the gender essay continues to be a productive genre today. Alongside the outpouring of scholarly writings on women, texts like Julieta Kirkwood's *Ser política en Chile* (To Be a Political Woman in Chile, 1986) and Heleieth Saffiotti's *A Mulher na sociedade de classes* (Women in Class Society, 1969) have their roots in the tradition of public discourse I am trying to identify here.

I described the gender essay as running parallel to the identity essay in Latin American letters. Both are associated with the figure of the public intellectual who writes fiction and poetry but also engages actively in journalism and public affairs. Often, as with the male tradition, gender essays began as public oratory. One of the many instances is Matto de Turner's "Las obreras del pensamiento," originally delivered at the Academy of Buenos Aires to a huge and affectionate public there to welcome her following her exile from Peru in 1895. Teresa de la Parra's "Influencia de la mujer en la formación del alma americana" originated as a series of acclaimed public lectures she delivered in Bogotá in 1930.

Amanda Labarca gave an address on women to the UN General Assembly in 1946. And of course there are the radio talks by Ocampo.

Obviously the parallels between the criollo identity essay and the criolla gender essay do not mean the two can be read or analyzed in the same way. Reading paradigms for the gender essay have not been widely developed. Indeed, the most basic kind of scholarly mapping has yet to be performed on this corpus of texts. One or two generalizations can be risked at this point, however. To begin with, as the titles above suggest, the gender essay typically draws very little on the categories of the *national*, at least until the post–World War II period. Traditionally, its writers tend not to speak either *to* or *as* subjects of particular nations, though they are very likely to be concerned with the status of women in modern nation-states in general. Second, among the materials I have examined, at least two conspicuously different discursive models seem to be at work. On the one hand, many gender essays take the form of a historical catalogue, in which the writer enumerates examples of women who have made significant contributions to society and history. Analytical commentary on women's social and existential condition is interspersed among these vignettes. Matto de Turner's "Las obreras del pensamiento" takes this form, enumerating a panorama of women creative writers of her day. Acosta de Samper's *La mujer en la sociedad moderna* (1895) is an astonishing book-length instance, cataloguing the contributions of dozens of women revolutionaries, charity workers, missionaries, moral thinkers, doctors, politicians, artists, writers, and educators throughout Europe and the Americas, starting from the French Revolution. The contemporary vitality of the historical catalogue is attested by such recent encyclopedic volumes as Lydia Sosa de Newton's *Las argentinas de ayer y hoy* (Argentine Women Yesterday and Today, 1967) or Angeles Mendieta Alatorre's *La mujer en la revolución mexicana* (Women in the Mexican Revolution, 1961).

At times the historical catalogue does little more than assert the presence and participation of women in history, culture, and public life. Often, in the celebration of *mujeres ilustres* (outstanding women) it provides little more than a distaff complement to criollo class privilege. This tends to be a literature more of fact than of ideas, yet its task must not be underestimated. Under the aegis of positivism, women's subordination is often legitimized by what are claimed to be objective observations about her natural capacities and limitations. Obviously it has been essential to combat such ideologies with documentation of what women in fact did. At the level of the social imaginary, the historical catalogue also insists on the reality of women as agents of history, a role denied them by official historiography. Within the hegemony of positivist thought, it makes the argument for women as agents of progress or human evolution rather than as regressive elements that need to be patronizingly brought up to par. In what is one of the richest instances of this genre, Teresa de la Parra's "Influencia de la mujer en la formación del alma americana" combines the historical catalogue with a profound meditation on the process of recovering submerged histories through imagination. The vitality of the historical catalogue in contemporary writing is scarcely a cause for unambiguous rejoicing. Historical catalogues of women's achievements are still being produced because the basic gesture they make is still necessary. In the face of an overwhelming androcentrism in the official institutions of knowledge, it is still necessary to assert, over and over again, the simple fact of women's social agency and their capacity for purposeful activity.

A second discursive practice within the gender essay is the analytical commentary on the spiritual and social condition of women. Here women writers challenge men on the intellectual terrain that has always been considered the domain of the essay, the terrain of *pensamiento* (thought). Among the texts I have mentioned, Gómez de Avellaneda's gender essays exemplify this mode, as do those of Manso, Moreau de Justo, Labarca, Portal, Ocampo, and Castellanos. Rather than seeking to reproduce male *pensamiento*, however, the analytical gender essay often proposes alternative forms of intellectuality that challenge the male prerogative to define thought. The first of Gómez de Avellaneda's essays on "La mujer" supplies an interesting nineteenth-century example of this intervention. Its main thrust is to strategically construct an alternative epistemological foundation from which to refute both the supremacy of secular rationality and the relegation of women to maternity. She opens her essay by distinguishing herself from "an elegant Spanish publicist" who has authored a recent volume on "the history of the fair sex." She asserts, "The idea does not enter our mind to accompany him over the vast terrain of his philosophical exploration, nor to lend him new and unknown data to enrich and support his theories" (285). Rather, she says, she will begin with the subject of sentiment, an area in which, she argues, the supremacy of women remains unchallenged. To clear a space for her own authority, she concedes certain forms of male superiority—but only provisionally:

> *We concede without the slightest reluctance that men received from nature a superiority in physical strength; we will not even dispute in the space of this brief article the intellectual superiority that he so immodestly bestows on himself. The conviction suffices us, and we say so sincerely, that no one can in good faith deny our sex supremacy in . . . the immense sphere of sentiment.*
> (IBID.)

Lest her readers devalue sentiment, Avellaneda immediately insists that lofty sentiments are the key to all great souls, particularly the capacity for sacrifice, which women possess most fully. In an obvious response to the secular rationalism that underwrote male intellectuality, she goes on to anchor women's social and intellectual authority in two entirely different sites: the Bible and the body. The pain of childbirth establishes the divine right of woman as "queen . . . of the vast dominions of sentiment" (287). The monarchic vocabulary here is a clear challenge to the republican values that disenfranchise women. Men corrupt the divine right of women: only by reproducing *on her own* could Mary produce a divine child, in contrast with Eve, whose relations with Adam produced "descendencia corrompida" (corrupt descendants). The "bloody pages of religious heroism," Avellaneda argues, readily dispel any notion of women as weak or unequipped to participate in public affairs. She returns to the Bible and offers what today would be called a feminist reading of the story of Christ. Her textual commentary presents a polarity, juxtaposing male obtuseness with female wisdom. While Jesus moves around Judea performing miracles and converting the poor, she observes,

> *The doctors of the law pursue and accuse him of disturbing public order.*
> *The ignorant women follow him, blessing the womb that conceived him.*
> *The Pharisee who receives him does not offer him water for the required ablutions.*
> *The sinful woman arrives to wash his feet with her tears.*
> (288)

The juxtapositions go on. Pilate orders Jesus beaten; Pilate's wife, "disturbed by mysterious presentiments," sends messengers begging for his life. The chosen (male) disciples disappear (all but one) at the crucifixion, while three women remain to become the privileged witnesses of the resurrection.

It is worth underscoring here that Avellaneda's tool for legitimizing woman's social and epistemological authority is her literary power as a reader and interpreter of texts, in this case the Bible. The high point of her argument is a purely textual observation:

> Woman! here is your son *says the Redeemer to
> Mary, symbolizing all men in Saint John. Note it
> well: he does not call her his mother, because the
> Queen of the martyrs does not represent simply
> the august Mother of the Messiah; she represents
> woman—the rehabilitated woman, the sanctified
> woman, woman the coredeemer, whose great heart can
> contain the maternity of the universe.*
> (290)

Though the point is easily lost on contemporary readers, Avellaneda's argument is a radical one in the context of dominant views of women and citizenship in her time. For her reading insists on an absolute separation of *womanhood* from *motherhood*. She insists the former must be privileged over the latter—the Bible itself says so. Implicit is an aggressive repudiation of republicanism's highly successful program of defining women's social value solely in terms of maternity.

The second essay in the series takes the challenge a step further, addressing the question of whether there are any grounds for considering women weaker than men, and whether women's superiority in matters of the heart necessarily implies their inferiority in matters of intelligence and character. Eventually, Gómez de Avellaneda openly lays claim to the domain of *pensamiento* (thought): "Not only are we disposed to declare, with Pascal, that *great thought is born from the heart*, but we are struck by the idea that the most glorious deeds . . . have always been the work of sentiment" (293). This argument provides the basis for the third essay, which arrives at the heart of the matter, the capacity of women "to govern peoples and administer public interests" (298). Avellaneda's interest is not, and never was, to establish an alternative sphere of action for women; what she seeks are alternative points of entry into spheres of action over which men were illegitimately claiming a monopoly, such as the Spanish Royal Academy, from which she was excluded solely on the basis of her gender.

Some seventy years later, in *La mujer y su expresión*, Victoria Ocampo likewise begins by evoking and enacting a gender-conscious female intellectuality distinct from the male tradition. Unlike Avellaneda, however, she seizes possession of the key term *pensamiento* right from the first sentence. "Lo primero que *pienso* al hablaros," (emphasis mine) she begins (The first thing I *think*),

> is that your voice and mine are conquering my great enemy, the Atlantic. . . . I have always seen the Atlantic as a symbol of distance. It has always separated me from beloved people and things. If it was not Europe, then it was America that I was missing.
> (9)

When she returned from the United States via the Panama Canal, she similarly "gave thanks to heaven" that the long separation imposed by the Pacific had also been "defeated." In complete contrast with the Americanist and, in this period, frequently nationalist identifications of the identity essay, Ocampo poses herself as a resolutely global subject for whom the mediation of distance is a primary task. Lest anyone think she is speaking only of geographical and not social distance, her oceanic image leads into an anecdote of a transatlantic telephone call she overhears in Berlin. An Argentine businessman calling his wife in Buenos Aires opens the conversation with the phrase "No me interrumpas" (Don't interrupt me). The miracle of transoceanic communication becomes a silencing. This anecdote leads into the discussion of male monologue quoted above. Ocampo's female *pensadora* (thinker), on the other hand, knows the world through dialogue and mediation. "Interrupt me," she says to her listeners. "This monologue does not please me. It is to you I wish to speak, not to myself" (12). She poses women's expression as a struggle first and foremost against the enforced male monologue, and against women's conditioning to "offer herself as a holocaust." Nowadays, says Ocampo, the woman on the other end of the phone call is daring to say, "This men's monologue does not relieve me either from my sufferings or *from my thoughts*. Why resign myself to repeating it? I have something else to say. Other sentiments, other pains have torn my life, other joys have illuminated it for centuries" (14). Like Avellaneda (and Parra), Ocampo begins with a preamble leading into a three-part essay, the first on women's subjectivity, the second on maternity and social reproduction, and the third on public and national life.

As a tradition and a praxis, the gender essay is inextricable from the vast journalistic literature on women and the gender system that has formed a conspicuous and continuous aspect of Latin American public discourse since the 1820s. Few themes have a more continuous presence across the vast range of periodical literature. For many women writers, from Clorinda Matto de Turner and Delmira Agustini to contemporary novelist Isabel Allende, short journalistic pieces on women were their point of entry into print; for many, from Juana Manso and Juana Manuela Gorriti to Marta Brunet, Alfonsina Storni, and Rosario Castellanos, such writing was an ongoing source of income and a way to maintain a public presence in print. Rosario Castellanos' noted *Mujer que sabe latín . . .* is a compilation of such journalistic articles, as is Amanda Labarca's 1946 *Feminismo contemporáneo* (Contemporary Feminism). I will be discussing men's contribution to this literature below.

CONTEXTUALIZING COUNTERCANONS

As with any effort to read marginalized writing into a discursive field dominated by a canon, there is a strong momentum to read the gender essay strictly as a response to male intellectual authority in general and to the criollo identity essay in particular. I would like to suggest, however, that such a move is justified only if it runs both ways. The criollo identity essay, that is, must also be read as a response to the demands of women and other marginalized groups for full inclusion in society. This may seem a radical notion, and perhaps it is. It requires reading the claims of the criollo essayists not as sui generis expressions of a particular imagination but as *contested* claims arising out of a profound and ongoing legitimation crisis. "Do I really have to think about *women* when I read the Jamaica letter, *Ariel, The Labyrinth of Solitude?*" the reader asks. Yes! You do! You have to (learn to) think about Bolívar's letters in the context of the ones Manuela Sáenz wrote, where she assumed a political and historical authority that was later denied her. You have to demand that Rodó's Ariel and Retamar's Calibán explain themselves to Miranda and to Sycorax. You have to think of the problem people like Magda Portal and Alicia Moreau posed for Mariátegui. You have to ask Paz what he was afraid of when he reduced Mexican women to the role of La Chingada, and what Elena Garro and Rosario Castellanos have had to say about that. Hegemonic writing, so the argument goes, must be seen as constituting itself in response to the counterhegemonic claims of those it subordinates, just as counterhegemonic writing must be read in relation to hegemony. The difference is that the hegemonic writers do not always have to name their others (in this case, woman) in order to constitute a discourse, whereas subalterns usually must do so in order to challenge the institutions of knowledge.

Three adjustments are required to prevent the argument here from being excessively reductive. First, the two categories I proposed at the beginning, the gender essay and the criollo identity essay, do not begin to exhaust the essayistic production of either sex. Both men and women wrote about everything under the sun. This fact is much better known about men than about women, however. As women are read back into Latin American literary and intellectual history, their overall intellectual production must be sought out and granted serious reflection.

Second, though women are absent from the canon of the criollo identity essay, it would be a complete mistake to say that women never wrote on the criollo identity question or never undertook to speak for the social whole. They did, though they were rarely canonized as legitimate interlocutors on the issue. Where but in the literature of identity are we to put Gorriti's *Panoramas de la vida* (Panoramas of Life, 1876), Matto de Turner's *Cuatro conferencias sobre América del Sur* (Four Lectures on South America, 1985/1909), Mistral's *Recados: Contando a Chile* (Messages: Telling About Chile, 1957), Sosa de Newton's biographical essays on the generals of the independence wars, or short pieces like Marta Brunet's article "Americanismo también es obra femenina" (Americanism is Also the Work of Women) in *El Repertorio Americano* in 1939?

In addition to their work specifically on the identity question, there exists of course an enormous and largely unexamined range of social and civic writing by women in Latin America. History, education, religion, and morality were all areas of general social inquiry on which women intellectuals regularly wrote. In the nineteenth century, in addition to her articles on women, Peruvian Mercedes Cabello de Carbonera wrote book-length studies on Cuban independence and on *La influencia de las Bellas Letras en el progreso moral y material de los pueblos* (The Influence of Letters on the Moral and Material Progress of Peoples). Her compatriot Clorinda Matto de Turner wrote a collection of *Bocetos al lápiz de americanos célebres* (Pencil Sketches of Renowned Americans). In addition to her essay on "The liberties, rights, and duties of women," Puerto Rican socialist Luisa Capetillo wrote books on *La Humanidad en el futuro* (Humanity in the Future, 1910) and *La influencia de las ideas modernas* (The Influence of Modern Ideas, 1916). Magda Portal wrote essays on "América Latina frente al imperialismo" (Latin America in the face of Imperialism) and "Defensa de la revolución mexicana" (In Defense of the Mexican Revolution, 1931). The list is endless and, so far, little read. Women writers were also prolific in the genre of civic poetry, while their autobiographical works, from Gorriti's *Peregrinaciones de una alma triste* (1876) to Eva Perón's *La razón de mi vida* (1951), often offer decidedly alternative visions of national reality and the national good.

The third corollary is that whether or not they participated in the gender essay as I have specifically defined it, men did, of course, write essays about women and about feminism; in fact they did so endlessly, perhaps obsessively. In the face of women's activism, their sheer numbers, and the manifest contradictions between democracy and gender inequality, an intense, ongoing propaganda effort was required to maintain women's subordination and to control their place in the social imaginary. This was particularly so during the 1920s and 1930s when the level of participation in all manner of women's organizations escalated and women's political activity began to focus on the demand for suffrage. During these decades, published writing by men about women increased startlingly, and a few male intellectuals more committed to democracy than to their gender privilege wrote in support of women's equality and emancipation. While only Hostos' "La educación científica de la mujer" (Scientific Education of Women, 1873) has entered the essay canon, scholars have now begun to attend to the writings of Sarmiento and Echeverría on women and women's education (Garrels 1989), the gender manifesto that is Mármol's essay on Manuela Rosas (Masiello 1992), González Prada on "El problema de la mujer," (Kristal 1987), Vaz Ferreira's *Sobre feminismo* (Moraña, n.d.), and others. In three recent books examining debates on gender in Colombia (Jaramillo, Roldedo, and Rodríguez-Arenas 1991), Argentina (Carlson 1987), and Chile (Santa Cruz et al. 1978), the bibliographies show that about a fourth of the books about women published between 1910 and 1940 were written by men. Needless to say, this literature runs the full breadth of the ideological spectrum, from Jesuits defending the Catholic order to socialists envisioning a gender revolution.

Here too, then, is a large corpus of writings needing to be sorted, sifted, and incorporated into scholarly accounts. Men's writings on the gender system, it seems, have been forgotten for the same reason women's have: women, and the gender system, have not been regarded as significant subject matter for real *pensamiento*. In its encylopedic treatment of major male essayists, Earle and Meade's (1973) history of the Latin American essay completely elides all mention of their writings on women. No matter which gender does it, apparently, writing about gender remains "women's work"! And of course indifference and neglect in this instance mask a serious interest in preventing the question of gender inequality from becoming a central issue in the arena of social understanding.

These bodies of largely unexamined essayistic literature suggest that an important dimension of Latin American intellectual history has been omitted from scholarly consideration. The debate on gender, as carried on by women and men, across the ideological and social spectrum, and across the whole of Latin American history, should hold as central a place in Latin American intellectual history as the identity debate does. It should be recognized as central to the ongoing self-creation and self-understanding of society. The gender essays of such writers as Gómez de Avellaneda, Ocampo, Labarca, Parra, Kirkwood, and Castellanos should be in the essay anthologies and on the syllabi alongside those of their male contemporaries. Women should be present as both the objects and subjects of *pensamiento*. It is a matter, as this volume attests, of both recovering the work and learning how to read it.

WORKS CITED

Acosta de Samper, Soledad. *La mujer en la sociedad moderna.* Paris: Garnier, 1895.
Cabello de Carbonera, Mercedes. "Influencia de la mujer en la civilización moderna." *El Correo del Perú* (1874).
Carlson, Marifran. *Feminismo! The Woman's Movement in Argentina from Its Beginnings to Eva Peron.* Chicago: Academic Publications, 1988.
Castellanos, Rosario. *Mujer que sabe latín . . .* Mexico City: Secretaria de Educación Pública, 1973.
———. *Sobre cultura femenina.* Mexico City: América/Revista Antológica, 1959.
Earle, Peter G., and Robert G. Mead, Jr. *Historia del ensayo hispanoamericano.* Mexico City: Ediciones de Andrea, 1973.
Foster, David William. *Para una lectura semiótica del ensayo latinoamericano.* Madrid: Porrúa, 1987.
Garrels, Elizabeth. "La Nueva Heloisa en América." *Nuevo Texto Crítico* 4 (1989), 27–38.
Gómez de Avellaneda, Gertrudis. "La Mujer." In *Antología, poesías y cartas amorosas.* Ed. Ramón Gómez de la Serna. Buenos Aires: Espasa Calpe, 1945.

Guillén, Pedro. *El ensayo actual latinoamericano.* Mexico: Ediciones de Andrea, 1971.

Jaramillo, María Mercedes, Angela Inés Roldedo, and Flor María Rodríguez-Arenas. *¿Y las mujeres? Ensayos sobre literatura colombiana.* Antioquia, Colombia: Universidad de Antioquia, 1991.

Kirkwood, Julieta. *Ser política en Chile.* Santiago: FLACSO, 1986.

Kristal, Efraín. *The Andes Viewed from the City.* New York: Peter Lang, 1987.

Labarca Hubertson, Amanda. *¿A dónde va la mujer?* Santiago: Editorial Extra, 1934.

Manso, Juana. "Emancipación moral de la mujer." *La Ilustración Argentina,* 1858.

Marting, Diane E., ed. *Spanish American Women Writers: A Bio-Bibliographical Source Book.* New York: Greenwood, 1990.

———. *Women Writers of Spanish America.* New York: Greenwood, 1987.

Matto de Turner, Clorinda. "Las obreras del pensamiento en la América del Sud." In *Boreales, miniaturas y porcelanas.* Buenos Aires: Juan del Asina, 1902.

Mendieta Alatorre, Angeles. *La mujer en la revolución mexicana.* Mexico City: Institución Nacional de Estudios Históricos, 1961.

Moraña, Mabel. Carlos Vaz Ferreira: Hacia un feminismo de compensación. Unpublished ms., n.d.

Moreau de Justo, Alicia. *El feminismo y la evolución social.* Buenos Aires: Ateneo Popular, 1911.

Ocampo, Victoria. *La mujer y su expresión.* Buenos Aires: Sur, 1936. [Also published in *Testimonios,* 2a. serie, 269–286. Buenos Aires: Ediciones Sur, 1941.]

Parra, Teresa de la. "La influencia de la mujer en la formación del alma americana." In *Obra.* Caracas: Biblioteca Ayacucho, 1982.

Portal, Magda. *Hacia la mujer nueva; El Aprismo y la mujer.* Lima: Atahualpa, 1934.

Rey de Guido, Clara. *Contribución al estudio del ensayo en Hispanoamérica.* Caracas: Academia Nacional de la Historia, 1985.

Ripoll, Carlos. *Conciencia intelectual de América: Antología del ensayo hispanoamericano.* New York: Las Américas, 1966.

Saffioti, Heleieth. *A Mulher na sociedade de classes.* São Paulo: Quatro Artes, 1969.

Santa Cruz, Lucia, Teresa Pereira, Isabel Zegers, and Valeria Maino. *Tres ensayos sobre la mujer chilena.* Santiago: Editorial Universitaria, 1978.

Skirius, John, ed. *El ensayo hispanoamericano del siglo XX.* Mexico City: Fondo de Cultura Económica, 1981.

Sosa de Newton, Lily. *Las argentinas de ayer a hoy.* Buenos Aires: Zanetti, 1967.

Urrello, Antonio. *Verosimilitud y estrategia textual en el ensayo hispanoamericano.* Mexico City: Premiá, 1986.

Vitier, Medardo. *Del ensayo americano.* Mexico City: Fondo de Cultura Económica, 1945.

Jill S. Kuhnheim

PARIAH / MESSIAH
THE CONFLICTIVE
SOCIAL IDENTITY OF
FLORA TRISTAN

Flora Tristan's relation to the Latin American essay tradition is problematic. In approaching Tristan's oeuvre, difficulties arise not only in the generic classification of her works, which straddle the line between autobiography, travel writing, theoretical treatises, and social criticism, but also in even specifying her national identity. Born in 1803, she was the illegitimate daughter of don Mariano Tristan de Moscoso, a Peruvian aristocrat, and a Frenchwoman of little social status, Thérèse Laisnay. Raised in France, Tristan traveled to Peru in 1833–1834 to claim her inheritance and meet her deceased father's family. In the introduction to her first book, however, *Mémoires et pérégrinations d'une paria* (*Peregrinations of a Pariah*, 1838), a semiautobiographical account of her travels, she introduces herself not as French but as a "fellow Peruvian," while many of her observations that follow in fact situate her as an outsider to Peruvian society. Marked as a "pariah" in France because of her need to escape from a disastrous marriage, she does not find a place in Peru and proclaims herself excluded from all society. Her very exclusion gives Tristan an international perspective that will become clearer in her later books, *Promenades dans Londres* (*London Journal*, 1840) and *Union ouvrière* (*The Worker's Union*, 1843).

Because of this lack of precise national positioning, Tristan has recently been reclaimed by both French and Latin American traditions. She is cited as an early feminist and socialist whose concept of a universal working class predates that of Marx. Her importance as an early female voice in Latin American history and literature is made evident by the attention of Magda Portal in her book, *Flora Tristán, precursora* (1944), Silvina Bullrich in *Flora Tristán, la visionaria* (1982), and Rosario Ferré's essay "La flor del aire" (in *Sitio a Eros*, 1980), and by her inclusion in Francesca Miller's new collection, *Latin American Women and the Search for Social Justice* (1992).[1] At the same time, Tristan's work has often been read as either sociological observations of the early nineteenth century or in purely biographical terms (it is difficult to find an author who does not value her contribution to the world of art as grandmother of Paul Gauguin).

In this essay I will shift the focus from life to literature, tracing the theme of women's emancipation through three texts in order to demonstrate that the generic shifts in Tristan's writing are linked to the author's own struggle with issues of gender, class, and nationality. In her foreword to *The Barthes Effect*, Michèle Richman notes the post-Montaigne bifurcation of the essay form into two distinct modes: the biographical essay, which is characterized by an informal, intimate style, and the critical essay, which is "dogmatic, impersonal, systematic, and expository" (x). I am proposing that Tristan begins with the more personal style and moves toward the expository, while never entirely removing biographical traits. In each case Tristan constructs her self in terms of predominating notions of subjectivity while modifying the masculinist models. Following Susan Kirkpatrick's excellent explication of the three major archetypes of Romantic subjectivity (the Promethean subject, the socially alienated subject, and the self-divided subject), I will show that Kirkpatrick's commentary about gendered inflections of these different subject positions is also pertinent to Tristan. Like George Sand's Lélia, Tristan increasingly characterizes herself as a "superior soul" but also as a transgressor with "no place in the patriarchal economy" (32). In the three works treated here, Tristan's changing subject positions allow her progressively more participation in nineteenth-century society as her critique draws nearer to European centers of power.

The author ties her story to that of Peru in the combination of autobiography and travel writing she chooses for her first book. *Peregrinations of a Pariah* is a narrative of self-exploration that is always relational, for Tristan's observations of Peru center on human beings, on populated places and human interactions, rather than on the surrounding scenery. Her ambivalent position in Peru permits her to vacillate (as narrator) between the perspectives of foreigner and niece as she chooses between identifying with the powerful, aristocratic Tristan family and taking the more distanced perspective of an outsider. Speaking from this shifting position, Tristan's narrator undermines masculinist Romantic models of subjective authority.

In the title of the book she identifies herself as an outcast, a pariah, and looking for a new social identity in Peru she feels alternately French, Peruvian, and even Spanish, according to changing interests and circumstances (Cuche 23). Like her marital status, which also shifts according to social exigencies,[2] the distance from her past and her society allows Tristan to redefine herself continually. The book charts her increasing detachment from Europe through her voyage to Valparaiso on the *Mexicain*, her journey and stay at her uncle's residence in Arequipa, and subsequent months in Lima. As her journey progresses she becomes freer in her social commentary. Tristan uses this opportunity to express herself as an ex-centric subject. She is both a victim of society and superior to it, demonstrating traits of the alientated Romantic subject.

Speaking from this outsider position, Tristan's narrative voice shields her from social criticism, allowing her to address traditionally "nonfeminine" subjects such as politics and war. While in Arequipa her interest in and commentary on the civil war is prolific.[3] Tristan watches the war like theater from the top of her uncle's house, proffering political background and analysis, describing the tactics employed in battle, but she does not remain an observer. Her clear-sightedness enables Flora to offer sage advice to her cousin Althaus and her Uncle Pío. In the chapter entitled "The Republic and the Three Presidents," Flora first gives her uncle advice about how to handle the changing political situation: "When he had gone Althaus approached me in his turn and said: 'Florita, I do not know what to do. Which of these rascally presidents should I support?' " (154).[4] Here creative self-portraiture overtakes journalistic veracity in one of many scenes that challenge our credulity. Tristan is teaching these Peruvian men how to play their own game. We are inclined to read these episodes as *pura literatura*, an example of how Tristan places herself at center stage not just as recorder of events nor in terms of her personal experiences, but as a participant in history. She makes herself into a behind-the-scenes heroine, an image that coincides in some respects with the paradigm of the Romantic hero, overstepping prescribed bounds in her social and political function. No "angel of the house," Tristan can be read as antidomestic in her dismissal of spousal and maternal responsibilities in *Peregrinations*.

We see this transgressive desire to obtain a position of historical influence again when Tristan considers a possible alliance with Colonel Escudero, "the only man in Peru capable of seconding my ambitious plans" (231). Escudero's interest offers Tristan the possibility of combining love and power and is an enormous temptation, an aspiration forcefully expressed but checked by Flora's fear of "the moral depravity that invariably accompanies the enjoyment of power" (232). After experiencing the strength of her ambition one wonders if she isn't paying lip service to conventional values here, strengthening her moral stance in order to avert the reader's attention from the fact that a union with Escudero would be bigamous. This episode foreshadows Tristan's meeting with doña Pencha Zabiaga de Gamarra, whose tacit power is "seconded" by her weaker husband, the president. In terms of her social role and the blatant admiration Flora expresses, we might read Pencha Gamarra—the patriotic heroine—as Tristan's alter ego.

Tristan and "la Mariscala" meet on board ship as Gamarra is about to depart, exiled from Peru by the change in powers. Flora is struck by this woman's superiority, her willpower, and her intelligence. She is also a casualty of her society:

> *her heroic endurance in the face of suffering made her*
> *appear larger than life to me, and it wrung my heart*
> *to see one of God's elite, herself a victim of the very*
> *qualities that set her apart from her fellow creatures,*
> *forced by the fears of a cowardly people to flee her*
> *country, abandon her family and friends, and go,*
> *stricken with the most frightful infirmity [epilepsy],*
> *to end her painful existence in exile.*
> (302)

In Tristan's description of Gamarra's situation we hear a curious echo of her own plight. The narrator is also "exiled" at both the beginning and end of *Peregrinations*, on the way to transforming herself into a citizen of the world. Her identification with this powerful woman presages Tristan's role as social heroine, a part she will play more overtly in *London Journal*.

Peregrinations of a Pariah is a prose text with a very personal perspective. Tristan offers her opinions, judgments, and incipient theorizing about social ills with a didactic intent (clearly stated in her introduction), for she wants her work to contribute to social progress in Peru. Her desires in this case are in keeping with the early nineteenth-century European Romantic tradition, in which insight in the personal realm "necessarily" translated into an insight into society as there was not yet a distinct separation between society and self (Williams 30). Employing a hybrid discourse that allows her to create a heroic self while maintaining

values appropriate to women of her time, Tristan uses the autobiographical essay to unite personal and public concerns.

Tristan's *London Journal* crosses other generic boundaries, for these essays are even more thinly disguised as travel writing.[5] As in *Peregrina-*
tions, once again there is little picturesque description of the city itself;
background scenes serve to highlight social conditions in the century's
center of industrial capitalism.[6] An examination of the chapters "Prostitution" and "English Women" allows us to see that here, although Tristan employs a more objective narrative stance, she is indirectly shaping
her own identity in relation to the women she observes. She and the
prostitutes she regards are subsumed under the larger category of
Women; linked by gender they share positions as victims of the social
order. The difference between Tristan's position and that of the prostitute
is one of degree, for the prostitute embodies the "ugliest of all the sores
produced by the unequal distribution of wealth" (72).

The situation of the prostitute represents the degraded feminine;
forced by a lack of job opportunities into selling her body, the poor
woman loses her *self*, suffering an irrecuperable moral death. Flora Tristan constructs prostitution as a question of economics, not virtue, because in order to have virtue, she reminds us, one must have freedom
(75). These powerless, voiceless women are "victims of vice," tortured
in scenes Tristan describes with the authority of an eyewitness (in-
duced to vomit, the women pass out and are splattered by remnants of
drunken men's drinks). Tristan's witnessing is a courageous act for an
early nineteenth-century woman, demonstrating her moral authority and
her willingness to encroach on male territory. The missionary rhetoric
with which she presents her evidence combines socially sanctioned values
for women (protecting the family, upholding morality) with the author's
desire once again to take center stage.

In her treatment of women Tristan clearly distinguishes between conditions ascribed to nature and those ascribed to culture; corruption does
not result from a "natural" weakness in women but a weakness in Western society that permits the wealthy to exploit the weak.[7] Expanding her
treatment of prostitution beyond gender, Tristan situates it as an issue of
class by calling attention to the children (male and female) who are kid-
napped or coerced into brothels, exposed by economic circumstances
to the dangers of the streets. Focusing on juveniles is also a rhetorical
strategy to increase her readers' sympathy and awareness of victimiza-
tion, indirectly strengthening her case for women. Tristan supports her
personal testimony with long quotes from the Society for the Prevention

of Juvenile Prostitution's reports and "Dr. Ryan's book,"[8] employing research methods that are beyond the purview of travel or journal writing. These are the traits of the analytic essay that Réda Bensmaïa associates with rhetorical "complicatio," a tactic producing theory or critical combat (rather than "inventio," associated with creation, or "dispositio," with ordering) (13). Tristan is no mere traveler but, like the Owenite reformers of her day, engages in "combat" by proposing a new international social order through her critique of London.

Her contentious style continues in "English Women." Here Flora notes the natural intelligence and sensibility of English women but bemoans their stifling education, their lack of civil rights, and the fact that in England, as in France, a married woman is virtually the property of her husband. This last observation is reinforced through the example of aristocrats Lady Bulwar and Sir Lytton, an estranged couple whose situation parallels Tristan's own personal history. Both Bulwar and Lytton are authors, he quite successful, she increasingly so, and as a part of the resulting rivalry, he slanders her character. Upon their separation Tristan observes that he produced "nothing worthy of note" (199), indicating that he had been abusing his more powerful position and plagiarizing his wife's work. Tristan hopes that, in spite of his acrimony, Lady Bulwar might "escape the assassin's bullet" (199). Once again Tristan has found a means to circuitously recount her own story, making oblique reference to the very public assassination attempt against her by her husband Chazal (September 1838). The attention paid to the event made Tristan a real-life Romantic heroine, augmenting the popularity of her first book, *Peregrinations*, which sold out after the shooting and went into a second edition (Strumingher 65).

This technique of doubling, in which the author's individual experience is reflected in another woman's, recurs in Tristan's treatment of Mary Wollstonecraft. She is very attentive to her *Vindication of the Rights of Woman*, which she characterizes as a national achievement, demonstrating British women's intelligence and resources. Tristan paraphrases and quotes extensively from the work, published fifty years prior to Tristan's visit, to reinforce the urgent need for reform in England. Wollstonecraft becomes a kind of second self for Tristan, augmenting the force of her own ideas. Through her link to the British feminist, Tristan situates herself as a coparticipant in a history of challenge to patriarchal hegemony. Tristan recognizes Wollstonecraft's principles as forerunners to the better-known ideas of Saint-Simon in a way that ironically foreshadows

her own lack of public recognition as an early advocate for the working class. The increasing class consciousness throughout her works comes to
fruition in the internationalism of *The Worker's Union*, the text that most
clearly falls within the tradition of the expository essay. Here Tristan
speaks most directly, most forcefully, and with the greatest authority, for
she is not speaking for herself but for the proletariat. The undisguised
shift in genre and breadth of perspective signal her transformation into
the "Mujer Mesías," a Female Savior. In *The Worker's Union*, Flora Tristan comes closest to a Romantic, Promethean presentation of the self, a
conversion that ironically requires that the author's individual subjectivity be most concealed.

   The Worker's Union is loaded with religious imagery. In her preface to
the first edition of the book, Tristan proclaims that her religion is to love
her brothers, to serve God in humanity (25).[9] She makes herself into a
Christlike figure whose exemplary self-sacrifice, her ceaseless travel to
speak for workers' rights (which would result in her premature death), is
part of a larger mission to unify the working class. Like Christ she is
both redeemer and intercessor; the latter trait is also associated with her
maternal stance. Laura Strumingher suggests that Tristan's leadership was
influenced by the "maternal metaphor" and notes that she wanted "to be
part of the workers but she did not want to relinquish control of their
development; she felt that they were not yet ready to push forward without her guidance and nurturance" (113). The family metaphor is appropriate in this instance because Tristan's goal in writing this "little book"
was to convince workers of the need to organize, to give them tools to
facilitate their association, and to demonstrate their essential unity by
addressing them as members of an extended family.

   Tristan's plan is both visionary and pragmatic. Her book includes
"self-help" letters that workers might use to gain the ear of the powerful
(king, nobility, clergy, etc.), an account of the struggle that surrounded
the book's publication, where funds were ultimately obtained, and a list
of subscribers. Any money received was to be reinvested in "the cause."
Tristan also recognizes her readers' role in the process of publication by
including letters responding to her ideas in the second and third editions
of *The Worker's Union*. In her mother/preacher role she seeks to activate
her readers; she does not want a passive audience but an engaged, participating community. She begins her text directed to working men and
women with the exhortation "Listen to me" (37), engaging the phatic

function of language to focus attention, to communicate the urgency of her message, and to speak directly to the workers. This opening address, like many moments in *The Worker's Union*, has a straightforward, oral quality. With a low literacy rate among her anticipated audience (lower still among its female members), Tristan's antiliterary style seems directed to aural consumption—to be read aloud or discussed at meetings.

Tristan is always gender specific in her general addresses in this book, so it is significant that in her chapter on women she directs herself to the men: "Workers, you my brothers" (75). "Why I mention women" is the explanatory title of this third chapter, which argues in a conversational tone that for six thousand years the "female race" has been treated as a *"true pariah"* (76). Italicized in the original text, this expression demonstrates how the author has again transformed her individual experience into a communal one. Tristan proposes that woman's inferior place in society is a "judgment" that can be "appealed" (76–77); their status, like that of the pre–French Revolution proletariat, can be changed and must be changed by men since it is the "lawyer, philosopher, and priest" who legislated it in the first place. Although women are different from men (hearts made for love, organs for motherhood, 76), they should be equal. It is the responsibility of the male workers to act in solidarity with their female companions to emancipate the last slaves remaining in French society (88).

This strong link between women's and workers' interests characterizes Flora Tristan's later works. In her earlier, biographical essays we saw how she created herself—as victim/heroine, French/Peruvian—through her social commentary; in *The Worker's Union* her personal experience has merged with that of the public. This integration is not a change but a culmination, for Tristan is always interested in those who occupy a marginal position, a position consistently analogous to that of women. As the "Mujer Mesías," she has a pseudodivine role that is in many ways the result of her own textual self-representation but is also a mask—a mask converting her into humanity's savior yet still marking her gendered specificity. The appellation broadens Tristan's audience and permits her full entrance into public discourse, calling attention to how she has rewritten the roles available to her. While a conventional masculine Promethean hero would strive toward a place one step away from God, Tristan's feminine Promethean hero reclaims rights that bring the dispossessed one step closer to Man, transforming women and workers into human beings.

NOTES

1. Another excellent recent addition to Tristan scholarship is Mary Louise Pratt's *Imperial Eyes: Travel Writing and Transculturation* (New York: Routledge, 1992). Pratt reads *Peregrinations* as travel writing that participates in and yet deviates from male-authored examples of an imperialist project in the contact zone. Out of all of Tristan's work, Pratt considers only *Peregrinations*. The trajectory of Tristan's writing changes the reader's impression of her project, making it clear that its primary focus is not imperialistic but aimed toward reformation with consistent attention to women's and workers' concerns.

2. Although separated from her husband, Tristan still had two children in France, and it was in part her sense of financial responsibility to her children (resulting from her bad marriage) that stimulated her voyage, a fact Tristan makes explicit in her introduction to *Peregrinations*. On her trip to Peru, however, she presented herself as single, widowed, or a single mother, depending on the situation.

3. These are the civil wars of 1833–1834 in which Agustín Gamarra, who came to power in 1829, lost control of the presidency. His hand-picked successor, Bermúdez, was not accepted by the people and his authority was directly challenged by General Orbegoso.

4. Since translations exist for all the works by Tristan cited in this essay, I will refer directly to the English editions, making reference to the French only when there is a discrepancy in the translation. It is often very difficult to find Tristan's works in their original language; *Peregrinations*, for example, has recently been republished in English, and I encountered several contemporary editions in Spanish (another indication, perhaps, of the degree to which Tristan plays a role in the Latin American tradition). There is only one copy of the book in French in U.S. libraries, however, so access to the original is available only through one of a few microfiche copies.

5. The English translation of the title is confusing since the French, *Promenades dans Londres*, does not suggest the usually private connotation of the English term "journal." *Paseos en Londres* is the Spanish version, which more closely approximates the original.

6. This book, published in 1840, is often considered a precursor to Engel's *The Condition of the Working Class in England* (1845).

7. In her constructivist view Tristan differentiates herself from influential theoreticians (such as Rousseau) who had proposed that the physical "inferiority" of women implied a concomitant intellectual and moral inferiority (Baelen 151).

8. She refers to a book by Michael Ryan, an evangelical physician's early treatment of the subject: *Prostitution in London, with a Comparative View of That of Paris, and New York* (London, 1839).

9. Although beyond the scope of this essay, the religious elements present in

The Worker's Union suggest a comparison to similar traits in the later essays of José Carlos Mariátegui.

WORKS CITED

Baelen, Jean. *Flora Tristán: Feminismo y socialismo en el siglo XIX*. Madrid: Taurus, 1973.

Bensmaïa, Réda. *The Barthes Effect: The Essay as Reflective Text*. Trans. Pat Fedkieu. Minneapolis: University of Minnesota Press, 1987.

Cuche, Denys. "El Perú de Flora Tristán: Del sueño a la realidad." In *Flora Tristán: Una reserva de utopía* by Magda Portal et al., 29–54. Lima: Tarea, Centro de la Mujer Peruana, 1985.

Kirkpatrick, Susan. *Las Románticas: Women Writers and Subjectivity in Spain, 1835–1850*. Berkeley: University of California Press, 1989.

Michaud, Stéphane. "En un espejo: Flora Tristán y George Sand." In *Flora Tristán: Una reserva de utopía* by Magda Portal et al., 101–116.

Richman, Michèle. Foreword to *The Barthes Effect* by Réda Bensmaïa, viii–xxi.

Strumingher, Laura. *The Odyssey of Flora Tristán*. New York: Peter Lang, 1988.

Tristan, Flora. *Flora Tristán's London Journal, 1840*. Trans. Dennis Palmer and Giselle Pincetl. Charlestown, Mass.: Charles River Books, 1980.

―――. *Peregrinations of a Pariah*. Trans. Jean Hawkes. Boston: Beacon, 1986.

―――. *The Worker's Union*. Trans. Beverly Livingston. Chicago: University of Illinois Press, 1983.

Williams, Raymond. *Culture and Society, 1780–1950*. New York: Harper & Row, 1966.

<table>
<tr><td>

Claire

Emilie

Martin

</td><td>

SLAVERY IN THE
SPANISH COLONIES
THE RACIAL POLITICS
OF THE COUNTESS
OF MERLIN

</td></tr>
</table>

The development of women's writing in the nineteenth century has been closely linked to the social and political changes that allowed women to bridge the distance from the private to the public domain, and to graft their unique experiences onto the margins of power and society. Still confined to the discourse of the self (autobiography, travelogs, memoirs, poetry), these writers started to venture into the fields of human knowledge and theoretical speculation in an effort to push back the limitations of such "womanly" genres. The trespassing act that the essay implied for women writers in the nineteenth century allowed them to recreate a literary *persona* that would assimilate facets of their individual life stories.

THE BIRTH OF A NATION:
THE PERSONAL AS POLITICAL

Nineteenth-century autobiographical narratives have given us a curious perspective into the early manifestations of Latin American writing as well as into Latin America's emergence from colonial status to nationhood. Sylvia Molloy in *At Face Value* maintains that the autobiographical works of these new nations became a form of historical account, a personalized insertion of the I/(eye) witness/protagonist/author in the historical process (82–83). Thus, the personal, the private history of the individual, functions metonymically within the national discourse.[1]

The works of Cuban-born María de las Mercedes Santa Cruz y Montalvo, Countess of Merlin (1789–1852), constitute a shrewd and engaging blueprint of a life in the making, not unlike the process of birthing of the new nations. The countess' autobiographical collection of essaylike letters, *La Havane* (Havana), represents her most conscientious effort as a Creole to carve an intellectual position amidst the Parisian intelligentsia.[2] In a cumulative impulse toward a compendious literary assessment of Cuba's economic, social, political, and ethical situation, the countess grafts onto her life story the dramatic events that would result in the infamous period in Cuban history known as the Conspiracy of "La Escalera" (the ladder) in 1844.[3] Merlin explored the most controversial issues of the time, and in the process she acquired a certain amount of authorial prestige and political clout. In addition to these very tangible rewards, Merlin fashioned a Creole self, deeply implicated in the political turmoil surrounding the future of the slave trade in the colonies and the threat of the abolitionist movement led by Britain. The unabashedly political, social, and ethical undercurrent in Merlin's ambitious *La Havane* exemplifies the development from women's personal narratives to the traditionally male territory of the essay, and consequently it constitutes a passage from the private domain to the public.

THE CREATION OF A
LITERARY TRIPTYCH

Between 1841 and 1844 Merlin published a tripartite account of her 1840 trip to Cuba. "Observations de Madame la Comtesse de Merlin sur l'état des esclaves dans les colonies espagnoles" (Observations by the Countess of Merlin on the Conditions of Slaves in the Spanish Colonies), *La Havane*, and *Viaje a La Habana*, (Trip to Havana)[4] were articulated as autonomous yet intimately related versions of the same experience tailored to satisfy the interests and demands of different publics. Thus, the publication of parts of the voluminous *La Havane* before its completion suggests the urgency of the political situation on the island and Cuba's strained relations with the Spanish Crown and with foreign powers in the Caribbean. Sensing the volatile nature of her assessment of the situation in the colony, Merlin fragmented her narrative to capture the goodwill of the Spanish readership, the Cuban intellectual circles that welcomed her return to the island, and the European public who would have access to the translations of her works. Given the wide range of differences in readership and interests that she hoped to reach, it becomes clear that the publication of interrelated materials during this short period followed her ambitious goal of engaging the international community in the debate around abolition and the cessation of the slave trade and Britain's leading role in both matters.

In June of 1841 Mercedes Santa Cruz y Montalvo published the controversial essay "Observations" in the *Revue des Deux Mondes*, the official voice of the French Romantics. The text would be also part of *La Havane* and appear as letter XX addressed to Baron Charles Dupin. A Spanish translation appeared in Madrid in February 1842 entitled "Los esclavos en las colonias españolas" (The Slaves in the Spanish Colonies).[5] This essay differs from the two other texts in that it is solely concerned with the political and economic aspects of slavery and it advances possible solutions to the problems of the colony.

The three-volume work *La Havane*, published in Paris by the Libraire d'Amyot in 1844, stands as a literary homage to her homeland and a search for her identity as an exiled Creole in France. Merlin undertakes the writing of her impressions of the island after returning from her 1840 trip. The full text includes thirty-six letters and an appendix containing letters on the slave situation in Cuba by the British consul, Mr. Turnbull, and by several influential Cubans. The letters that comprise the three volumes (over twelve hundred pages long) shape a multilayered discourse that entangles itself in the profusion of historical narrative, essays on the political, economic, and social systems governing the colony, and anecdotal and pictorial narratives. While unfolding the "petite histoire" with its charming scenes of colonial life, the text reflects a well-defined political agenda espoused by the countess herself and many of the Cuban intellectuals of the time.

The same year, a translation of her work *La Havane* was published in Madrid in a much abridged form with a preface by her compatriot Gertrudis Gómez de Avellaneda. *Viaje a La Habana* includes only ten of the thirty-six letters, and the appendix was omitted along with the name of the person to whom the letter was addressed. The resulting text was a diluted version of the original; it transformed the politically volatile issue of slave emancipation and slave trade into an uneasy absence. Merlin characterized this Spanish version as "divertida" (light and amusing; Figarola 136); it was in nature a piece of exoticism to delight the senses. However, in reading *Viaje a La Habana*, the reader cannot fail to notice the constant preoccupation with the role of blacks (slaves or freed) within Cuban society. There is also a singular attempt to erase any fears the Spanish readership harbored concerning the violent disposition of blacks

and the possibility of a general uprising such as the one in Santo Domingo. The dilemma of the black element in Cuban society became the
matrix subtext of all three works. In both its conspicuous absence as well
as in its obsessive presence, blacks (slave, *cimarrón* [fugitive], or freed)
were in the limelight of the political and philosophical debate in the
island.

SLAVERY IN CUBA:
OBSERVATIONS FROM PARADISE

The ideological inner workings of the literary
triptych are laid open in "Los esclavos en las colonias españolas." The
text is imbued with ambiguity, vagueness, and contradictions. The essay
demonstrates that the dilemma Merlin faced between her Romantic ideals
on individual freedom and her mercenary interests was tied to slavery.

Merlin starts her polemical essay by addressing the scarcity of studies
on the Caribbean colonies and, more importantly, the lack of knowl-
edgeable debate over slavery. She boldly confronts her readership by stating what would become her main argument: "Nothing is more just than
the abolition of the slave trade; nothing is more unjust than the emancipation of the slaves" (2). She bases her assertion on the principle of freedom and natural law. While the slave trade is an attack against natural
law, the emancipation of slaves would constitute a violation of property
rights. This clearly establishes the pragmatic nature of her allegations.
There is nothing "sentimental" about her position, nothing veiled, nothing philanthropic. Merlin speaks solely on behalf of the interests of the
Cuban sacharocracy to which she and her family belong and stubbornly
defend. She weaves her arguments on a historical base to persuade her
readers to judge the situation with their minds, not their hearts.

Merlin's position contrasts sharply with the sentimental and heartfelt
account of the plight of the slaves by Gertrudis Gómez de Avellaneda in
Sab (1841). Curiously, the countess expressed a very similar vision to
that of Avellaneda in an autobiographical narrative she wrote in 1831,
Mis doce primeros años (My First Twelve Years). In this work Merlin attacks the institution of slavery as a repugnant offense against individual
freedom and the dignity of humankind. Her revolt against the situation
of slaves acquires all the nuances of the sentimental narrative in which
the black character becomes an idealized and faceless replica of the Romantic sensibility. However, in "Los esclavos," as well as in the other

two versions, Merlin distances herself from the human drama of slavery
to argue the case of a slave owner whose economic well-being is tied to
slavery. In order to prepare an "objective" argument, the countess becomes a historian and blames the most "enlightened nations" for engaging in the slave trade: "England held a monopoly on the slave trade for
more than half a century" (3). If the most advanced and civilized nations
protected the trade, she asks, why should they now bow before the very
suspicious motives of the English abolitionist forces? Why indeed, since
the plight of Africans is much worse in their native lands where they are
systematically killed to be eaten: "if the miserable blacks were given the
choice of being eaten by their own or remaining in slavery among a civilized people, without a doubt they would choose slavery" (6). In addition
to her calculated use of the shocking practice of cannibalism, the countess
stresses the economic nature of abolition (and the thus hypocritical posturing of England and France). She points out that since Cuba produces
better quality and greater quantity of sugar than the English colonies,
"the island of Cuba is the only true rival of the English colonies" (7).
The cards are on the table. Abolitionist England is in reality a facade to
subvert the economic domination of the Spanish colonies. Merlin accuses
England of promoting and instigating uprisings among the slaves: "Almost all black uprisings in the island's plantations have been instigated
by English agents and some by French" (7). She further notes that no
one has tried to eliminate slavery in other parts of the globe, victimizing
only the rich Spanish colony. In exposing the hypocrisy of these "civilized" nations, the countess strives to weaken the moral grip they have
held in the debate over slavery. She shifts the tone and the rhetoric of the
issue. She positions Cuba as a victim of a purely economic coup by the
European powers under the guise of humanitarian principles.

Merlin takes refuge in history to validate the presence of slaves in
Cuba. In a singularly twisted rationalization, she justifies slavery by tracing the origin of the slave trade in America to Fray Bartolomé de las
Casas, and in what would appear to be a cynical remark, she states,
"Love for humanity introduced the germ of slavery in America" (12).
Then she introduces a relativist perspective on good and evil: "Today the
world is in such disarray that slavery should be seen as a relative good"
(13). Cuba, argues the countess, is sowing the bitter seeds of slavery,
which prove to be rooted in the economic life and survival of the island.
Moreover, the government is unlikely to stop a trade that has proven
extremely profitable. Between these half-truths lies the tragic impasse of
a successful economic system based upon colonialism and slavery.[6]

The countess then turns to a discussion of the cultural aspects of the slavery system, addressing the biases against the black slaves and the resulting dread of whites toward manual labor. Here, she overtly criticizes Europeans of low socioeconomic class who in order to distance themselves from the despised black slaves become the most cruel masters and most unproductive members of society. Merlin peppers her discourse with cases and examples drawn from her childhood experiences and from sources close to her entourage. She then stresses the impossibility of harmonious relations between the two races and bluntly dismisses the likelihood of a multiracial and equal society: "One could say that nature has signed with her own hand the incompatibility between the two races" (22).

The condition of slaves in Cuba, argues Merlin, is one blessed among the slave populations of the world. In a disgraceful attempt to paint slavery in Cuba as a benign system ruled by strict laws to protect the slaves from abuse, Merlin distorts reality to fit the argument. She illustrates her point by referring to the multiple advantages enjoyed by the Cuban slaves: the right to complain about mistreatment to the "royal defender of the slaves," "the right of a slave to buy his freedom in small payments," the right to own and sell the produce from the *conuco* (small patch of land to cultivate); in short, Merlin describes an illusory paternalistic society in which the slaves can change their luck by simply working hard and being responsible for their destinies. Surely Merlin knew her readership had undoubtedly heard or read about the condition of slaves in the colonies, but clinging to her newfound authority as a Creole, Merlin blamed the slaves themselves for their predicament: "The slave, object of exalted pity among Europeans, deprived of future and ambition, calm, indifferent, lives for the day, lets his master be in charge of his preservation, and, if he falls ill at twenty he will have the rest of his life taken care of, even if he lives for a century" (49).

Merlin continues with an arsenal of observations on the "natural" characteristics of the slaves: slaves used as domestics possess every chance to better their lives, but they are by nature lazy and vice-ridden (49). Slaves are beggars that abuse the generosity of the masters (50). They often prefer slavery after having bought their freedom and having suffered the rigors of living without the paternalistic tutelage of their master (53).

She then compares the laws that control and punish runaway slaves in Cuba, France, and England to prove the benign nature of Cuban slavery (53–54). In comparing the work of a European journeyman and a slave, she finds that the latter shows fatigue, discouragement, and weakness while the former expresses happiness, vigor, and intelligence. In the European worker Merlin finds the fruits of civilization and good institutions (59).

At this point, Merlin changes strategies by asserting the political purpose of the essay. Her solution to the island's ills lies in the massive immigration of European labor to replace the slave. In order to attract the European worker Merlin has to dispel certain notions about Cuba. She concedes that life in the plantation is fraught with disease and violence in spite of the good care and special attention the slaves receive from their masters (60–63). She attempts to explain the high mortality rate in the plantation as a direct result of the "natural constitution" of the Africans who "are sensitive to atmospheric changes" (63). The problem is compounded by epidemics of yellow fever and cholera that Merlin assures readers only affect blacks. White Creoles and foreigners need not fear disease and climatic troubles: "There are numerous examples of the benefits and positive influences that our climate bestows upon foreigners" (67). She then asserts, "so, without any fear, foreigners can come to cultivate our virgin fields that offer incalculable and yet unexploited treasures" (67). Merlin seems to be writing a travel brochure to lure Europeans to invest and work in the island and, of course, to increment the white population. To reassure prospective settlers about the benign relationship between master and slave, Merlin unabashedly constructs a fairy tale in describing the master/slave relationship: "The kindness of the Cuban slave-owner inspires in the slave a respect that approaches a cult"; "the master is for the slave his fatherland and his family"; "(the slave) is passionate in his hatred as in his love; but almost never is the master the object of his revengeful wrath" (68). And to complete this picture of harmonious bliss in colonial Cuba, Merlin adds, "The inhabitants of Cuba not only favor slave emancipation by providing them with ways to get money, but also sometimes they give them their freedom" (74), and "Blacks identify with their masters' interests" (78).

Merlin oscillates between extreme positions regarding the character of slaves: they are either savages easily dominated by the intelligence of masters or simple and kind souls forever indebted to their benefactors. Examples of the inner beauty of slaves abound, creating a nonsensical sequence of narratives that contribute to the self-serving portraiture of slavery in Cuba. Merlin appears to be torn between articulating an "enlightened," humanitarian, and paternalistic view of slavery and representing the more pragmatic concerns of colonial landowners on the brink of losing the foundation of their wealth through the emancipation of slaves. This juggling act is a poignant display of the conflictive and complex forces within Creole society in Cuba. The countess embodies the dilemma of a society torn between its alliance to Spain and the impulse toward independence; a society uneasy about the racial imbalance of the island; an economy at once dependent and tied to the traffic of slaves to build itself and prosper; a sacharocracy facing the looming threat of being destroyed by the same forces that constituted its wealth.

Merlin espoused the ideas of her compatriots Domingo Del Monte and Antonio Saco, among others, to effect a change in the Spanish policies in the colony. Using threats, both veiled and overt, luring her readership to believe in a paradisiacal land, and confirming their prejudices about blacks and slavery, Merlin attempted to change the destiny of her island. However ill-conceived and self-serving this literary and political adventure proved to be, the countess of Merlin left a revealing testimony of a woman's perilous journey into the political essay.

NOTES

1. Molloy observes that "la petite histoire"—that is, the personal narrative of childhood and family life—is relegated during this period to the margins of the autobiographical discourse. The first autobiographical works of Mercedes Santa Cruz y Montalvo illustrate the inclusion of the self into the history of the island in order to weave a national/personal identity that will evolve throughout her works.

2. Several critics have noted that the financial gains derived from the publication of these volumes and their possible translations were the principal reason for their existence. In her private correspondence with her lover, Philarète Chasles, Merlin bitterly complains about her financial woes. However, to reduce the countess' production of literary works to a mercenary cause would be to overlook the early attraction that literature and the world of ideas held in Merlin's life.

3. Refer to Robert Paquette's *Sugar Is Made with Blood* and Murray's *Odious Commerce* for a detailed discussion of the different views on the violent suppression of the uprising and its political consequences.

4. It is interesting to note that Merlin's works were translated into Spanish without delay. Her *Les loisirs d'une femme du monde* was translated into English as *Memoirs of Mme. Malibran*. The countess herself was in the process of translating the *La Havane* into English and considering a German version, according to her correspondence with her lover and collaborator Philarète Chasles. Domingo Figarola-Caneda, in his volume dedicated to the countess, *La condesa de Merlin* (Paris: Editions Excelsior, 1928), lists the translations and editions of Merlin's

works he consulted in the libraries of Madrid, Paris, Brussels, London, Milan, and Berlin.

5. This account found itself almost immediately translated into English and reproduced in the form of an extensive quote in the work of the abolitionist George William Alexander, *Letters on the Emancipation*, published in London in 1842. All the English translations here of "Los esclavos en las colonias españolas" are my own.

6. The slave trade had been encouraged and protected by all European nations. The great influence of abolitionist societies on the British government was a development few had foreseen, and one that was not to last more than a couple of decades. The expansionist and annexationist designs of Britain and the United States, however ill founded, determined the political path of both the Spanish and the Cuban leadership. The terror and utter paranoia that pervaded the 1830s and 1840s in Cuba point to the delicate balance that the Spanish government had to strike between a protectionist position toward the colony and the implementation of the slave trade laws of 1835. These laws were considered unjust and an offense to the autonomy of the Spanish monarchy.

WORKS CITED

Alexander, G. W. *Letters on the Emancipation.* 1842. New York: Negro University Press, 1982.

Figarola-Caneda, Domingo. *Correspondencia íntima de la Condesa de Merlin.* Madrid, Paris: Industrial Gráfica Reyes, 1928.

Molloy, Sylvia. *At Face Value: Autobiographical Writing in Spanish America.* Cambridge: Cambridge University Press, 1991.

Murray, David R. *Odious Commerce: Britain, Spain and the Abolition of the Cuban Trade.* Cambridge: Cambridge University Press, 1980.

Paquette, Robert L. *Sugar Is Made with Blood: The Conspiracy of La Escalera and the Conflict between Empires over Slavery in Cuba.* Middletown, Conn.: Wesleyan University Press, 1988.

Santa Cruz y Montalvo, María de las Mercedes (Countess of Merlin). *Los esclavos en las colonias españolas.* Madrid: Imprenta de Alegría y Charlain, 1841.

———. *La Havane.* 3 Vols. Paris: Amyot, 1844.

———. *Mis doce primeros años.* 1831. Havana: Imprenta El Siglo XX, 1922.

———. *Viaje a La Habana.* 1844. Havana: Editorial de Arte y Cultura, 1974.

Nancy

Saporta

Sternbach

"MEJORAR LA CONDICIÓN DE MI SECSO"

THE ESSAYS OF

ROSA GUERRA

U ntil Argentina's most recent dictatorship (1976–1983), historians had tended to concur that the nineteenth-century dictatorship of Juan Manuel Rosas was the cruelest and bloodiest in that country's history. Even deflected against the atrocities of the 1970s and 1980s in Argentina, Rosas' twenty-year reign of terror over the Argentine population can hardly be understated. All aspects of cultural life, including freedom of speech and freedom of the press, came to a halt— both for men and, naturally, for women. In a country that had only just begun to forge a national identity, this paralysis virtually brought intellectual life to a standstill. When Rosas fell in 1852, the political gap that suddenly appeared gave birth to a liminal moment: Argentines found themselves in the position of being able to create the nation that they had imagined forty years earlier. In no small measure, such an imagining was enabled by the sudden proliferation of periodicals of every kind and every political persuasion.[1] Many of those often short-lived, always urgent newspapers or journals not only contained articles by women but were founded, headed, and run by women who used the periodical press as a means to further their cause, voice their opinions, and break the silence of political and sexual oppression.[2] These women essayists took advantage of the fissures in the political system in order to create, foment, and position their uniquely female voices as political subjects. But not all of them were willing to embark upon such a radical undertaking openly since, as we shall see, a woman writer was not only an anomaly and aberration but also a threat. Thus, in order to negotiate the reality of their culture (patriarchal, in spite of its new democracy) with the urgency of their female voice (feminist, in spite of the lack of the term), women essayists often embedded within their concern a "double-voiced discourse," which "embodies the social, literary, and cultural heritage of both the muted and dominant" groups (Showalter 263).

Two writers in particular whose names continually appear in these journals are Juana Manso (sometimes known as Juana Manso de Noronha, 1819–1875) and Rosa Guerra (early 1800s–1894). That most contemporary readers—especially outside of Argentina—have never heard of them is hardly surprising given all the factors that have historically contributed to silence women's voices. Because of space constraints, in this essay I will concentrate solely on Rosa Guerra's essays in spite of some similarities between the two women. They both began as schoolteachers, as it was one of the only respectable professions for nineteenth-century women, and both worked on Sarmiento's education project (Fletcher 99; Hodge 50). Both of them struggled incessantly for women's rights through their activism and their writing while simultaneously insisting that women not make a profession of writing. Such a paradox in their own lives suggests that the double-voiced discourse was not a mere rhetorical device but rather one of the only recourses available to them.

In Guerra's case, such discourse mediates her lived experience as a woman writer with her unwillingness to submit to the harshness of patriarchal public scrutiny. In order not to alienate her potential audience, Guerra *appeared* to adopt what Linda Alcoff has called an "essentialist" definition of women, that is, one that salutes her "identity [as a woman] independent of her external situation" (433), an identity in this case consisting of moral superiority, virtue, and her saintly mission of motherhood.[3] One of the problems with such a definition, as Alcoff points out, is that it is grounded on principles of androcentrism and misogyny and pretends to "define, delineate, and capture" womanhood in categories that anyone would find unthinkable if applied to men (406). For that reason, it hardly seems consonant with a radical proposition of the transformation of government, revolution, and change that these writers also espoused, once the black cloud over the horizon—their metaphor for Rosas—had finally disappeared (*La Camelia*). Yet I will argue here that this essentialist notion was only the veneer for another, ultimately more important framing of the concept of woman, a subject positionality that "makes her identity relative to the constantly shifting context, to a situation that includes a network of elements involving others, the objective economic conditions, cultural and political institutions and ideologies" (Alcoff 433). While decidedly not contradicting the essentialist rheto-

ric, and even appearing to embrace it, Guerra also established and determined a mid-nineteenth-century Argentine identity politics for women.
Yet what she truly does is not only deconstruct the essentialist definition
altogether but position herself to imagine and create her own concept of
womanhood.

Guerra negotiates this task through a rhetoric of negation and false
modesty, which pretends to conform to the mid-century (essentialist)
ideal of womanhood. Yet by her own example and by scripting another
clearly readable subtext she also manages to create a space for women's
writing in the new democracy. Put another way, Guerra (as well as
Manso, who wrote the first Argentine history to be used in the public
schools) uses and ultimately appropriates this literary space so that
she—or any woman—could become a writer. Thus, the legacy that they
leave our century is at least twofold: a woman's right to define and determine her own identity, including her not-to-be-underestimated right to
become a writer, and a tradition of sisterhood and foremotherhood that
would serve as a model to this day.[4]

But can we be so sure that Guerra and others even knew what they
were doing? Is a contemporary feminist theory of subject positionality
for a nineteenth-century woman writer another example of feminist cultural imperialism? By insisting that Guerra's intentionality was contradictory to her own claims of essentialism, I will attempt to show that
Guerra purposely used a double-voiced discourse in order to subvert the
patriarchal rhetoric and espouse the causes she so passionately embraced
without alienating her audience.

I believe that the symbols, metaphors, allegories, and rhetorical strategies of her periodical *La Educación* (1852) stand as a paradigm for both
her own work and that of future women essayists. Its first issue's subtitle
informs us that it is "religious, poetic, and literary," and is dedicated to
the "Honorable Charitable Society" (who had control of the school system) and the Argentine "bello sexo" (fair sex).[5] Guerra's main interest
here and elsewhere is education for women, but in order to engage her
readers, she employs a series of metaphors standard in the nineteenth
century, each of which triggers or leads to the next until she places herself
squarely in the living room of her readers and can take up the topic of
the family.

> *Education, gentlemen, is a flowing, inexhaustible*
> *fountain of good, of pleasure, the origin and begin-*

ning of all social delights.—From good education
emanates the peaceful and sweet union of marriage,
the calm of families in domestic life, tender relation-
ships between siblings, respect and love of children for
their parents, and parental love toward children.
From these small societies, nations, republics, king-
doms, and empires are formed.

Like many others of her day, Guerra posited the family as the metaphor for the nation, so it only took a small leap of imagination for readers
to make the connection (Sommer 20). In so doing, Guerra anticipates her
next argument, which is that poorly educated "men" do not make the
kind of citizens needed to populate the new Argentine democracy. Thus,
she shows how it is in the interest of families to educate their children for
the future of the nation. Yet in the first three paragraphs, in seeming
contradiction to the spirit of her dedication of the newspaper to women,
Guerra is careful only to mention men, reminding readers that "a meeting of evil men who will tear each other apart" could never be a nation
about to "constituirse" (constitute itself, make a constitution).

Finally, after this lengthy introduction, Guerra dares to speak the truth
that motivates her: "Without a doubt, when I speak about education, I'm
not just talking about men. I'm talking about education in general and
especially for women." For readers familiar with Guerra's style, the
many rhetorical questions that follow, coupled with Guerra's sarcasm
and distinctively feminist voice, are trademarks of her text, as in the remark: "But just who are these women who dare to raise their voices
demanding education?" Before answering in her own voice, Guerra gives
all the essentialist arguments and positions regarding education that were
commonly printed: "These unfortunate beings are considered slaves in
primitive societies or, among the Asians, flowers destined for gifts or
pleasure, but kept in chains just the same." In contradiction to such a
position, and in her capacity of creating an identity politics for the group
"woman-as-citizen," Guerra states, "Even in cultured places . . . women
are only considered capable of governing a family." Having established
in her introduction that nations are a series of families, Guerra has now
effectively undermined the discursive practice of her time by announc-
ing, or insinuating, that a woman who can govern a family can govern a
nation. Yet she knows that this radical discourse must be mitigated by
confirming the reality of women's lives—thus her next sentence: "How

awful to be a woman!" The irony of this and other passages penned by
Guerra underscores the need for women to maintain a sense of humor
coping with patriarchal injunctions.[6]

On yet another rhetorical level, recognizing that her own voice, that
of the woman who identifies herself as "redactora" in the next issue, is
too threatening to win readers over to her cause, Guerra employs a
strategy of reversing pronouns that also reveals her strength and ideological positioning. Thus, for example, because "strong" women were
universally equated with be(com)ing masculinized, Guerra removes herself as a possible example by employing either the third person singular
"she" or simply the word "woman." Such a tactic permits at least two
results. In the first instance, it separates Guerra, the writer, from self-
referentiality, as in the sentence "If she's smart she has to hide it." She is
decidedly not saying, but certainly implying, "I've had to hide my intelligence." Second, it transforms the notion of woman from the coy to the
rational, each of the positions that sparked the debates of her time. In yet
another subversive reversal, Guerra attempts, by use of the pronoun
"we," to include herself in the essentialist definition of woman as protest
against women's oppression and their weakened position in the political
structure, or the "outmoded custom." In this manner readers, both male
and female, feel that they are identifying with that first-person-plural
Guerra without having to consider her to be the horror of all women:
strong, masculine, and educated. Each time Guerra includes herself as
simply one more member of the "bello secso," as when she claims ironically to raise her "débil voz" (weak voice) simply to found the paper. In
fact, she actually reverses and reconstructs the category of "woman,"
redefining it outside the dominant patriarchal paradigm while appearing
to agree with the essentialist definition of "woman" in her culture.

Though her next tack appears to appeal to democracy, Guerra knows
her country too well to rely solely on democratic principles and thus
reverts to religion. By invoking the Creator rhetorically and ironically,
she not only questions male supremacy but also positions herself to question the construction of gender in her society: "Did the Creator of the
world institute some law from which it was deduced that woman was
inferior?" While her readers are still reeling from the affirmation that
Divine Rule endowed women with the same faculties as men, Guerra
moves on: "No matter how she is educated, a girl must not become a
lawyer, writer, or poet." In my reading of this, Guerra deliberately imi-
tates the repressive voice of patriarchal authority in order to criticize the
construction of gender in her society.

Recognizing the impossiblity of obtaining equal educational opportunities for women for their own sakes, self-improvement, or satisfaction, Guerra suggests that a policy be adopted for the good of the nation:
women will become *useful* members of their society, a goal to which she
herself aspires. For that reason, and given all we know about her, her
own voice, textually aligned to the first person plural, cannot be self-
referential when she entreats, "Wise and paternal Government . . . we
weak women unite ourselves with you from the bottom of our hearts to
help us carry out the arduous and difficult task of our political regeneration." Nor are her adjectives "wise" and "paternal" convincing, unless
one understands them ironically. What was true was that women's position both as subject and as citizen in the new government was bound to
change, or at least the women thought it should. But they would never
convince the men in the government of that unless they appeared to conform to accepted social stereotypes in which men were wise and paternal
and women the moral fiber of the society in their capacity as mothers:
"Male children receive their first impressions from women," who teach
them to protect women from tyranny in order to be worthy of their
love. Thus, education for women could be read as a preventive measure
against tyranny: "Educate your daughters, they will be the mothers of
that generation." Again the question is open: does she want to promote
women as active agents of education within the family, or is she recognizing that women already have this role and thus promoting a larger
public involvement for them? To press her point, Guerra reverts to the
common political practice of pitting rivals against each other, in this case
the new government against Rosas. Knowing their hatred for the tyrant,
and knowing that they would not want to be outdone by him, she closes
her argument reminding readers that even Rosas "knew full well . . . the
influence that women have, and the role they play . . . in revolutions and
change." And if women in Rosas' regime were involved citizens, why
not women like herself?

Anticipating the reaction of a conservative, patriarchal government,
Guerra knows that in order to make an argument for woman's role as
citizen, one must do so without appearing to jeopardize or even question
her role as mother. Thus she gives a simultaneous reading of her idealized new society: "Give women an education without altering the sweet
and tender sentiments of her woman's heart." The previous essentialist
remark, then, does not take precedence over her true concern: education
should teach her to understand "los deberes de ciudadana" (her responsibilities as a citizen). Since woman-as-citizen is also responsible for cre-

ating both female and male citizens, her role cannot be underestimated. But this does not appear to be as important to Guerra as assuring that women have the best chance to excel in her society:

> *I'm not saying that you should educate her for the forum, for war, for court, or for poetry or literature; but do educate her so that she be given full range for her inclinations and ideas, and if you should discover the spark of genius . . . protect her, give her means.*

Guerra immediately subverts her own text again, after saying that women need not be educated for war, by spelling out exactly what women did during the war—and this was without an education for it. What has been true for women across cultures and centuries also holds here: during time of war "we experienced the need to be given an education enabling us to fend for ourselves, our needs . . . wives without husbands, mothers without sons, sisters without brothers." Guerra describes the heroism of everyday women who worked to feed their families, who dressed as men, who slipped notes and money into the food baskets of jailed men, who subverted Rosas' spies, who accompanied men to the battlefields. A supposedly "weak and insignificant being" became self-sufficient, attempting afterwards, as did many women throughout history, not to lose the independence achieved during wartime. Thus the category of "woman" that began the essay ("weak" and "insignificant") has just gained new currency: notwithstanding Guerra's irony, she is now a person fit to rise to any occasion even with a meager education. Though an education would catapult her even further in the sociopolitical system, Guerra prefers to let her readers deduce this rather than to say so directly.

Guerra's last appeal is to the Minister of Public Education himself. Not only does she remind him that "no man has risen to a position of power, the height of glory, to the apogee of knowledge without having gone through the rudiments of primary education in the *mother* tongue" (my emphasis), she also adds that evil men come from mothers or nannies with "perverse instincts" while eminent men have had virtuous, educated mothers committed to the cause of the people. Thus, women should be educated not for their own good but for that of the republic.

Guerra's second issue of *La Educación* follows her previous pattern; once again she establishes the dichotomy between essentialism and subject positionality in her discussion of motherhood and women writers. Having devoted her entire first issue to education, here she develops her own voice as a woman writer, the "redactora" of the journal. With our twentieth-century perspective, we can see how she utilizes the coy strategy of camouflaging her strength in order to advance women's power in politics and women's possibilities as writers. If in the previous essay she identified herself as an insignificant woman with a weak voice, now she has taken the affirmative step of choosing her agency by declaring her role in the paper.

In this issue, then, her primary concern is to assure that she has company; what she advocates here is the practice of writing for women. In fact, this is so important to her that she is willing to go to any length, make any compromise, in order to achieve it. But again, she must straddle the line between the two positions she identified earlier. Therefore, while complaining about the "old, deeply rooted routines" that bound women to an essentialist position, she is careful to assert that she has no desire for a literary reputation, which would attract "criticism and ridicule," as it inevitably did in Manso's case in the next decade.[7] Even with the literary reputation Guerra had established by the time she published the paper in 1852, she prefers for her reference to include other women in addition to herself, undoubtedly from her same social class and already literate. Although her readership is clearly not inclusive of the entirety of the nineteenth-century Argentine population, she directs her discourse to the new generation of young mothers who will educate future citizens. While she exalts motherhood as the most sacred of female professions, what harm could it do if this young mother jotted down a few lines while rocking the cradle?

> *Ten or twelve lines written at the foot of her child's cradle, rocked as she writes, under that divine influence as mother, in one of those ecstatic moments so frequent in motherly love, don't make a housewife waste time nor do they distract her from the sacred obligations she has as mother of the family.*

Guerra knows woman's "place" in her culture, but she is also willing to subvert and transgress its borders by conflating political action and motherhood.[8] When she claims that this writing would most certainly not be given to the public or be taken as a profession for women, Guerra appears to reassign women to that traditional place. She even goes so far as to say that husbands should welcome this activity, for it could actually make a man "poseedor" (owner) of his wife's thoughts. Considering that men already owned women's lives and bodies, by appealing to their egos to control women's imagination as well, Guerra accomplishes a way for women to write and men to live with it. Thus, the same discourse of appearing to conform to her culture's definition of woman simultaneously undermines it.

Conjugal bliss, however, is not what motivates Guerra; rather, she sees herself and all women as citizens of this great new nation. With a new generation of educated mothers, everything "brusque and rude" would disappear, and the world would cease to speak of Argentina as an insignificant society. Women like herself, writing essays, founding newspapers, have no "guide" or "advice" and no foremothers. Yet, her aim is modestly expressed as "el solo y único deseo de ser útil con mis pocas luces a mi país y mejorar la condición de mi secso" (the one and only desire to be useful to my country with my limited education and to improve the condition of my sex).

Clearly, Guerra was not a woman of "pocas luces," and improving the condition of her sex meant going far beyond simply obtaining an education for women. But Guerra and others, including her adversaries, knew that education (in conjunction with motherhood) was the first step in establishing women's agency in their culture, an agency that would eventually prepare them for the forum, the court, literature, and poetry. If the mid-nineteenth-century Argentine public was not prepared for radical reform in women's education—a women's revolution from the trenches—that revolution would have to take place from within those selfsame institutions of the culture that oppressed women in the first place. Here, then, is where Guerra registers her double-voiced discourse: appearing to speak from the dominant discourse that assigned women to designated roles as submissive wives and sweet mothers, she also uses every conceivable argument to get women educated, to get them to write. That she needed to establish such a discourse evidences the immutability of gender roles in nineteenth-centry Argentina and the vested interest her readers had in having them remain so. In my reading of Guerra's essays, the double-voiced discourse was merely a foil to establish her own feminist voice. By reading these short journal and newspaper articles as essays, I hope to show that we can indeed identify a woman's voice and subject positionality as early as 1852 in Argentina. Though it would take quite some time for the same to emerge in fiction and poetry, voices such as Guerra's serve as a paradigm for Latin American women writers who established a program for women, women's rights, and women's education against all odds.

NOTES

Much of the initial thought that went into this essay originated in a coauthored feminist project with Lourdes Rojas (Rojas and Sternbach, 1993). Many of the insights that appear here come from those brainstorming sessions when we first started to unravel this topic. My debt to her is immeasurable.

1. I am referring to Benedict Andersen's concept of imagined communities for both the idea of nationalism and that of a print vernacular.

2. June Hahner has used the term "the women's free press" to designate this phenomenon in Brazil. Some of the Argentine periodicals that proliferated during this time were *Album de Señoritas, La Camelia, La Ilustración,* and *La Siempre-Viva.* While some took up the topics of the day, many used the printing press to bring women's issues to the fore. Education for women was a major theme in both mainstream periodicals and the women's alternative ones.

3. This is also the case for twentieth-century essayists such as Gabriela Mistral. Clearly, we begin to note a tradition in Latin American women's writing that draws upon the same strategies regardless of the epoch of the writer. I am grateful to Alberto Sandoval for bringing the case of Mistral to my attention and for his careful reading of an earlier draft of this chapter.

4. We might add that this tradition of foremothers was begun by none other than Sor Juana Inés de la Cruz who, according to Josefina Ludmer, also employed "the tricks of the weak" in order to accommodate or at least appear to accommodate herself to her audience.

5. Guerra uses both spellings, "secso" and "sexo," in the same issue. Because of the brevity of the essays, some only consisting of one page and lacking titles, I have not included page numbers or titles. All citations are from the two short essays in question.

La Educación began publication on 24 July 1852 and ceased publication after six issues for lack of funds to continue.

6. Readers no doubt will also be reminded of Sor Juana's strategies here. Although we have no way of knowing if Guerra ever read *La respuesta,* we can see that the strategies and tactics that she employs here might be considered typical for women writers living within the confines of patriarchy.

7. Because of her writings, Manso was accused of lunacy and of not being in control of her senses.

8. It is tempting here to read Guerra's suggestions as a precedent for the political actions of the Mothers of the Plaza de Mayo.

WORKS CITED

Alcoff, Linda. "Cultural Feminism versus Post-Structuralism: The Identity Crisis in Feminist Theory." *Signs: Journal of Women and Culture in Society* 13:3 (Spring 1988), 405–436.

Andersen, Benedict. *Imagined Communities: Reflections on the Origin and Spread of Nationalism.* London: Verso, 1983.

La Camelia. Buenos Aires. 1:3 (15 April 1852).

La Educación. Buenos Aires. 1:1–2 (24 July 1852, 31 July 1852).

Fletcher, Lea. "Patriarchy, Medicine, and Women Writers in Nineteenth-Century Argentina." In *The Body and the Text: Comparative Essays in Literature and Medicine,* 91–101. Ed. Bruce Clarke and Wendell Aycock. Lubbock: Texas Tech University Press, 1990.

Guerrero, César. *Mujeres de Sarmiento,* 75–105 (refers to Juana Manso). Buenos Aires: Artes Gráficas Bartolomé U. Chiesino, 1960.

Hahner, June E. *Emancipating the Female Sex: The Struggle for Women's Rights in Brazil, 1850–1940.* Durham: Duke University Press, 1990.

Hodge, John E. "The Formation of the Argentine Public Primary and Secondary School System." *The Americas* (1987), 45–65.

Masiello, Francine. "Between Civilization and Barbarism: Women, Family and Literary Culture in Mid–Nineteenth Century Argentina." In *Cultural and Historical Grounding for Hispanic and Luso-Brazilian Feminist Literary Criticism,* 517–566. Ed. Hernán Vidal. Minneapolis: Institute for the Study of Ideologies and Literature, 1989.

Rey del Guido, Clara. *Contribución al estudio del ensayo en Hispanoamérica.* Caracas: Academia Nacional de la Historia, 1985.

Rojas, Lourdes, and Nancy Saporta Sternbach. "Latin American Women Essayists: 'Intruders and Usurpers.'" In *The Politics of the Essay: Feminist Perspectives,* 172–195. Ed. Ruth-Ellen Joeres and Elizabeth Mittman. Bloomington: Indiana University Press, 1993.

Showalter, Elaine. "Feminist Criticism in the Wilderness." In *The New Feminist Criticism,* 243–270. Ed. Elaine Showalter. New York: Pantheon, 1985.

Shumway, Nicolas. *The Invention of Argentina.* Berkeley: University of California Press, 1991.

Sommer, Doris. *Foundational Fictions: The National Romances of Latin America.* Berkeley: University of California Press, 1991.

Nina M. Scott | # SHORING UP THE "WEAKER SEX"

AVELLANEDA AND NINETEENTH-CENTURY GENDER IDEOLOGY

Gertrudis Gómez de Avellaneda (Cuba, 1814–1873) is not known as an essayist: she was principally a poet, novelist, and playwright, famous in her lifetime—at times even notorious for her unconventional love life—and best known today for her radical two first novels, *Sab* (1841) and *Dos mujeres* (Two Women, 1842), some plays, and her earlier lyric poetry.[1] Avellaneda had traveled to Spain in 1836, and by means of her talent, her striking physical appearance, and her astuteness in marketing herself and her writing, had come to be a noteworthy figure in the Madrid literary scene. As the stormy Avellaneda aged, she also mellowed in character: in time her initial radicalism gave way to greater piety and conservatism. "La mujer" (Women), the essay Avellaneda published in 1860 and the focus of this study, is thus an anomaly in a number of ways: the essay was not a genre she habitually cultivated, it was published in Cuba and not in Spain,[2] and though it was a late piece, it is openly critical of male privileges and as radical as works she had composed much earlier in her life.

"La mujer" appeared in the pages of the *Album cubano de lo bueno y lo bello* (The Cuban Album of the Good and the Beautiful), the women's magazine Avellaneda founded in Cuba in 1860; it was later republished, with slight variations in the wording, in the 1914 edition of her complete works. Rather than look only at the essay itself, however, I want to study it within its context, i.e., the pages of the journal in which it was first presented. The twelve issues of the *Album*, published biweekly before its demise six months later, offer a fascinating frame for women's roles in nineteenth-century literary production, for Avellaneda's own involvement in this sphere, and ultimately for the essay itself.[3]

In 1859 Avellaneda returned to Cuba for the first time since her departure twenty-six years earlier; her second husband was a Spanish officer who had been assigned a post there, one he would hold until his death in 1864. As she was by then a very famous writer, Avellaneda was given a triumphant reception in her homeland, although some of the younger intellectuals who aspired to Cuban independence frowned on Avellaneda's association with Spanish officials (Portuondo, *Capítulos* 224). The Royal Academy of Spain had denied her admission seven years earlier (a rebuff she never got over), but the Lyceum of Havana lionized her, and in late January 1860, at a glittering ceremony in the Teatro Tacón, she was honored for her literary achievements by being crowned with a diadem of gold laurel leaves. Tula, as her friends called her, had definitely arrived in Cuba.

We don't know if Avellaneda planned to launch a women's magazine before she returned to Cuba, but the date the first issue came out had undoubtedly been carefully orchestrated: February 18, 1860. Everyone would be sure to recall her recent honor: lest they forget, however, one of the features of the publication was a gossipy "Revista de la Quincena" (The Fortnight's Review), the author of which made much of the ceremony in his column, in spite of claiming that his editor had given him strict orders to the contrary: "Because of modesty, Tula forbade me to mention the festivities celebrated on January 27 in the Tacón theater, and I will follow those orders. But I won't mention Tula: I'll speak of Madame Avellaneda" (28). Another clever touch in this first issue was an adulatory sonnet to the Countess of San Antonio. I initially asked myself, Who is this lady and why is she being profiled in this way? Read the gossip column. The Countess of San Antonio, magnificently coiffed and surrounded by Spanish officials, presided over Avellaneda's coronation from her box at the theatre. Another tidbit: one of the two ladies chosen to place the crown on Avellaneda's head was Luisa Pérez de Zambrana, Cuba's reigning woman poet; she and her husband later published extensively in the *Album* and Avellaneda wrote the preface to Pérez de Zambrana's book of poetry (1860). Networks are networks.

Avellaneda was very familiar with journalism in Spain, not only through her own frequent publications in the press, but because as early as 1845 she had been asked to direct a women's magazine in Madrid, a venture that ended after only one issue appeared (Kirkpatrick 77; Miller 204). During the nineteenth century, Spanish women had begun to participate more and more actively in the production as well as the consumption of literature: they progressed from readers to contributors and finally to editors of their own magazines and journals. Many of these publications were short-lived, just as the *Album cubano* proved to be, but the very involvement of women in this sphere was an important step in their personal and artistic emancipation.

The content of the *Album* was standard fare for female readers of the time: serialized fiction, poetry, some essays, music commentary, edifying pieces on moral deportment, social gossip, letters to the editor, and lengthy pieces on fashion. Another feature was the "Galería de mujeres célebres" (Portraits of Famous Women), brief biographies that focused on the lives and achievements of illustrious women of the past, a time-honored ploy to legitimize women's activities in the present. Christine de Pizan had used this tactic in the Renaissance and Sor Juana Inés de la Cruz in the Baroque, and it was popular again in Avellaneda's own day. "The general female readership seems to have been much interested in women of the past who had become part of literary history, for throughout the 1840s articles on Sor Juana Inés de la Cruz and Saint Teresa of Avila as well as on Sappho turned up in illustrated magazines and women's journals" (Kirkpatrick 326, n.9). A wide range of women are profiled in the *Album*; the portraits are not limited to Spain or even Western Europe but include a Persian ruler and a Chinese intellectual of the first century A.D. Critics tend to assume that Avellaneda wrote all of these biographies herself, but she signed only the sketches of Queen Isabella I, Aspasia Miletia, and Catherine the Great of Russia.[4] The piece on the Greek poet Sappho is one of the best and in style and content bears Avellaneda's stamp, but it was published without any signature, just as it had originally appeared in a Madrid journal in 1842 (Kirkpatrick 337).[5] The information about famous women of the past is not only interesting in and of itself, but, as we shall see, dovetails with similar catalogues Avellaneda used in her essay on "La mujer."

The first issue of her *Album* sets the stage for the ones to follow and is worth examining. Avellaneda led off with an introductory statement in which she declared her intentions for the publication: an essentially religious focus on works that would be morally uplifting as well as artistically rewarding, an aid to the human spirit in its striving toward God. In a more strident tone she addressed possible male detractors from her aims: "Oh yes! Know this once and for all, frivolous or *positivist* men, who judge art a futile human invention of mere entertainment!" (4). The two other contributions the editor made to her fledgling journal are a poem, "A las cubanas" (To Cuban Women), and the first part of a Swiss legend, "La montaña maldita" (The Cursed Mountain). In the poem she greets her Cuban sisters and states her happiness at her return and her gratitude for the affection that has tempered some harsh personal experiences.[6] This is one of the few contributions I have noted that Avellaneda directs at her Cuban environment; for the most part she tended to focus on European culture and indeed often recycled material either she or Spanish colleagues had already published in Spain. In the annals of the *Album* there are contributions by many illustrious Spanish literati whom she counted among her friends: Hartzenbusch, Fernán Caballero, Nicasio Gallego, Emilio Castelar.[7] Naturally she also featured pieces by the leading Cuban intellectuals such as Ramón Palma, Juan Clemente Zenea, José Ramón Betancourt, and so forth. Her journal thus became the meeting ground for a number of important writers on both sides of the Atlantic. As literary historian Portuondo observed, during her brief stay in her homeland Avellaneda played a significant role in the improvement of nascent Cuban literature (*Bosquejo* 30).

In terms of her own contributions to the *Album*, the twelve issues feature a number of poems by the editor that by their content seem to indicate that many of these, too, had been written at some earlier date.[8] One of the early issues also includes a lengthy eulogy to one María Verdejo y Durán, a great admirer of Avellaneda who died at the age of twenty, when she had just begun to write creatively. Avellaneda must have been very fond of María. A number of works by Verdejo appear in subsequent issues of the *Album*, showing that, contrary to her usual aloofness in Spain, in Cuba Avellaneda followed in the footsteps of what Kirkpatrick calls the "lyrical sisterhood": women actively furthering the literary efforts of other women (82–83). The same can be said of her support of Luisa Pérez de Zambrana and of her sister, Julia Pérez y Montes de Oca, who was also a poet.

Like many Romantics, Avellaneda was fond of collecting folk legends, and she contributed three to the *Album*, two of them Basque and one Swiss in origin. One of the two Basque legends is fairly conventional, but "La montaña maldita" and "La dama de Amboto" (The Lady of Amboto) are quite different. In the Swiss tale, Marta, an aged mother, is treated with cruel indifference by her son Walter. Whereas he is one of the richest men in the canton, she lives alone and in poverty. The reason for the rift between mother and son is that Walter is an illegitimate child who has never ceased blaming Marta for the circumstances of his birth, while the mother is consumed by lifelong guilt for her past error. Indulgent, loving, forgiving, and humble, Marta is the quintessential "angel in the house"—until her son refuses her pleas for shelter and turns her out into the cold. Then the mother curses her son, his riches, and the mountain on which he lives. "She says no more; no one dares reply; all is wrapped in dreadful silence, and she leaves the inhospitable house without a glance at the perverse son whom she has just given over to divine retribution" (46). Marta dies from exposure, but when morning comes the entire mountain is white, its flanks encased in ice and strewn with boulders, while Walter's body lies crushed beneath the ruins of his once flourishing farm. So powerful is the mother's curse that the mountain remains forever barren.

"La dama de Amboto" tells of Pedro and María de Urraca, aristocratic siblings who live in a castle in the Basque mountains. Whereas Pedro dotes on María, the beautiful and ambitious sister feels only bitterness for the position in which her gender has placed her:

> *Her pride rebelled against the perpetual dependence*
> *to which the smallness of her fortune condemned her,*
> *for all the possessions and domains of their luxurious*
> *house were the property of one who owed the preroga-*
> *tives of his sex to chance. The young woman railed*
> *against the injustice of such privileges, and the brother*
> *who enjoyed them became the target of her hatred.*
> (110)

When the two go off on a boar hunt, Pedro is ostensibly killed by an accidental fall into a gorge, leaving María free and rich, but eventually the memory of her fratricide drives her to madness and a fall into the same abyss.

Both of these folk tales focus attention on the roles that society dictated to women and the destructive power that is unleashed when the women break out of them. In both stories rage and violence are very close to the surface and may well reflect emotions the author had felt. Avellaneda had battled gender privilege for many years, both in her family and in her profession. In her 1839 *Autobiography* she spoke of her brother Manuel's self-interest and insensitivity toward her, and of the galling economic dependence on the stepfather she disliked with such intensity. The injustice of gender privilege is also a leitmotif in "La mujer."

The essay appears in three parts in the *Album* and in four in the 1914 edition of Avellaneda's complete works. Her intent, Avellaneda says, is to study the role of women in four areas: religion, history, government, and intellectual life and the arts. Her examination of prevalent gender ideology illustrates to perfection just how nineteenth-century social norms divided the sexes, and how Avellaneda both accepted these "gendered blinkers" and fought against them.[9]

Running through all four of these essays is Avellaneda's desire to redefine the expression "the weaker sex."[10] Judging by the open sarcasm of her tone, this was a label that had irritated her for a long time: "We concede without the slightest reluctance that, given the duality that marks our species, Nature endowed man with superior physical strength, and we will not even dispute that he has greater intellectual prowess, which he appropriates for himself with little modesty" (34). Nevertheless, Avellaneda claimed that women excelled in matters of sentiment and feeling, and that therein lay the "weaker sex's" greatest strength, an opinion that was completely in tune with prevailing constructs of gender in nineteenth-century Europe. As Virginia Woolf said, "in the nineteenth century, a woman lived almost solely in her home and her emotions" (46).

In the first part of the essay, in which Avellaneda considers woman in the sphere of religion, she begins by underscoring a woman's accepted role as "angel in the house," always there to sacrifice herself for the sake of others. As daughter, wife, and mother, a woman habitually renders "three-fold tribute of unnoticed sacrifices" (35). Avellaneda focuses on Biblical women in the domestic sphere, examining Eve and Mary principally in their roles as mothers. As such they represent dialectic poles of motherhood: one with sinful progeny, the other the progenitor of the Savior. If Eve indeed bears the guilt of original sin, Mary's purity has expiated all humankind (the Eva-Ave dyad), but as long as we're on the topic of original sin, maintains Avellaneda, let's not forget that Adam sinned right along with Eve, whereas Mary's triumph is hers alone. Avellaneda also underscores the fact that women treated Christ far better than men did, and that in recompense the message of the Resurrection was first communicated to women. Mary Magdalene is singled out as a particularly loyal Christian, which is interesting, because as a former courtesan she represents the opposite of self-abnegating motherhood. For Avellaneda, Mary and Magdalene, spotless Virgin and repentant sinner, together symbolize "the glorious sex to whom the Eternal granted sovereignty in all feelings, and, through the merits of all [their] sacrifices, the first fruits of all victories" (37). In the final analysis, then, in religion the "weaker sex" prevailed over the "stronger."

I find it significant that this initial part of her essay should appear not
in the first but in the second issue of the *Album*, as though Avellaneda
wanted to avoid being too militant too early. She also structured the
progression of her four topics from the most conventional (woman as
mother) to the least (woman as intellectual). Furthermore, Part 1 is
framed by two carefully orchestrated companion articles: a very conventional piece by Luisa Pérez de Zambrana entitled "Charity in Women,"
exhorting her readers to be "simple as doves, sweet as children, good as
angels, and charitable and adorable as God's mother" (34), followed by a
letter from her husband Ramón Zambrana, the rector of the University
of Havana, who chides the male sex for excluding women from anything
weighty or transcendental and states his admiration for Avellaneda's
"natural propensity to choose serious, philosophical topics in her poetry"
(39). While Luisa's piece focused on the sanctity of the home, Ramón's
approbation enhanced Avellaneda's status outside of the purely domestic
sphere.

In Part 2 of "La mujer" Avellaneda examines the role of women in
history, and again returns to the alleged weakness of the feminine gender:
"It piques us somewhat to determine if the greater delicacy of our physical frame is an insurmountable obstacle that Nature placed in opposition
to intellectual and moral vigor; and whether, [though] enriched by treasures of the heart, Providence on the other hand cut us off from inherit-
ing the great faculties of intelligence and character" (226). Avellaneda
postulates that all great thoughts must of need spring from the
heart—already established as a predominantly female domain—and then
returns to deconstructing the stereotype of the "weaker" sex. Women are
capable not only of great acts of love but of valor, as shown by an extensive list of brave women of the past; the latter are especially to be admired
since women were not trained for this kind of activity. Avellaneda then
anticipates the charge that whereas women may perform isolated acts of
valor, they are incapable of sustained enterprises. No better example of
sustained enterprise exists than that of the government of nations, she
says, which becomes the theme of Part 3. After a long catalogue of illustrious women rulers, Avellaneda ends with some defiant statistics:

> *I think that we can throw down the gauntlet to the*
> stronger sex *and force it into this decisive contest: we*
> *women steadfastly maintain that of any ten queens,*
> *we can point out at least five who are deserving of*

respectful memory; dare [men] to show us fifty out of
any hundred kings who deserve the same honor?
(260)

Part 4, in my opinion, is the one closest to Avellaneda's heart, for it
addresses the issue of women's intellectual competence. With thinly disguised rage Avellaneda had previously alluded to a serious male scholarly
dispute as to whether or not women could even be classified as rational
beings (259); she now takes the opportunity to establish proof of their
rational and moral achievements in literature and the arts. The sciences
were a different matter, for as women were barred from the universities,
access to this field was automatically denied them. Given a chance,
women could also excel in science and mathematics, as several women
she cites had already done. Exclusion from male academies was as sore a
point with Avellaneda as it was with Virginia Woolf: as men have to
relinquish more and more of their prerogatives every day, she snapped,
being able to grow a beard has become the determining prerequisite for
admission to those hallowed halls. In spite of this exclusion, Avellaneda
proudly cites the names of a number of women who have distinguished
themselves in literature and the arts. Among them is Anacaona, the indigenous poet/priestess mentioned in chronicles of exploration of the
Caribbean and the only American woman included in her essay. Surprisingly, Avellaneda omits Sor Juana, though the two women had much in
common, most of all the battle for intellectual freedom in the face of
societal gender expectations. Although Avellaneda concludes her essay
by saying, "Far be it from me to present myself to my dear readers as
the worthy champion of our common desire" (262), she goes on to claim
both the intellectual and the moral high ground: only in countries where
women are honored is there genuine civilization and progress. Places
where the opposite is true are condemned to bondage, barbarism, and
moral decay.

Just as Avellaneda had done earlier, she was careful in placing Part 4
of "La mujer." This time her essay was inserted between two male-
authored articles that would do much to legitimize its message: "La razón
y la voluntad" (Reason and Will), which underscored the fallibility of
human reason without the intervention of God, and a letter from a ge-
ologist who excused himself for his numerous scientific digressions, but
stated that there was no reason to deprive Avellaneda's readership of
some knowledge of the earth's crust—a calculated swipe at those who

denied women access to the sciences. Thus, both in content and in textual strategy Avellaneda again used every means in her arsenal to debunk the classification of the "weaker sex."

Why did Avellaneda write this essay and why did she choose to publish it in Cuba? I can but speculate. The irony and sarcasm with which she addresses gender prejudice in this text indicate that this was a long-festering issue with her. She had already railed against it in her *Autobiography*, and Avellaneda's rejection from the Royal Academy had further wounded her pride and ambition. Beth Miller quotes from a number of her letters that attest to this bitterness (211–212). Avellaneda was doubly angry because exclusion from this body affected both her status as a writer and her purse, as the Spanish government often granted economic benefits to the *académicos*. Cuba's enthusiastic welcome of its distinguished daughter must have assuaged her feelings a good deal and given her the impetus to express resentments she had felt for so long. Her recognition as a major writer at the highest official levels in Cuba explains to me why she felt able to complete and publish the militant "La mujer" at this stage in her life. It is a pity that Avellaneda did not cultivate the essay further, for the scope and quality of this piece, not to mention her articulate defense of women's achievements, certainly merit her inclusion among the essayists profiled in this particular book.

NOTES

1. Susan Kirkpatrick, who has done some of the most perceptive and in-depth scholarship on Avellaneda to date, is of the opinion that after 1845, although she wrote prolifically, her lyric poetry at least is not of significant value (207).

2. Part 1 of "La mujer" was published in Madrid in the 1850s (Miller 213), but the essay appeared in its entirety in Havana.

3. The *Album* was only the second journal in Cuba to be directed by a woman (Greenberg 184–185). Avellaneda's journal probably died for lack of subscribers. For an in-depth look at women's activity in the field of journalism in Latin America, see Greenberg.

4. Avellaneda chose to highlight the empress' economic and social reforms; of Catherine's prurient sexual activities she says primly, "Let us piously draw a veil over those revealing flaws of human nature" (360).

5. Miller definitely attributes it to her (213), as does Bravo-Villasante, who views it as a mini-autobiography of Avellaneda herself (194).

6. She may have been referring to her husband Verdugo's stabbing in 1858. During the production of one of Avellaneda's plays, a wag had put a cat onstage in order to disrupt the performance. Verdugo met the perpetrator on a Madrid street a few days later, insults were exchanged, and the man stabbed Avellaneda's husband in the chest. Although Verdugo lived, his health was permanently impaired, leading to his early death.

7. Surprisingly, Avellaneda even republished an 1840 poem by Gabriel García y Tassara, her former lover and the father of her illegitimate daughter, who had abandoned both mother and child.

8. Another interesting item in the *Album* is an announcement that offers several of Avellaneda's works for sale. *Sab* and *Dos mujeres* had been banned in Cuba, one because of its attack on slavery and the other because its heroine was an adulteress. Nevertheless, one of the books Avellaneda was openly selling was precisely *Dos mujeres*.

9. Jill Ker Conway used this felicitous phrase in her recent talk on "Women's Studies and the Education of Women" at the celebration of the first anniversary of the Five College Women's Studies Research Center, South Hadley, Mass., Mount Holyoke College, 2 October 1992.

10. I have taken some liberties in translating the original "el sexo débil"; its literal meaning is "the weak sex," but as the expression "the weaker sex" is more common in English, I have used it instead. I have correspondingly translated "el sexo fuerte" as "the stronger sex." In my opinion this change has no effect on the thrust of Avellaneda's essay. All translations in this essay are mine.

WORKS CITED

Avellaneda, Gertrudis Gómez de. *Album cubano de lo bueno y lo bello: Revista quincenal de moral, literatura, bellas artes y modas. Dedicada al bello sexo y dirigida por Doña Gertrudis G. de Avellaneda.* Havana: Establecimiento Tipográfico La Antilla, 1860.

Bravo-Villasante, Carmen. *Una vida romántica: La Avellaneda.* Madrid: Instituto de Cooperación Iberoamericana, 1981.

Greenberg, Janet. "Toward a History of Women's Periodicals in Latin America: An Introduction" and "Toward a History of Women's Periodicals in Latin America: A Working Bibliography." In *Women, Culture and Politics in Latin America,* 173–231. Berkeley and Los Angeles: University of California Press, 1990.

Kirkpatrick, Susan. *Las Románticas: Women Writers and Subjectivity in Spain, 1835–1850.* Berkeley: University of California Press, 1989.

Miller, Beth. "Gertrude the Great: Avellaneda, Nineteenth-Century Feminist." In *Women in Hispanic Literature: Icons and Fallen Idols,* 201–214. Ed. Beth Miller. Berkeley: University of California Press, 1983.

Portuondo, José Antonio. *Bosquejo histórico de las letras cubanas.* Havana: Ministerio de Relaciones Exteriores, 1960.

————. *Capítulos de literatura cubana.* Havana: Editorial Letras Cubanas, 1981.

Woolf, Virginia. *Women and Writing.* Ed. Michele Barrett. New York: Harcourt, Brace, Jovanovich, 1979.

Francine

Rose

Masiello

LOST IN
TRANSLATION
EDUARDA MANSILLA
DE GARCÍA ON POLITICS,
GENDER, AND WAR

With his pathbreaking *Facundo* (1845), Sarmiento explained the ills of Argentina and proposed a course for the nation's future. Dismayed by the backwardness that haunted his country under Rosas, Sarmiento advanced a program for modernizing the state and for bringing the virtues of European civilization to bear upon barbarism at home. It is paradoxical, nonetheless, that the text considered to be the paradigm of nineteenth-century Latin American intellectual thought was marked by hybridization: a prime example of the excesses of the Romantic imagination, *Facundo* is both fiction and essay, narration and political treatise. Appearing first in the Chilean newspaper *El Progreso*, in the space usually reserved for serialized fiction, Sarmiento's masterpiece provides a clear example of those prepositivist impulses working against the limits of genre and absolute narrative form. In this way, civilization and barbarism as binary opposites were terms metaphorically crossed in the free form of the text, subjected to constant inversions of narrative structure and language.

Sarmiento's desire to conquer barbarism, as expressed in *Facundo*, continued long after the defeat of Rosas at Caseros and well into the period of Sarmiento's presidency, when he sought to consolidate national frontiers and repress the inhabitants of the pampas. In these years, the debate between federalists and unitarians had been altered considerably, changing the terms of meaning assigned to the conflict of "civilization against barbarism." Thus, the factionalism within the unitarian cause and the assertive stance of federalist intellectuals against the conscription of gauchos led to a reconsideration of the neat formula that Sarmiento had set in place in 1845.[1] Boundaries were occluded once again and the limits of meaning were tested.

In this context of muddled ideological goals and outcries over the forced recruitment of gauchos, it is not surprising that Eduarda Mansilla de García (1834–1892) questioned the presumptions of *Facundo* and issued a challenge to the military program set in operation by Sarmiento. This critique was set forth in a hybrid text, combining both essay and fiction, and made its debut in French a year before its appearance in Spanish.[2] *Pablo ou la vie dans les pampas* (Pablo, or Life in the Pampas, 1869) is startling not only for its structure, which evokes the impure forms of *Facundo*, but also for the resounding contestatory statement issued to Sarmiento, who was president of Argentina at the time of its publication.

Along with Juana Manuela Gorriti (1819–1892), Eduarda Mansilla de García was the most important woman writer of nineteenth-century Argentina. With an elegant style clearly linked to the mannerisms of the generation of 1880, Mansilla dedicated her life to musical composition, theatrical scripts, children's literature, novels, and journalism, and covered issues ranging from the early conquest of America to travelog reflections on modern North American culture.[3]

Unlike Gorriti, who was allied politically with Sarmiento in the struggle against Rosas and who lived the years of early federalist rule in political exile, Eduarda Mansilla carved another route through federalist and unitarian terrain. Niece of Rosas and brother of Lucio, of the Argentine generation of the 1880s, Eduarda's pure federalist origins were put in question by her marriage to Manuel Rafael García, an ambassador of unitarian persuasion who had achieved recognition for both international diplomacy and his writings on political economy and the law. A member of the Argentine privileged elite, García married Eduarda, forming a match that was likened to the union of Romeo and Juliet, owing to the opposing political forces that set the two families in conflict (Sosa de Newton 41). The contradictions of the nation's political debates also surfaced in Eduarda's writings as she alternately voiced criticism of unitarian military policy and severely chastised federalist inaction in the areas of education and civic reform.

Beyond the courtly refinements of her style, which often expressed a nostalgia for a perfect world no longer accessible to elites, Eduarda Mansilla de García, like her sisterly colleagues Juana Manso de Noronha and Juana Manuela Gorriti, also linked her identity as a writer to her interventions in national politics. Her project was to question the guiding principles of the modern state and to reshape narratives of the historical past in order to find a voice of her own. Her novel *Lucía Miranda* (1882), for example, recuperates legends of women engaged in the settlement of the Spanish territories. Other stories and theatrical works address the modernization of Argentine society and the need for changing mores and a public voice for women.

Her dilemmas as a woman writer surface even in the presumed authorship and gendered interests of her texts. Mansilla de García's early works were signed with the pseudonym "Daniel," a name belonging to one of her sons; her first novel, *El médico de San Luis* (The Doctor of San Luis, 1860), was dominated by a masculine narrator who surveyed and explained the lives of women; many of her later books, especially those of a more overtly political theme, were written in French. Anticipating a tradition that later would rise to prominence with Victoria Ocampo, here the Argentine woman writer assumed a voice in political discourse by using a language other than her own.

Pablo ou la vie dans les pampas provides an exemplary case of a counter-discourse to official programs of state, an incursion into political debates emerging from dissatisfied Argentine intellectuals in the decades following Caseros. Published in French and almost immediately translated into German and Spanish, *Pablo* was designed as a commentary on the modern Argentine nation. Drawn from Mansilla de García's perspectives abroad, it voices a clear resistance to President Mitre's (1862–1868) recruitment of gaucho labor to serve in the war with Paraguay and questions Sarmiento's subsequent military expansion during the years of his presidency (1868–1874); it also condemns federalists for their inaction in areas of civic reform. Ironically, Mansilla's textual strategies closely follow those of Sarmiento insofar as she situates national debate in the plains of Argentina and relies upon the figure of the gaucho outlaw to indict government policy.

Offering a broad panorama of the pampas, the text appeals to an exoticist view of Argentina while also serving as a corrective for a national political program gone astray. Mansilla's work narrates the trials of the gaucho Pablo, who is forced to leave the pampas when conscripted for military service in the border wars with Paraguay. Pablo is surprised by police in a roundup of peasants in the countryside; he is pressed to fulfill his military obligation and abandon his romance with Dolores. When he attempts to desert, he is captured and shot as an outlaw. Set against this primary plot is a secondary narrative about the women who organize the households of the pampas and search for their lost lovers and sons who have been taken off to jail or war. Mansilla thus tracks the sufferings of Dolores and of Micaela, Pablo's mother, exposing the disasters that befall Argentine women in the name of military expansion. Daughter of a federalist supporter and deeply in love with the gaucho Pablo, Dolores is attacked and killed in an Indian raid. Meanwhile, Micaela, widow of a unitarian, follows the troops to Buenos Aires in search of her son. When she learns of his death, she loses her sense of reason and wanders the desert in madness.[4]

Against this thinly lined plot, Mansilla de García weaves a number of interpolated essays on the nature of militarism and war and the future development of the country. As in Sarmiento's *Facundo*, the opening pages of *Pablo* track the immensity of the pampas with special attention to its vegetation, resources, and primitive beauty. Likened to the writings of Humboldt and Tschudi for its treatment of the American landscape, Mansilla de García's text extends a panoramic gaze over the nation's natural wealth.[5] But what especially commands attention and reminds us unequivocally of the opening pages of Sarmiento's masterwork is the positioning of human figures—the tracker, the *gaucho malo*, the *payador*—who roam the pampas. Mansilla de García is careful to underscore the precious quality of human labor, showing the talents and achievements of country folk who can better account for the nation than even the most able statesmen. Rationality, she claims, lies not in the emerging state but in the souls of its inhabitants and in those who have invested human resources in building a modern Argentina.

Although Mansilla was rarely swayed from her aristocratic pretensions, her sympathies toward the ignorant gaucho are expressed with great compassion. Pablo is described as an untutored savage, deprived of the benefits of civilization; nonetheless, he is richly endowed with feelings: "What could his poverty be—he asked himself—compared to absence, that most dreadful of evils that leads to the death of the soul? . . . How could he live apart from his beloved? And with that cruel reflection, his blood surged toward his heart threatening to explode" (28).[6] Mansilla sets out to humanize the gaucho and thus to make a case against the practice of military conscription that would take him from his home.[7]

In this respect, Mansilla is allied ideologically with writers such as José Hernández, who, shortly following the publication of *Pablo*, took up the defense of the gaucho in his *Martín Fierro* (1872, 1879). And like her brother, Lucio, in his *Excursión a los indios ranqueles* (1870), she maintains a focus on the pampas, attempting to give a literary version of the rural inhabitants of Argentina, who certainly held an exotic attraction for an audience of European readers. Nevertheless, in the French edition of the text (whose contents later would be modified for publication in Spanish), Eduarda expresses reservations about Argentine partisan politics and repeatedly notes the confused agenda belonging to both unitarians and federalists. Both sides have erred, she explains, in their exploitation of the gaucho and in depriving rural peoples of the civilizing benefits of education and literacy.

Mansilla's concern for the conflicts between civilization and barbarism, certainly one of the great themes of nineteenth-century intellectuals, is here rewritten as a condemnation of the faulty perceptions of urban elites whose "civilizing" military machines have unleashed their own form of barbarism.

> *How odd! In our cities, "authority" almost always refers to civilization, superiority, refinement, and culture. In the shadow of that authority, political theories grow and develop that are more or less the most up-to-date expression of the ideals held by man with respect to matters of governance.*
>
> *A surprising contrast! If you are in our cities and travel to the countryside, you will see that this very authority represents something quite different: there, brutality reigns and the only law is force itself.*
>
> *Nevertheless, despite what may be said, the gaucho is not ferocious by nature; he is only indolent and untutored.*
>
> *Our legislators are horrified by the idea of conscription; but when the government wants it, when it finds itself in need, the poor gaucho is subject to that voice of authority that takes him prisoner by law. He must then go to fight for a form of liberty that ends for him at the moment he begins to defend it. With this attitude, rural folk formulate two sets of laws: one for themselves and another for the military campaigns.*
>
> *Who knows? . . . Perhaps from their point of view this makes sense.*
>
> *Oh! Civilization always appears before their eyes*

> *cloaked in military garb. Can we be surprised, then,*
> *that rural people despise it so?*
> (18 – 22)

In this context, the gaucho is a captive, entrapped by a misguided government policy that endorses military recruitment.[8]

Beyond her efforts to humanize the gaucho, Mansilla also draws attention to the role of women in the wars of the pampas. Here, Mansilla rehearses the *cautiva* legends that are designed to set gaucha women and African slaves against natives, thus reminding us of the plot of Mansilla's *Lucía Miranda*.[9] Indeed, in this struggle the intervention of gaucho and African women is shown to resist the ferocity of Indians. In *Pablo,* women identified with gauchos are described for their valor in battle, and Mama Rosa, the African servant, is especially tenacious in protecting her ward, Dolores, against Indian advances. Nevertheless, as a consequence of war women are left abandoned or widowed, and the unmarried mother is a commonplace sight on the plains.

Mansilla's critiques are directed toward policy issues regarding *both* unitarians and federalists, who have refused to honor the interests of women. A strategy reminiscent of the narratives of Juana Manuela Gorriti and Juana Manso, who attacked Rosas but also undermined the blindness of unitarian men, Mansilla here collapses both sides of the partisan debate by calling attention to the masculine disregard of the female population in matters of national governance. "Man, in a halfway civilized environment, enjoys advantages denied to women," she explains (122).[10]

In particular, Mansilla signals the literacy campaigns that have neglected the training of women and points to the silence of native-born women in speaking their mind in public. It is not surprising, in this respect, that Dolores, the female protagonist and daughter of an untutored federalist, rarely speaks except for what Mansilla calls the "silent language of love"; by contrast, Mama Rosa, the African servant, initiates all discussion and decries the abuse of women. It is as if the speech of slaves could find expression in Argentina while native rural women were forced into silence. Similarly, Mansilla observes the ignorance of foreigners in the city and the multiple subaltern languages that proliferate on the urban frontiers: "one can hear many languages at once. Foreigners who arrive from all parts of the world swear in just as many foreign tongues" while "black vendors of porridge challenge the foreigners by lashing out with hybrid tongues uttering African and Spanish expressions" (227–228).

Here the excesses of language, unrestrained by any national educational program, appear to have escaped the control of partisan politics and the local laws.[11]

Mansilla's book offers an extended meditation on the authority of print traditions and on the promotion of female literacy in building the modern nation. However, even Eduarda Mansilla's authority was tested through the publication of *Pablo* and through the translation to which her own work was subjected by her brother, Lucio. The serialized publication of *Pablo* within the newspaper *La Tribuna* (November–December 1870) is therefore fundamental to an understanding of the relationship between female authorship and politics in Argentina of the late nineteenth century.

It raises the problem of where and how to speak of the state and, of course, the problem of the authority of female language. Sarmiento, in *Facundo*, had already taught the uses of apocryphal citation; errors in his translations from French repeatedly marked a schism between America and Europe.[12] Moreover, this mimetic anxiety evokes questions about building a nation from the traces of foreign languages and cultures. In the French publication of *Pablo*, Eduarda Mansilla positions herself as a bridge between two worlds; her lexicon and footnote citations clarify her knowledge of local uses of Spanish, gaucho, and Indian lore, and the cultural distinctions marking Argentine rural life. Hers is the voice of the multilingual woman who translates as she writes, bringing diverse cultures under her control and exposing the connections between them. At the same time, she bridges the gap between unitarians and federalists by issuing a severe critique to both camps for their failure to modernize Argentina.

This topic is reshaped when Lucio Mansilla translates *Pablo* from French into Spanish and situates the text as a *folletín* in *La Tribuna*, the most important Argentine newspaper of the time with an estimated circulation of thirty thousand. A newspaper marked by its decidedly federalist agenda, especially in the hands of editor Luis V. Varela, *La Tribuna* organized a critique of the unitarian government. This project becomes apparent both in the headline stories and the *folletines* printed in the pages of the daily. Thus, the news items carried reports from the wars in Europe, the annexation of Alsace, the dangers of the Paris Commune, and the struggles for Italian unification, topics considered relevant for the internal discussions about Argentina's future. News of public disorder at home also occupied considerable attention in *La Tribuna*; thieves, delinquents, and urban loan sharks were frequently noted. Moreover, *La Tribuna* carried fashion reports and printed a travelog column, commonly written in French, to inform readers of feminine styles and customs abroad. Authored by "Daniel," who was later identified as Miguel Cané but whose name also evokes the pseudonym taken by Eduarda Mansilla, this column described female fashion in London, the character and taste of Italians, and the achievements of literacy programs in Germany and France. Finally, a human interest page, authored by "Orion" (later revealed to be Hector F. Varela), reported social events in Buenos Aires and issued caveats to women lest their eagerness for independence bring danger to the world of elites. Above all, *La Tribuna* issued a challenge to the unitarian government and demanded correction of the political situation and an end to internal strife. It is not surprising in this context that the serialized texts of 1870, which anticipated the book publication of the translated version of Mansilla's *Pablo*, included Ponson du Terrail's narratives of crime in urban Paris and Lucio Mansilla's *Una excursión a los indios ranqueles* (May–September 1870). Clearly, the concerns of Argentine journalists were reflected in the *folletines*, especially in the representation of delinquents, Indians, and gauchos.

Mansilla de García's work is situated appropriately within this context insofar as she directs a critique against the institutions that fail to represent adequately the disparate populations of Argentina. This point notwithstanding, Eduarda's text is rewritten in the hands of her brother Lucio, with attenuated criticism of federalists and a more severe attack on unitarian programs. Specifically, the unitarian army, in the Spanish version of the text, is seen as effete and corrupt, led by unlearned officials who fail to honor principles of justice, while the federalists, who were criticized in Eduarda's French version of *Pablo*, are represented as less seriously offensive. In addition, the Spanish translator criticizes his sister's text and appends a number of footnotes that bring Eduarda's legitimacy into question. As an example, he corrects the use of the noun *chañar* with the following note: "The author describes 'chañar' as a small thorny tree. She is wrong; the 'chañar' is a corpulent tree, lasting for centuries" (30 November 1870). Here, Lucio challenges his sister's linguistic authority and her access to the indigenous world while also asserting his superior knowledge based on his own experience with the Ranquel Indians. Referring to current politics, he also intervenes with a note: "The lamentable conditions painted by the author have improved considerably in recent years in this part of the world" (29 December

1870). Translation, in this instance, serves as a corrective to the author's vision and ideology; it also serves to refute the author's claim to originality and voice.

The basis of this vengeful translation was most clearly acknowledged in Lucio's prologue to his sister's work, in which he reproduced a letter addressed to Eduarda:

> *Dear sister:*
> *As I translated your book, I felt as if I had been conversing fraternally with you nearby. . . . I tried to respect the integrity of your text insofar as the agility of both tongues allows it;*
> *Carlos Guido y Spano, our excellent and dear friend, in an effort to be diplomatic, spoke to you one day about your first literary project:*
> *Même quand l'oiseau marche*
> *On voit q'il a des ailes*
> *You, playing a bit, improvised a response that you may not recall:*
> *Même quand le lion caresse*
> *On sent q'il a des griffes*
> *Now speaking with complete candor, I don't believe that my feathers can ever adorn that person who, since the days of her youth and before she learned how to fly, already held such vengeful fantasies.*
> *I can only beg you to ignore the errors of a translation whose page proofs I will not be allowed to correct.*
> (28 – 29 NOVEMBER 1870)

Following Eduarda's metaphor cited in French, Lucio here bares his own lion's claws in the act of translation. Through correction and emendation, he mutilates his sibling's text and presents himself as the final authority on Argentine rural life.

Eduarda Mansilla reminds us of other Argentine women writers such as Juana Manso, whose novel *Los misterios del Plata* was rewritten by a man in the years following her death. Her plight also recalls the fears expressed by Victoria Ocampo, who distrusted the effects of translation upon her texts and upon her image of self. A victim of sibling rivalry in the literary field, Eduarda Mansilla's hybridized work exhibits the urgen-

cies of the translator's political agenda and a quest for narrative appropriation. It also reveals the kinds of textual unweavings that have been en-
acted upon women writers in Argentina and begs contemporary critics,
once again, to restore a lost feminist tradition. In this context, *Pablo*
stands as the vibrant expression of a political project initiated by a
woman writer determined to be heard in public.

NOTES

1. On the debates between federalists and unitarians as they took shape after
1852, see Tulio Halperín Donghi and David Rock (118–137).

2. Néstor Tomás Auza notes that Eduarda began her writing career with
publications in French and in imitation of French thinkers such as Fedon (141).

3. Her most important prose works include *El médico de San Luis* (1860),
Cuentos (1880), *Lucía Miranda* (1882), *Recuerdos de viaje* (1882), and *Creaciones*
(1883).

4. This type of narrative plot is fairly common in the women's fiction of
mid-nineteenth-century Argentina. Gorriti, for example, often situates her heroines in the pampas, where they wander bereft of reason and dazed by the consequences of political tragedies that have befallen them and their lovers and children. The clash of federalists and unitarians, according to writers like Gorriti,
can bring no positive result for women. See, for example, "El guante negro,"
included in Gorriti's *Sueños y realidades* (1865).

5. See the review by Doctor José F. López, included in the human interest
column "Cosas," *La Tribuna* (5 August 1870), 2.

6. All translations are based on Mansilla de García's French edition of *Pablo*
unless otherwise noted. In subsequent pages of this chapter, I will address the
inconsistencies of the Spanish translation of this text as rendered by Eduarda's
brother Lucio, but for the moment it might serve us well to note that while
Eduarda presents the gaucho as a tormented soul, Lucio reduces this scene of
Pablo's suffering to an example of uncontrolled barbarism: "His thoughts are
twisted and disfigured; horrible phantasms of death and voluptuousness cross
through his weakened brain" (1 December 1870).

7. Mansilla de García's defense of the gaucho may be contrasted to her obvious contempt for European immigrants, whose arrival in Argentina is described as an "excess population that Europe relentlessly pushes toward the New
World" (186). For Mansilla de García's discussions of race in the United States,
in which she refers in particular to African slaves and indigenous populations, see
her *Recuerdos de viaje* (1882).

8. Josefina Ludmer (21) has noted the categorization of the "gaucho paisano"
(he who works, respects the law and authority, and fulfills his military service)
and the "gaucho neto" (the dissolute wanderer who refuses discipline and takes

refuge among the Indians). Interestingly, Mansilla would appear to confuse these two categories, representing Pablo as the good gaucho who nevertheless deserts the army. This shifting of terms coincides, I believe, with Mansilla's larger project of calling into question the ideological differences that organize partisan politics in Argentina. In this respect, it is worth paying heed to Ludmer's astute observations when she writes that the very topic of the gaucho brings about a confusion of generic form; like *Facundo* and Echeverría's "El Matadero," Mansilla's work about the gaucho also defies categories of genre.

9. In *Lucía Miranda*, Mansilla places the Spanish heroine Lucía as a captive of the indigenous warriors. Because of her virtue and unyielding respect for her husband, Lucía refuses to surrender to the sexual demands of her Indian aggressors. It is of importance here that Lucía defends herself through her ability with words; as an orator, she protects the Spanish Crown, performs baptismal rites for Indians, and ultimately defends her honor. In *Recuerdos de viaje* (1882), Mansilla's travelog account of her journey through the United States in the 1860s, the author speculates on the poor treatment accorded indigenous populations in the United States and on the ideological premises of the U.S. Civil War. Curiously, Mansilla expresses great sympathies for North American Indians and perceives the full extent of their abject situation; in *Pablo*, by contrast, she sustains a clearly hostile vision of indigenous populations in Argentina.

10. This is not to say that Mansilla pursued an active defense of women's issues; rather, Mansilla's feminism was restricted to a conventional endorsement of republican motherhood through which values of maternity and family might generate proper citizens. In an article published in *La Nación*, Mansilla wrote, "I am not in favor of the emancipation of woman in the sense of believing that she can compete with man in the sciences and professional development. . . . I believe that nature has disposed of things differently and that woman is destined to carry on her breast the child who will become a man" (28 July 1883).

11. Note that African populations were typically identified with the programs of Rosas, and hence the federalist project, whereas the European immigrants reaching Buenos Aires were seen as part of a unitarian initiative. Note, too, that as Mansilla comments on the situation of women who were denied access to education, she remarks on the proliferation of female language engendered through sexuality and eros.

12. On the question of translation in *Facundo*, see Ricardo Piglia.

WORKS CITED

Auza, Néstor Tomás. "Eduarda Mansilla: Escritora y mujer de su tiempo." In *Mujer y escritura*, 140–144. Ed. Mempo Giardinelli. Buenos Aires: Editorial Puro Cuento, 1989.

Gorriti, Juana Manuela. *Sueños y realidades*. Buenos Aires: Casavalle, 1865.

Halperín Donghi, Tulio. *José Hernández y sus mundos.* Buenos Aires: Sudamericana–Instituto Torcuato Di Tella, 1985.

López, José F. "Cosas." *La Tribuna* (5 August 1870).

Ludmer, Josefina. *El género gauchesco: Un tratado sobre la patria.* Buenos Aires:
Sudamericana, 1988.

Mansilla de García, Eduarda. *Creaciones.* Buenos Aires: Juan A. Alsina, 1883.

——. *Cuentos.* Buenos Aires: Imprenta "La República," 1880.

——. "Educación de la mujer." *La Nación* (28 July 1883).

——. *Lucía Miranda: Novela histórica.* Buenos Aires: Juan A. Alsina, 1882.

——. *El médico de San Luis.* 1860. Buenos Aires: Eudeba, 1962.

——. "Pablo o la vida en las pampas." Trans. Lucio Mansilla. *La Tribuna*
(28–29 November–30 December 1870).

——. *Pablo ou la vie dans les pampas.* Paris: E. Lachaud, 1869.

——. *Recuerdos de viaje.* Buenos Aires: Juan A. Alsina, 1882.

Piglia, Ricardo. "Sarmiento the Writer." In *Sarmiento, Author of a Nation*, 127–
144. Ed. Tulio Halperín Donghi, Gwen Kirkpatrick, and Francine Masiello.
Berkeley: University of California Press, 1993.

Rock, David. *Argentina, 1516–1987: From Spanish Colonization to Alfonsín.* Berkeley: University of California Press, 1987.

Sosa de Newton, Lily. "Eduarda Mansilla de García en el recuerdo." *Feminaria*
3:5 (April 1990), 41.

Mary G. Berg

WRITING FOR HER LIFE

THE ESSAYS OF CLORINDA MATTO DE TURNER

Burned in effigy, excommunicated, the presses of her feminist print shop smashed and her manuscripts burned by mobs just before her hasty flight from Lima in 1895, Clorinda Matto de Turner may have been the most controversial woman writer of nineteenth-century Latin America. As the editor of a series of newspapers, she wrote and published hundreds of essays and editorials during her lifetime as a crusading journalist; she clamored for improved civil and legal rights for all, better education and working conditions for women and Indians, and enforced moral standards in government. She denounced corruption and indifference wherever she encountered them. Blasted as an enemy of the Church, celebrated as a Peruvian Harriet Beecher Stowe for her 1889 novel *Aves sin nido* (*Birds without a Nest*), she was both hated and admired for being a prototype of the modern woman. In later life, she was extensively praised for her long years as an enthusiastic and combative journalist (Burgos Seguí 6) and for her many achievements.

Matto's forty years of essays reflect and celebrate her passionate commitment to social reform. They reveal her varying relationships to political, social, and religious conventions as well as her shrewd sense of who her readers were at each stage of her writing career. Most of her essays were hastily written, and there is no perfect masterpiece among her hundreds of published editorials, speeches, memoirs, and short biographies, but their liveliness and sincerity remain attractive a century later and their subject matter continues to be of great interest. As glimpses of Matto's own dramatic life, they are fascinating.

Clorinda Matto was born in Cusco, Peru on 11 November 1852. She was brought up on a family estate nearby where she played with Indian children and learned both Quechua and Spanish, thus beginning a familiarity with Quechua culture that would be of continuing importance to her. She was educated in Cusco at the school later renowned as the Colegio Nacional de Educandas, and she often mentioned this experience as formative of her lifelong advocacy of better schools for all women. Married at age eighteen to an English physician and business entrepreneur who encouraged her interest in writing, Matto wrote and published poems, legends, historical vignettes, and essays about injustices to Indians and the need for education and rights for women. These early pieces were published under various pseudonyms in local newspapers.

In 1876, with the encouragement of her husband and her father, Matto founded a weekly magazine in Cusco, *El Recreo*, to which she contributed extensively.[1] She was acclaimed as an outstanding young writer of *tradiciones* (short historical fictions) at Juana Manuela Gorriti's salon in Lima in 1877, and she continued to publish essays as well as fiction throughout the difficult years of the war with Chile. Matto wrote many pieces in support of the cause of Andrés Cáceres who, with his army of Indian soldiers, defended the Peruvian Andean region. She turned her home into a field hospital, organized an ambulance service, raised funds for the war effort, and spoke to the troops in Quechua. In print, she exhorted Peruvians to exhibit patriotic strength during the war and energetic recuperative strategies afterward. Her essays deplore national chaos and sloth and suggest following the model of French postwar recovery, with emphasis on industrialization and education: "Thus we will see progress on a national level and on the home front under the benign auspices of education and of *national industry*" ("La industria nacional," 1882 in *Perú* 250).

When her husband, Joseph Turner, died in 1881, leaving his business affairs in Tinta in disarray and bankruptcy, Matto tried to pay his debts by running a wheat grinding mill and other businesses, but in 1883, she moved to Arequipa and became the editor of a daily newspaper, *La Bolsa*, thus becoming the first woman in the Americas to head an important daily paper. Many of her first articles and editorials are exhortations to all Peruvians to unite, elect honest leaders, and resolve their postwar problems, but she went on to write about business and agriculture, immigration, Indian problems, and education, particularly education for women.

Matto's interest in women's lives, dilemmas, and opportunities is revealed in a series of publications in the 1880s. Two books of her *tradiciones* and legends appeared in Huarás in 1880, *Hojas de un libro* (Pages of a Book) and *Cusiccoillor*, and two more were published by La Bolsa press in 1884: her first extensive collection of essays and historical sketches, *Perú: Tradiciones cuzqueñas* (Peru: Cusco Traditions), and a literature textbook for girls, the first of many textbooks produced by Matto for the education of female students. Her first play, *Hima-Sumac*, a melodrama that portrays the life dilemmas of a young Indian heroine with great empathy, was premiered to great acclaim on 16 October 1884, at the Teatro de Arequipa. Matto's essay "La mujer, su juventud y su vejez" (Woman, Her Youth and Her Old Age) also speaks of the complexity of women's roles and the impossibility of making the right choices without "a complete and solid education" (*Perú* 246). Matto's feminism is evident in one of her Holy Week essays of that same year, "El gólgota y la mujer" (Golgotha and Women), which comments on how unenlightened the Romans were about women until Jesus came along and proclaimed the equality of women, "and ever since then, women have been recognized as equal to men in intelligence, superior to them in faith and in tenderness of heart" (*Perú* 234).

On 30 December 1885, Matto published her farewell editorial in *La Bolsa* and moved to Lima. She had paid her husband's debts and established herself as a writer of prominence as well as a capable editor. By the end of 1887, she had published two biographies of prominent Indian citizens of Peru: one of Juan de Espinosa Medrano, a seventeenth-century Catholic priest, and the other of statesman José Domingo Choqquehuanca. Both were included in her 1889 *Bocetos al lápiz de americanos célebres* (Pencil Sketches of Renowned Americans), a collection of biographical essays. During the next twenty years Matto would write hundreds of biographical sketches, thus bringing to the attention of her reading public vivid depictions of women and men whose achievements she found exemplary.

Matto was invited to become a member of the most prestigious literary societies of the Peruvian capital, the Círculo Literario and the Ateneo. She addressed the Círculo Literario on the subject of the Quechua language (*Leyendas* 91–111).[2] A few weeks later, on the occasion of Manuel González Prada's inauguration as president of the Círculo Literario, Joaquín Lemoine read a tribute to Clorinda Matto, referring to her as the most Peruvian of Peruvian writers, a true Joan of Arc of intellectual enterprise whose energy had not always been appreciated (*Leyendas* vii–xxxiv).[3] In November of 1887, Matto began to gather Lima intellectuals at her home for regular meetings to discuss the future of Peru and plan both social reforms and cultural improvements. The meetings included programs of literary readings, musical performances, and exhibitions of art, but their emphasis was on social change. Matto's speech when she was inducted into the Ateneo on 6 January 1889, later included as an essay in the collection *Leyendas y recortes* (Legends and Clippings), reflects her concern that Peruvian public morals were in a state of disrepair and decadence, and that Peru desperately "needs more free schools, industrial establishments, factories, . . . that is, practical items rather than dissident theories or rhetorical flourishes" (89). She felt that it was women who would be most capable of transforming Peru, of reestablishing "moral and religious principles" and of combatting materialism and greed, and she called on Peruvian women to get busy: "it is up to women, the mothers of Peru, to sweep away the shadows that obscure our sun and cloud our days" (90).

Later in 1889, Matto was named editor and director of the most prestigious Lima literary periodical of its day, the weekly *El Perú Ilustrado*. Again, she controlled an immediate forum for her crusade for ethical public institutions, the improvement of education, and the encouragement of the best writers. She published a series of biographical sketches, many of them of women, collected in the 1889 *Bocetos*. The major Lima literary event of 1889 was the publication of Matto's first novel, *Aves sin nido*, which dramatized the chasm between social classes, the exploitation of Andean Indians, and the corruption of the Church, the state, and the army in their dealings with highland people. The novel met with immediate acclaim and notoriety and quickly sold out in several editions.

On 23 August 1890, *El Perú Ilustrado* published a story by the Brazilian writer Henrique Coelho Netto about the life of Christ that outraged many readers who felt that it defamed Christ by portraying him as sexually attracted to Mary Magdalene. Matto claimed repeatedly that she had been ill and had not made the editorial decision to publish the story, but the controversy escalated after the archbishop of Lima issued an edict prohibiting, under penalty of mortal sin, anyone from reading, selling, or discussing any issue of *El Perú Ilustrado*. The archbishop also banned Matto's novel and excommunicated her. In Arequipa, crowds burned Matto in effigy, shouting "Death to Clorinda Matto! Long live God!"[4] Large crowds in Cusco burned Matto's effigy and piles of copies of the magazine and her novel, and listened to speeches condemning her. The Unión Católica of Cusco demanded that the government close down *El Perú Ilustrado* and punish Matto, and that she never again be allowed to return to her native city. The bishop of Arequipa prohibited the reading

not only of *El Perú Ilustrado* but also of her novel.[5] The matter was discussed in the Chamber of Deputies. Matto and *El Perú Ilustrado* had many
defenders, and the archbishop of Lima finally lifted his ban on the periodical on 7 July 1891, in return for extensive promises on the part of the
paper's owner that there would be more rigorous editorial vigilance.
Matto resigned four days later.

    She published a second controversial novel, *Indole*, that year, and early
in 1892 she launched a feminist print shop enterprise, La Equitativa,
staffed by women. In addition to books by and about women, La Equitativa printed Matto's new weekly political magazine, *Los Andes*, which
began publication 17 September 1892. In the pages of *Los Andes*, Matto
made explicit her political commitment to Andrés Cáceres and his new
Constitutional Party, which opposed Nicolás Piérola, the leading con-
tender for the Peruvian presidency. *Los Andes* contained substantial literary contributions as well as political articles, but its Constitutional
Party affiliation was evident in every issue. When fighting broke out in
Lima on 17 March 1895 between the supporters of Cáceres and those of
Piérola, Matto's house was looted, and she and her brother barely escaped being killed. In April, the La Equitativa print shop was demol-
ished, its presses smashed and manuscripts destroyed by Piérola's troops.
La Equitativa had published a collection of Matto's essays, and a third
novel of hers, *Herencia*, had been issued by another Lima publisher in
1895, but the manuscripts of several of her books, including two more
novels, were lost. Hastily, on 25 April 1895, Matto left Callao for Chile
and then Argentina, never to return to Peru.[6]

    Matto settled in Buenos Aires, welcomed by her many literary friends
and admirers, and she immediately began to publish articles in Argentine
newspapers. On 14 December 1895, Matto was made the first woman
member of the Ateneo, and she gave a speech, "Las obreras del pensamiento en la América del Sud," (Women Workers of Thought in South
America), which was widely reprinted, in which she celebrated the
achievements of women writers of the Americas (*Boreales* 245–266).
Exiled now from political involvement, Matto devoted her immense
energies to women's education. She taught at three different schools in
Buenos Aires (the Escuela Normal de Profesores Número Uno, the Escuela Normal Norte-Americano, and the Escuela Comercial de Mujeres),
lectured extensively, translated books of the Bible into Quechua, and
wrote textbooks and newspaper articles. As in Peru—where her eagerness for access to an immediate outlet for her written opinions had resulted in a series of publications that she edited single-handedly, and to

which she contributed extensively—so, too, in Buenos Aires she almost immediately founded a periodical where she could publish her essays, biographies, and commentaries about current events. The first number of *Búcaro Americano* appeared on 1 February 1896, and it was published at regular intervals until just three weeks before her death in 1909. Although it included many contributions by other writers, each issue of *Búcaro Americano* was dominated by Matto's presence: she wrote the editorials, the short biographies, and many of the sections of social commentary. The essays, stories, and poems by others reflect Matto's ongoing interests in women's education, internationalism, and women's rights. She frequently included letters and poems written to her and many pages of favorable reviews of her own books, reprinted from other journals.

For thirteen years, *Búcaro Americano* loomed large in literary Buenos Aires, analyzing ideas, people, and events and introducing new writers, featuring and acclaiming even the voices of Modernist writers such as Rubén Darío and Leopoldo Lugones, whose deliberate provocations are startling in the context of earnest articles about educational methods and industrial development. Matto's own voice is one of steadfast insistence on women's need to assert themselves. In "La mujer y la ciencia" (Woman and Science), 1 January 1898, she points out that women cannot hide behind sentimental notions of motherhood because 60 percent of women are not in fact actively engaged in the roles of mother or wife. She analyzes the statistics of women's great success in the German university system and encourages Argentine women to insist upon their rights to equal education and equal suffrage, which will be beneficial to all of society. Statistically, women do better in school than men, and women must outmaneuver any "egotistic and retrograde individuals" who do not wish to acknowledge the capabilities of women.

In many of her essays she distinguishes between "the woman as *object*" and "the woman as *person*" (9 July 1899), the former a social construct of composite male views of how a woman should look and behave, the latter an identity built on individual values, refined and articulated through education, practical experience, and the development of self-confidence. Matto applauds the gradual acceptance of women in medicine in "¿Avanza la mujer?" (Are Women Advancing?, 15 February 1899). Her admiration of the United States and England is evident in many essays, and she is euphoric about the progress of society in general and women's lives in particular ("La mujer avanza," 25 March 1901) once women moved out of their nineteenth-century passive roles as consumers into their twentieth-century identities as active producers.[7] Matto writes often of the success of the Escuela Comercial de Mujeres, which as of 1901 had been "during its eleven years of operation, a true revelation that Argentine woman shares the energy of the North American woman to forge her own liberty, for only the self-sufficient are free" ("Escuelas comerciales" [Commercial Schools], 15 June 1906, 624). Matto is ecstatic about new banking and insurance policies that allow women to be assured of self-reliance. One of the few companies from which Matto accepted advertising for *Búcaro Americano* was La Dotal, which provided dowry insurance for women; Matto felt strongly that this would facilitate "marriages of young women who could not otherwise have fulfilled their dreams, and would have been left weeping, silent and sad not to have been able to marry their hearts' choices" ("Ahorrar es virtud" [Saving is Virtuous], 15 June 1906). Matto's optimism about the twentieth century extended to a belief that peace-loving women could resolve disputes between nations and end war forever ("La Mujer," 25 June 1907). Her positive view of the future was also demonstrated in lectures that she gave in Spain in 1908 about Argentina and Peru, later published as *Cuatro conferencias sobre América del Sur* in 1909. This volume also included the text of "La obrera y la mujer" (Women Workers and Women), a controversial antistrike speech delivered at the Consejo Nacional de Mujeres in Buenos Aires on 8 December 1904, which applauded the dissemination of theories of social Darwinism not because women were not always capable but because Matto believed that "the doctrine of evolution, which is the synthesis of the Spencerian system, . . . must bring incalculable benefits to the cause of the *woman as a person*" (54). Matto speaks out in favor of professions and jobs for all women. Working women are not only self-sufficient but also happier and better off than those who are idle. Even working women should take care not to imitate men: their role should be a peaceful one—extending their gift for creating "domestic peace" into the public sphere—and they must oppose strikes and violent political upheavals. Women are steadier and wiser than men, and it is essential to "entrust the future of young America to the sensible effort of women" (57). Constant vigilance is necessary to make sure that, although men and women perform tasks differently, their accomplishments are recompensed equitably; it is important to insist on opportunities for women and crucial to demand that "their work should be duly remunerated, for industrial magnates exist who despite their doing equal work, pay women less, just because they are women" (57).

Matto's last essays were a series of descriptions of her experiences and observations during six months in Europe in 1908, a trip financed by the Argentine Consejo Nacional de Mujeres so that she could study European education for women. Her travel essays describe schools and workshops as well as her impressions of the women she met in six countries. She became increasingly aware of the differences between her American way of thinking and that of her European hosts. To her own surprise, she particularly admired English and German straightforward practicality and disliked French social attitudes and customs. She reflects proudly that "in America we really do have liberty, equality, and fraternity" (68) whereas the French do not. While most Parisian women live only for immediate sensual gratification, America can claim "the cradle rocked by the fairy godmother of feminism, that is, of the woman-person, of the conscious and free being" (69). These essays, published as *Viaje de recreo* (Pleasure Trip) just after her death in 1909, constitute Matto's most personal book, the least polemical, and the most optimistic, as she foresees and celebrates the "glorious future of the feminine cause" (47). More self-reflective than many of her previous writings, the commentaries and observations of *Viaje de recreo* are an appropriate final summary of the views of a woman who was a lifelong feminist and crusader for reforms.

NOTES

1. In one of her first editorials (1877), she proclaimed the idealistic educational purpose of journalism: "it is the calling of journalism to instruct the various elements of society as well as to widely preach about morals and civic virtues" (*Perú* 222). "Provincia de Calca" (Province of Calca), published by El Recreo in installments in September and October of 1876, is a vivid description of rural landscape, Indian traditions, and personal anecdotes (*Perú* 223–230).

2. In this 5 October 1887 speech, as on other occasions, Matto argues eloquently and forcefully that Quechua is "the proper and true language of Peru" (*Leyendas* 100) and that if Peru values its heritage, its national unity, and the representation of all its citizens, the state should choose "Quechua, that language that should be the permanent bond of unity for the Peruvian race" (99). She extolls the advantages of Quechua, its expressiveness and its qualities of condensation and descriptiveness that are so appropriate for Peruvian reality. At the very least, asserts Matto, "it is not possible to write Peruvian history worthy of being called such without knowledge of the language" (107).

3. Lemoine points out that although she has manifested her personal courage and has persevered in outspokenness—"Mrs. Clorinda Matto de Turner . . . has

not been silent a single day, either during the war or afterward" (x)—she does tend to remind people of what they would rather forget, and thus it will be only someday in the future that "then, yes, then, more justice will be done than today to the Peruvian writer. Her country will view her with national pride" (xxxix).

4. For more information about these incidents, see Berg, De Mello, and Küppers.

5. It was apparent to Matto that her novel and her feminism were the true subjects of the attack on her; as she wrote in an editorial in *El Perú Ilustrado* on 1 November 1890, "we should recognize that 'Magdala' has been the pretext, probably deliberately set up, and the novel the objective of all the persecution." Ricardo Palma wrote in *El Perú Ilustrado* on 11 October 1890 that clearly it was not acceptable to the Church for women to concern themselves publicly with controversial issues; he comments that Matto was excommunicated as a warning to other women: "Clorinda Matto . . . has been the victim chosen to intimidate any members of the fair sex who might feel tempted to flee the confessional or desert the choir of the faithful." Matto says in her journal that when she met Coelho Netto in Río in 1908, she told him that the scandal was a political strategy, "a campaign of priests who have taken the habit for mercantilistic reasons; . . . in religion as in politics, there are patriots and patrioteers" (*Viaje* 12). Matto comments on the irony of meeting Coelho Netto just as she is on her way to Rome to see the pope.

6. Even after her death in 1909, she was unwelcome in Peru. Despite her family's efforts over the years, her remains were not returned to Peru until 1924.

7. What a wonderfully civilized step it is, says Matto, to recognize that "woman could be converted from being essentially a consumer into being a dignified producer" ("Escuelas comerciales," 1 July 1906). Matto's rhetoric is often effusive, as in "La mujer trabajadora" (15 April 1899), where she celebrates the number of women employed by a new department store and speaks at length of "how many women, what an infinite number of adolescent girls, have been saved from hunger and grief, within that human beehive that offers them the delicious honey of work properly recompensed! . . . This offers proof that official effort and individual energy have joined to unify the movement for the progress of women. And like the hands that are shown clasped on the proud Argentine coat of arms, amidst the laurels of yesterday's victories on traditional military battlefields, illuminated by the glorious May sun, today the heat of that same sun heralds the unstoppable chariot of women's progress."

WORKS CITED

Berg, Mary G. "Clorinda Matto de Turner." In *Spanish American Women Writers: A Bio-Bibliographical Source Book*, 303–315. Ed. Diane E. Marting. New York: Greenwood, 1990.

Burgos Seguí, Carmen de. "Femeninas." *El Heraldo* (Madrid, 3 November 1908). (Also in Matto de Turner, *Cuatro conferencias* 5–7.)

De Mello, George. A Literary Life of Clorinda Matto de Turner. M.A. thesis, University of Colorado, 1959.

Küppers, Gabriele. *Peruanische Autorinnen von der Jahrhundertwende: Literatur und Publizistik als Emanzipationsprojekt bei Clorinda Matto de Turner.* Frankfurt am Main: Peter Lang, 1989.

Lemoine, Joaquín de. "Clorinda Matto de Turner." In Matto de Turner, *Leyendas y recortes*, vii–xxxiv.

Matto de Turner, Clorinda. "Ahorrar es virtud." *Búcaro Americano* (15 June 1906).

———. *Aves sin nido.* Lima: Carlos Prince, 1889, and Buenos Aires: Félix Lajouane, 1889.

———. *Birds without a Nest: A Story of Indian Life and Priestly Oppression in Peru.* Trans. J. H. Hudson. London: Charles J. Thynne, 1904.

———. *Bocetos al lápiz de americanos célebres.* Lima: Peter Bacigalupi, 1889.

———. *Boreales, miniaturas y porcelanas.* Buenos Aires: Juan A. Alsina, 1902.

———. *Cuatro conferencias sobre América del Sur.* Buenos Aires: Juan A. Alsina, 1909.

———. *Herencia (Novela peruana).* Lima: Masías, 1895.

———. *Hima-Sumac: Drama en tres actos y en prosa.* Lima: Imp. "La Equitativa," 1892.

———. *Indole (Novela peruana).* Lima: Tipo-Litografía Bacigalupi, 1891.

———. "La mujer y la ciencia." *Búcaro Americano* (1 January 1898).

———. *Leyendas y recortes.* Lima: Imp. "La Equitativa," 1893.

———. *Perú: Tradiciones cuzqueñas.* Arequipa: "La Bolsa," 1884.

———. *Tradiciones cuzqueñas.* Vol. 2. Lima: Torres Aguirre, 1886.

———. *Viaje de recreo: España, Francia, Inglaterra, Italia, Suiza, Alemania.* Valencia: F. Sempere, 1909.

Sandra M.
Boschetto-Sandoval

THE SELF-CONSTRUCTING HEROINE

AMANDA LABARCA'S REFLECTIONS AT DAWN

> Never to be yourself and yet always—
> that is the problem.
> VIRGINIA WOOLF, "THE MODERN ESSAY"

Characterized by Chilean historians and biographers as "ahead of her time" (Mussa 47), Amanda Labarca Hubertson (born Amanda Pinto Sepúlveda, 1886–1975) is, after Gabriela Mistral, Chile's most readily acknowledged "femme savante." Incorporated among the already illustrious archive of Chilean women intellectuals as an outstanding educator and "scientific humanist," Amanda Labarca's celebrated career spans an interdisciplinary spectrum so extensive we cannot do justice to it here.

Labarca's writings in the educational and pedagogical field are numerous and varied and those which have caused perhaps the strongest polemic.[1] The search for an "integral education" at a time when Chile was coming of age as a nation was a daring adventure for the author, but perhaps no more so than her struggle to obtain legal and social equality for women. Postulating with feminism as well as with education the integration of praxis and theory, "the right *to express* and *to exercise* the authentic self in tangible acts that respond to genuine impulses" (*¿A dónde va la mujer?* 189, emphasis added), Amanda Labarca has also contributed a significant essayistic opus to the field of women's history and feminist thought. Her more acclaimed feminist writings include such texts as *Actividades femeninas en los Estados Unidos* (Feminine Activities in the United States, 1914), *¿A dónde va la mujer?* (Where Are Women Going?, 1934), *La mujer en la vida económica* (Women in Economic Life,

1938), *Feminismo contemporáneo* (Contemporary Feminism, 1947), and "Evolución femenina" (Feminine Evolution, *Desarrollo de Chile*, 1953). The latter essay, which incorporates material from previous texts and reflects Labarca's preference for framing her discourse in historical perspectives, is a richly significant compendium of Chilean feminist achievements. In the essay she cites a varied spectrum of women, otherwise lost to anonymity, dating from early Independence. This desire to place woman in history, to refute patriarchal monopoly of historical space, is further expressed by Amanda Labarca's claim that woman's destiny cannot be separated from that of the community, the environment, and history ("El imperio femenino" 107). With progressive foresight, Labarca also expresses the need to incorporate "the family unit, human relationships, ways of life, . . . the aspirations of the common people" ("El imperio" 109) into the masterdiscourse of history. This recognition that the private/domestic sphere is also historical and hence politically significant raises the notable thesis that *her own* life/story must be viewed and studied in an equally holistic way.

In addition to her pedagogical and feminist writings, Amanda Labarca was also a literary critic and the author of several fictional and "private" writings that have received scant if any critical attention to date.[2] As Gayle Greene and Coppélia Kahn have noted, male historians, in their first efforts to incorporate women into history, concerned themselves with "exceptional" women (13). If the task of feminist historians, however, is to reconstruct the female experience, to fill in the blank pages and to make the silence speak, then both public and private spheres of the so-called extraordinary woman—and her less famous sisters—must be viewed as interdependent. While recent critics of Amanda Labarca's work have taken to underscoring her more public writings, dichotomizing her opus into essay and fictional narration (Pinto, "Paradigma" 138–139), a closer look at lesser-known texts such as her journal, *Desvelos en el alba* (Restlessness at Dawn, 1945), and the essays published in *Atenea* as "Meditaciones breves" (Brief Meditations, 1924–1931) will uncover a dialogic interrelationship between a public masterstory and a private fiction.

Jean Franco, in her study of the Latin American "public woman," has theorized on the social construction of the feminist position. Franco sees female creativity as a desire for performance on a public stage (113). The "self-destructing heroine," according to Franco, projects her female fantasy as performance in order to "expose the painful contradiction that, to be creative, she must become a public woman, a public woman whose shame and failure are exposed to ridicule" (108). The implications of Franco's astute commentary may serve as an outline for our thesis here, namely that there is a need to evaluate the complex life/story of Amanda Labarca Hubertson in the context of the relationship between self-fabrication and self-realization and between private and public discourse/life.

Patricia Pinto, in her analysis of Labarca's essays, acknowledges the author's transgressive character and the construction of a subversive subject position with respect to her male audience ("Mirada" 64). Amanda Labarca was unafraid of controversy and in some instances proclaimed its provocation as the intent of her essay (*Bases para una política educacional* 24). Study of Labarca's earlier subjective discourse, however, uncovers another position: the yearning for a semiotic retreat outside the symbolic order of masculinist discourse.

The short essays that constitute *Desvelos* comprise a series of conflictive journal entries dating from 23 May 1922 to 14 September 1936. They appear intentionally to subvert chronological order and linearity.[3] The first entry is dated 16 April 1924; others are left undated. The text is divided, however, into seven groupings: "Opiniones" (Opinions), "Cultura y tradición" (Culture and Tradition), "El mundo se encoge" (The World Is Shrinking), "Del valor" (On Valor), "Descripción de Chile" (Description of Chile), "En España" (In Spain), and "Páginas personales" (Personal Pages).

Dates of the journal entries extend over a period of roughly fifteen years. This was a time of both triumph and struggle for the author. In 1922 Amanda Labarca was granted the chair of Professor Extraordinaire of Psychology at the University of Chile, the first Chilean woman to be so honored. In 1928 she was dismissed from the university post and, with her "anarchist" husband, exiled to Concepción by the government of Colonel Carlos Ibañez del Campo, who, through a series of military juntas, had inaugurated the "Difficult Years" (1925–1931) of economic and political crisis. The political repression of the time had even forced Labarca to author published writings under pseudonyms.[4]

The journal entries are preceeded by an extensive prologue by long-time friend and publisher José Santos González Vera, who provides an anecdotal summation of Labarca's life/story, including an intriguing physical description of the author.[5] Labarca herself refers to the entries as "fleeting nocturnal meditations" and "notations on the margins of a life" (25–26). The journal thus uncovers a disorderly collage of reflections: religious and metaphysical conflict, injunctions in favor of free love and a complete redefinition of sexual function (44–45), and diatribes against rational positivism (37) together with positive reflections on technological utopias (73–74).

Displayed in the entries are theme fragments that also appear in such texts as *Actividades femeninas* and *Feminismo contemporáneo*, as they relate not only to the "conjunction of the material and the spiritual, the mental and the instinctual" but to the dissolution of dysfunctional polarity: "The great periods of human flourishing are those in which both instincts are harmonized like the chords of a single instrument. The periods of decadence, on the other hand, are those in which one of those instincts tends to suppress or annihilate the other" (37–38). In these brief essays Labarca outlines in fragment form the key postulates of her feminist politics, including the subversion of strict divisions between female and male roles, as presented later in "El imperio femenino" (1949): "Only through extraordinary exception can one be 'all male' or 'all female.' The gradations, the nuances that intervene from one and the other are infinite" (112). In these disorderly meditations Labarca acknowledges that the oppression of women and men is both a material reality, originating in material conditions, and a psychological phenomenon, a function of the way women and men perceive one another and themselves. The utopic impulse for Amanda Labarca is to seek to reconcile intelligence with instinct, mind with sentiment, exclusive of gender boundaries.

It is difficult to read Labarca's journal without connecting it to the intentional optimism that her later essays communicate. The fluctuation, however, between the pragmatic optimism of the essays and the tragic thread that permeates the journal illustrates the "absence of system" that characterizes both the essay genre itself (according to Réda Bensmaïa) and feminism's own double-voiced strategy of submission and subversion. "And I am like unkneaded dough into which the water and flour have not yet been mixed. . . . My intelligence told me: this way! and this way I went until the resolution lasted; but I was distracted momentarily and my nature shot out on its own, taking its own paths, which were not those indicated by logic" (128–129). Opposed to the transgressive quality of Amanda Labarca's linear and historical masterdiscourse, *Desvelos* reflects a Montaignian "negative capability" (Kauffmann 223), a high tolerance for doubt and contingency, the desire to approach truth obliquely, and an openness to discarding or moving beyond "truth" insofar as it becomes constraining, disabling, or compromising.

Labarca acknowledged in several interviews that *Desvelos* portrayed her "true" self.[6] This confession, however, raises further questions concerning the dichotomy between public and private posture and Labarca's apparent desire to break free of conventional authorial constraints. If *Desvelos* was intended for public display (one way of reading González Vera's poignant reference in the prologue to Labarca's desire to go "house building" [7]), then the existential angst displayed in the journal recreates another fictional *persona*. At the same time, the reader must also take into account the age of the author at the time the journal was written; she was in her late thirties and forties. Anxieties and uncertainties brought on by menopausal depression punctuate the pages of *Desvelos*. The "Páginas personales" of the journal especially serve up to the reader a disturbing portrait of the author as an older woman. Not only is suicide contemplated (107–108), but the narrator also clarifies her personal motives for writing, with doubt expressed about public transcendence:

> *I write* because of subjective need. *I know that
> what I am jabbering lacks transcendence: the noise of
> leaves blowing in the wind. But I need to do it. I also
> understand that* one thing is to write for oneself
> and a very different thing to keep up the vanity
> of writing for the sake of literary prestige and
> the honor of humanity.
> (126, EMPHASIS ADDED)

Like other feminists, Labarca continually asks why she writes. What does she hope to achieve through her writing? For the "public woman," whose discourse privileges the conversation of men and their traditions, to write without regard to audience or purpose constituted a surprising and subversive maneuver.

At stake in these reflections is Amanda Labarca's often-quoted Socratic mandate: *gnoscete ipsum* (know thyself). Throughout her life Labarca acknowledged art (writing) as a "consoling window" through which one could gaze at the sky and, for at least a few moments, sense fulfillment (*La novela castellana de hoi* 13). In *Desvelos* she speaks of the function of art as not only transformative for both author and reader alike but as capable of providing the means "to transcend this three-dimensional prison in order to express-life in innumerable dimensions" (99). As acknowledged in both *Desvelos* and much later in an interview for *El Mercurio* (31 December 1961), Labarca's greatest utopian longing was to accomplish this transformation and transcendence of self through fiction.[7] Her early attempts at "pure creation," however, had led to negative, gender-biased reviews.[8] In *Desvelos* she appears to decry her "meagre talent; dull intuition, difficulty in finding the right word, cowardly imagination, poor vocabulary" (126), all of which were accusations raised by her critics.

The appearance of the journal in 1945—when the author had achieved considerable notoriety primarily as an essayist and educator—seems to inject these personal reflections with ironic intent, however. If the self-critique belies a divided self, "a perpetual coming and going between what is pleasing and what offends, between what one desires and what one attains" (115–116), then it may also do so duplicitously: "Externally, people see us from a perfectly contrary perspective, no doubt, to that in which we place ourselves in order to judge ourselves. And between what we are in reality and what we would like to be, who is capable of defining the borders?" (59–60). Labarca's struggle between "dispersion and continuity" (127) reflects a subversive disjunction between being and action, between inner desire and outer performance. "And all my life I have been struggling intimately between my natural mode of being, which shuns boundaries, and my intelligence, which forces me to understand that if . . . I do not dig a riverbed my energies will disperse in the wind" (127–128).

It is perhaps to offset "public exposure" that Labarca writes in 1907 of her "desire to have the soul of others be known, rather than to make my own works of art" (*La novela castellana* 10). By 1945, however, she had achieved considerable public success by accepting traditional notions of realism, of rationality, of mastery, of explanation; nevertheless, as exemplified by the publication of "Indefensa" (Defenseless) in the "Meditaciones Breves" (1928), she had also been able to enter into this symbolic order without rejecting a feminocentric semiotic discourse—that is, writing in which bodily drives survive cultural pressure and erupt, challenge, and fissure the symbolic order. *Desvelos*, thereby, must also be viewed as exhibiting a refusal to submit to the logic of patriarchal discourse, and, instead, as displaying a desire for the sensual, emotional, embodied, and experiental self.

In the prologue to *¿A dónde?*, entitled "La lámpara y el espejo" (The Lantern and the Mirror), Amanda Labarca had written of woman's conflictive, intimate history in the following terms: "To be or not to be. To express one's will or to renounce it. That is the dilemma" (12). In *Desvelos* she prefigures this assertion with a more private revelation: "Will? I don't think I have it. Ambition? . . . I don't know. Perhaps it is a subconscious energy. It looms whenever I feel most listless. And it forces me to

take up my cross" (113–114). It is noteworthy that while Labarca in-
veighs against "indecisive, defenseless, and weak feminine will" in *¿A
dónde?* (12), she herself speaks from a personal experience of "defense-
lessness," one brought on by the oppositions and paradoxes precipitated
by masculinist discourses: law, custom, and tradition.

As Rosemarie Tong has noted, the liberal feminism of the late nineteenth and early twentieth centuries, which called for the same civil
rights and economic opportunities for women as for men, celebrated rationality as both a moral and prudent virtue (17). The tendency to accept
as truth the priority of mind (i.e., the lantern of free will) over body (the
mirror of male vanity), however, is problematic not only because it leads
to a devaluation of semiotic functions but also because it usually steers
toward both political solipsism and political skepticism.[9]

The "instability" of *Desvelos* (120–121) and the implied dualism of
"La lámpara y el espejo" suggest the paradoxes that result when the
category of woman is inserted into a masculinist discourse on politics
and public life. It also underscores the fact that the discursive field of
Labarca's modern political theorizing, however much a critique of the
older suppositions of patriarchal politics, was nevertheless constituted by
a binary structure of oppositions: between public and private, state and
family, temporary and unchanging, discourse and silence, universal and
particular, culture and nature, rational and irrational, order and chaos,
power and morality, justice and love, knowledge and superstition, and
city and countryside. These terms constantly interpenetrate in Amanda
Labarca's writings, but indicated in the posing of a series of oppositions
is an uneasy relationship to a masculinist discourse, a theoretical tension
that results when she must acknowledge being both victim and agent
within a system of domination.

González Vera's anecdotal admonition that, had Amanda Labarca followed her inclinations, she would be "construyendo casas" (building
houses), directs the reader's attention toward the architectural, utopic
metaphor that circumscribes much of Labarca's life and work. The motif
of construction, of both home and self, of the self "centered" in a "new
order," is also significantly in evidence in her attempt to construct a new
mode of expression suited to a female aesthetic.

The convergence of both literary and scientific epistemologies, the
merging of both referential and figurative forms, is undeniable in
Amanda Labarca's writings. The balancing of the self-reflective and the
creative with more objective modes of discourse suggests not only an

attempt to offset masculinist opposition but also a cultural intertextuality, the creation of a "new discourse" mediated by the interpenetration of opposing terms. Labarca openly proclaims this "new genre" for the first time in *Actividades femeninas* (1914):

> *in the future everything is yet to be, even* finding
> one's own artistic expression, *because the work of*
> *art that should embody the nature of* [our] *gender*
> *doesn't exist either and it will be necessary to create*
> *it,* forgetting the models that men have created.
> *The feelings, the ideals, the feminine aspirations,*
> *will be expressed in the words, in the colors, in the*
> *strains of a new technique and spirit."*
> (19, EMPHASIS ADDED)

In the "Meditaciones" collection of essays, which coincides with the publication of the essays contained in *Desvelos* (1924–1932), Amanda Labarca inaugurates this "new discourse" by exploiting textual openings where referential and lyrical convergences can occur. Several of the entries, e.g., "La voz del paisaje" (The Voice of the Landscape), "Etica sexual" (Sexual Ethics), "Cultura y tradición" (Culture and Tradition), and "La materia conquistada" (Conquered Matter), reproduce, in some instances word for word, the personal meditations from *Desvelos*. Other entries, e.g., "Paisaje y educación" (Landscape and Education), "Ejemplos-Hábitos" (Examples-Customs), and "Sud-Americanos en Paris" (South Americans in Paris), which appear as veiled references to the political and social repression of the Carlos Ibañez government, conjoin ethnographic description with lyrical commentary and metaphor. In "La voz del paisaje," for example, Labarca desires "to strip away all patriotic sentimentalism" (61) and to reject temporarily ethnographic data (62) in order to portray the landscape with female eyes: "landscape that incites [one] to cultivate flowers, to conceive children, to live with all one's senses open and well nourished" (62). As a utopic site, however, the landscape also incites heroic projects yet to be realized: "I sense that this [Chilean] landscape is made for giants and not for the little dwarfs that inhabit it today" (63). Hence the landscape depicted by Amanda Labarca is also a site of conflict and contestation, an ambiguous and plurivocal one.

The essay, then, becomes for Amanda Labarca the means to articulate an integrative feminist discourse, almost literature and almost science. Transcending consideration as "minor" and "feminine," Labarca's journal is "an expression of the self thinking," an operation Alfred Kazin calls characteristic of the essay (x). In the very process of rethinking the self, *Desvelos* also constructs a new "self-centered" being, best defined perhaps as a fluid utopia. Roland Barthes has described the essay as a "utopia of language" with reference to its discursive discontinuity and play (8). Michel Foucault has cited the desire to "stray afield of oneself" as the motivation behind the essay (8–9). Finally, Georg Lukács maintains that the essayist expresses a messianic, unfulfilled longing that Lukács concludes is "a fact of the soul with a value and an existence of its own. . . . The essay is a judgment, but the essential, the value-determining thing about it is not the verdict (as is the case with the system) but the process of judging" (17–18).

Not unlike her culminating essay at the age of eighty-four, "Una mujer enjuicia al tiempo" (A Woman Passes Judgment on History, 1970), *Desvelos* is constructed so as to allay completion or closure. In the later essay Labarca faces life with the same gesture contained in *Desvelos*—at once fragmentary and holistic. What is most important for her is not the problem of invention, finding something to say; nor that of rhetorical disposition, putting in order what has been found, nor that of knowledge, speaking of Being, Truth, and other abstract concepts, but, finally, that of complication. For her, the complication was one of utopic reconstruction, both of world and of self: "The best state will be that which can guarantee the greatest individual development within the most just social harmony" (41). The construction of a new aesthetic and the feminization of culture implicated in her early essays are reasserted in her later work, where Labarca incites her contemporaries to set forth on a new path of self-exploration: "At the present time, woman feels it is her right to write in the journal of her life *her own poem*, that which can translate her aspirations, that which can elevate her, if she desires, toward the conquest of the universe" ("Una mujer" 17, emphasis added). Thus, with Amanda Labarca, the "self-destructing heroine" becomes the "self-constructing" one.

The particular art form or construction to which Labarca refers is, of course, a plural text made up of multiple networks, an "ideal" text that assumes neither absolute intentions nor covert significance. As readers, we gain access to her essays by several entrances, none of which can be authoritatively declared to be the main one. With her disorderly reflections Amanda Labarca engenders not only "her own poem" but, in architectonic and utopic terms, a new locus of hope for the self.

NOTES

1. There is no intent here to underemphasize Labarca's educational endeavors. Given, however, the limitations of this project and the somewhat comprehensive work of Catherine Manny Paul in this field, this chapter will focus attention on her more feminist writings.

2. Labarca's book *Impresiones de juventud* (1909) incorporates literary analysis on the Generation of '98, which she undertook as the focus of her doctoral dissertation. Among the authors studied in depth were Pío Baroja, Blasco Ibáñez, and Emilia Pardo Bazán. Throughout her life she was particularly fascinated with Scandinavian, Russian, and English authors, the last being her favorite. As an educational reformer, Labarca was most influenced by the work of H. G. Wells, William James, and John Dewey. Reading her literary criticism, the reader is constantly confronted with the coincidence of ideology of the particular authors studied and Amanda Labarca's own life experience.

Elena Aguila has begun a brief study of the fiction of Amanda Labarca. No in-depth examination, however, is made of *En tierras extrañas* or the literary incursions of 1928. Patricia Pinto refers overtly in her essays only to *La lámpara maravillosa*.

3. The publisher himself may have been primarily responsible for this rupture in chronology. González Vera does not provide an explanation in his prologue. It appears, however, that Labarca herself authorized the final version of the journal in unsequential form.

4. The essays bearing the pseudonyms Juliana Hermil or "Cenicienta" (Cinderella) were all published in the "Meditaciones breves" series in the journal *Atenea* of the Universidad de Concepción. Several of the essays had been directly transposed from *Desvelos*. Pseudonyms for public exposure (self-effacement) also underscore the interplay between destruction and/or (re)construction of self in Labarca's discursive praxis.

5. "Her words capture the profound attention of the audience and the atmosphere is filled with previously unawakened sentiments that, through her influence, come to life with new creative force. In that precise moment she is a mixture of girl and teacher. On the other hand, when she gives a lecture she is taken by the most extreme seriousness and one would like to tell her (so that only she could hear): Madam, you are not like that!" (*Desvelos* 18). González Vera's projection on Amanda Labarca of the woman/girl dichotomy provides evidence for the gender-biased environment with which the author had to contend.

6. Catherine Manny Paul provides the English translation: "Of all my writ-

ings," said the author, "these essays portray most genuinely my deepest thinking and my real self" (23 February).

7. "I would have greatly enjoyed two things: to write the novel of my time. A novel that would not be about one individual or another but rather would capture all this stormy Chilean history. And I would have liked to write vanguard theatre. To portray human and social phenomena in more than one dimension, from more than one angle, with more than one interpretation" (*El Mercurio*, 31 December 1961).

8. *En tierras extrañas* (1915) was read more as a novel of ideas, as opposed to the more conventional novel of "intrigue, . . . customs . . . passion" in vogue at the time. She was "publicly exposed," as it were, for her "tendentious observations" as well as her style, which was viewed "more properly that of a man than of a woman" (Parra 2, 5). The gender bias of her time explains a good deal of Labarca's self-doubts and hesitations.

9. According to Tong, who cites Alison Jaggar's *Feminist Politics and Human Nature*, "Political solipsism is the belief that the rational, autonomous person is essentially isolated, with needs and interests separate from, and even in opposition to, those of every other individual. Political skepticism is the belief that the fundamental questions of political philosophy—in what does human well-being and fulfillment consist, and what are the means to attain it?—have no common answer" (35). These philosophical dilemmas are not only sketched in *Desvelos en el alba*; they are also confirmed in interviews with the author later in life.

WORKS CITED

Aguila, Elena. "Amanda Pinto S./Amanda Labarca H. (1896–1975)." In Historia literaria de las mujeres en Chile: Narradoras chilenas (1900–1930), 19–25. Chile: World University Service. Unpublished manuscript.

Barthes, Roland. "Lecture in Inauguration of the Chair of Literary Semiology, College de France." *October* 8 (Spring 1979), 3–16.

Bensmaïa, Réda. *The Barthes Effect: The Essay as Reflective Text*. Trans. Pat Fedkieu. Minneapolis: University of Minnesota Press, 1987.

Foucault, Michel. *The Use of Pleasure*. Trans. Robert Hurley. New York: Random House, 1986.

Franco, Jean. "Self-Destructing Heroines." *Minnesota Review* 6:22, 105–115.

Greene, Gayle, and Coppélia Kahn, eds. *Making a Difference: Feminist Literary Criticism*. New York: Routledge, 1985.

Jaggar, Alison M. *Feminist Politics and Human Nature*. Totowa, N.J.: Rowman & Allanheld, 1983.

Kauffmann, R. Lane. "The Skewed Path: Essaying as Unmethodical Method." In *Essays on the Essay: Redefining the Genre*, 221–240. Ed. Alexander J. Butrym. Athens: University of Georgia Press, 1989.

Kazin, Alfred. "Introduction: The Essay as a Modern Form." In *The Open Form: Essays for Our Time.* Ed. Alfred Kazin. New York: Harcourt Brace, 1961.

Labarca Hubertson, Amanda. *Actividades femeninas en los Estados Unidos.* Santiago: Imprenta Universitaria, 1914.

———. *¿A dónde va la mujer?* Santiago: Impresa Letras, 1934.

———. *Bases para una política educacional.* Buenos Aires: Editorial Losada, 1944.

———. *Desvelos en el alba.* Santiago: Editorial Cruz del Sur, 1945.

———. "Evolución femenina." In *Desarrollo de Chile en la primera mitad del siglo xx.* Ed. Amanda Labarca Hubertson. Santiago: n.p. [1953].

———. *Feminismo contemporáneo.* Santiago: Editorial Zig-Zag, 1947.

———. "El imperio femenino." *Atenea* 93:286 (April 1949), 101–120.

———. [Juliana Hermil]. "La voz del paisaje" (Meditaciones breves). *Atenea* 5: 4–10 (June–December 1928), 61–63.

———. *Una mujer enjuicia al tiempo* (Discurso de Incorporación a la Academia de Ciencias Sociales, Políticas y Morales). Santiago: Editorial Andrés Bello, 1970. 5–17.

———. *La novela castellana de hoi* (Conferencia leída en la Universidad de Chile). Santiago: Memorias Científicas y Literarias, 1907.

Lukács, Georg. *History and Class Consciousness: Studies in Marxist Dialectics.* Trans. Rodney Livingstone. Cambridge: MIT Press, 1971.

Mussa, Moisés. "Amanda Labarca H. (La mujer, la educadora, la pedagoga)." *Occidente* (March–May 1956), 45–49.

Parra, Alejandro M. "En tierras extrañas." *Las Ultimas Noticias* July 15, 1916, 1–7.

Paul, Catherine Manny. *Amanda Labarca H.: Educator to the Women in Chile (The Work and Writings of Amanda Labarca H. in the Field of Education in Chile).* Cuernavaca, Mexico: Centro Intercultural de Documentación, 1968.

Pinto, Patricia. "Mirada y voz femeninas en la ensayística de Amanda Labarca: Historia de una anticipación chilena." *Nuevo Texto Crítico* 2:4 (1989), 57–67.

———. "El paradigma masculino/femenino en el discurso narrativo de Amanda Labarca." *Acta Literaria* 15 (1990), 133–146.

Tong, Rosemarie. *Feminist Thought: A Comprehensive Introduction.* Boulder: Westview, 1989.

Woolf, Virginia. "The Modern Essay." In *The Common Reader.* New York: Harcourt, Brace, 1925.

Doris Meyer

RECIPROCAL REFLECTIONS

SPECULAR DISCOURSE AND THE SELF-AUTHORIZING VENTURE

To recuperate the full history of female literary expression in Spanish America we must examine the ways in which women, particularly in the earlier periods, turned to writing to inscribe their own configurations of truth in a society that traditionally devalued the female intellect. The "cultural hall of mirrors" in Western societies has ideologically and aesthetically deflected women's attempts to find an authentic self-image (Friedman 38). For Spanish American women, whose life experiences have been ex-centric to the European and North American models favored by their culture, the mirrors were even more distorted.

The essay is a congenial genre for a woman seeking self-expression. As the original French term "essai" implies, the nonacademic essay is an individual attempt to make sense of a specific situation or subject. Unconstrained by systematic laws of style, it allows for a personal response to a particular circumstance without the pretension to establish permanent truths. Intellectually and aesthetically, the essay is reflective in its self/object relationship—rather like the work of a portraitist who, in rendering the likeness of an image, also inscribes a personal way of seeing and interpreting it. According to Graham Good, the essay is thus a "reciprocal characterization":

> *The heart of the essay as a form is this moment of characterization, of recognition, of figuration, where the self finds a pattern in the world and the world finds a pattern in the self. This moment is not the result of applying a preconceived method, but is a*

> *spontaneous, unpredictable discovery, though often*
> *prepared by careful attention and observation. This*
> *discovery can be about the self or about the world, but*
> *is mostly about a combination of both. Self and object*
> *are configured in a mutually illuminating way. But*
> *the insight is confined to that moment; the generaliza-*
> *tion cannot be separated from its particular circum-*
> *stances of time and space.*
> (22)

The contingency of the essay situation lends itself to the sense of transgression women may have upon entering the dominant male terrain of
literary expression. Its nonauthoritarian, personalized discourse facili-
tates the act of bearing witness so characteristic of the essay impulse just
as its malleability encourages a pattern of interwoven thoughts rather
than constructed arguments. In Good's words, it offers "aesthetic knowledge" or the possibility of a personal configuration of the truth, a pattern
that can be reconfigured in other essays as one's experience and perspective change (185).

Consider, for example, the early precedent of Sor Juana Inés de la
Cruz's *Respuesta a Sor Filotea*, written over three hundred years ago
(1 March 1691). In this feigned letter, which is truly an essay of self-
justification, Sor Juana employs the "tricks of the weak," as Josefina
Ludmer has pointed out, to protest the subordinate status of knowledge-
able women in Colonial Mexico and simultaneously to inscribe her autonomous self. She does this in the context of a response to the bishop
of Puebla ("Sor Filotea") in which she ostensibly capitulates to his
("her") ecclesiastical authority while dramatically foregrounding the issue of gender in Church practice. The occasion of the bishop's rebuke for
her intellectual aggressiveness opens a door to Sor Juana's clever strategy
to bear witness to her own condition and also evoke the biblical precedent of other learned women who were silenced in their endeavor to
teach and write. As Ludmer points out, women have historically dealt
with patriarchal repression by practicing their arts in private spaces; once
within those spaces, however, they have denied sexual limitations and
challenged proscriptive conventions (93).

Sor Juana's letter-essay also reflects the Baroque preference for layers
of interpretive meaning in a repressive, absolutist culture obsessed with
the illusions of truth. Her stated pretext was to accept "Sor Filotea's"
authority as spiritual counselor, but the subtext of her essay traces her

own intellectual autobiography, which resists that authority and finds self-justification in the context of a larger intellectual sisterhood. Sor Juana's reciprocal identification with women of earlier times is an example of "aesthetic knowledge" in which "the self finds a pattern in the world and the world finds a pattern in the self," to echo Graham Good. Her recognition of the centrality of socio-historical context for the interpretation of canonical texts is a example of her modernity, as is her impulse to produce a normative standard out of her own experience (Behler 3). Her specular discourse is actually part of a female tradition, from Christine de Pizan to the present, of women who have connected personal memory (identity) to social memory (history) in the effort to shape a female self-consciousness and reappropriate the right to interpret intellectual authority (McLeod 136–137).[1]

If we consider essays by other Spanish American women authors we can find many examples of specular discourse, essays in which women write about other women writers, thus giving to the notion of "reciprocal identification" a specific gender and vocational significance. Shared gender experience creates a bond between author and subject that refuses the distance of alterity, affirming an atemporal solidarity that is both intellectual and spiritual. Examples of this type of essay in twentieth-century Spanish American literature can be found in the works of such authors as Rosario Castellanos, Elena Poniatowska, and Rosario Ferré, women whose feminocentric works reveal a commitment to create new paradigms of female identity and to demystify traditional Hispanic gender mythologies. I would like, however, to focus attention on two earlier writers whose essays offer important precedents for this kind of reflective portraiture: Gabriela Mistral and Victoria Ocampo. Both of these authors became larger-than-life legends in their own time, and critical attention has often singled out the high-profile aspects of their literary *personae* (Ocampo as an influential Argentine literary figure and publisher, Mistral as a Nobel-prize-winning poet and Chilean cultural ambassador) while overlooking their merits as essayists.

In fact, Gabriela Mistral's oeuvre includes a number of essays written in portrait style. The fact that many more of these are about men than women is testimony to the gender imbalance among the consecrated cultural figures of her time; yet it may also be an indication of a generational dependency on the male intelligensia which women like Ocampo shared. Mistral's endorsement of traditional gender roles was culturally engrained, as evidenced by the selections she made for an educational reader, *Lecturas para mujeres* (Readings for Women, 1923).[2] When she

turns to writing sketches of other women, however, we see her awareness of the subordinate role of women in society and her recognition of
their efforts to define themselves intellectually. A collection of twelve of
these essay-portraits can be found in a posthumous volume entitled *Gabriela piensa en . . .* (Gabriela Is Thinking of . . .). With the exception of
Emily Brontë, all of the women she selects are twentieth-century figures,
including Selma Lagerloff, Alfonsina Storni, Teresa de la Parra, Victoria
Ocampo, and Carmen Conde. One of her most lyrical and revealing
portraits is of her mother, doña Petronila Alcayaga.[3] Written from Mexico in 1923, six years before her mother's death, it inscribes the intimate
voice of an adoring daughter entirely dependent on a mother who was
forty-four years old when she was born and who was abandoned shortly
thereafter by her errant husband. In the voice of her childhood self, the
young Lucila (Lucila Godoy Alcayaga was Gabriela's birth name) pays
tribute to her mother's self-sacrifice, evoking the gentle power of her
formative influence and exalting the nurturing role of motherhood. By
bringing her out of the shadows and casting herself in the dependent role,
Gabriela Mistral, the internationally respected writer and teacher, "authorizes" her mother's anonymous existence:

> *As I said before: I carry the gift of your flesh, I speak
> with the lips you made for me and I look with your
> eyes at strange lands. Through them, you too see the
> fruits of the tropics. . . . You enjoy with my eyes the
> shape of these other mountains, so different from the
> denuded mountain at whose foot you raised me!*
> (20)

The pretext of this specular portrait is to praise her mother, but its subtext is to mythologize motherhood itself and construct a public *persona*
for herself that could hide the anxieties and transgressions of her own
gender identity. The ennobled image of the nurturing mother in turn
envelops the adult daughter in a psychosymbolic relationship that suggests an inability to achieve full autonomy: "Then I became an adolescent, and later a woman. I have walked alone, without the shelter of
your body, and I know that what they call freedom is a thing without
beauty" (19).

Bell Gale Chevigny has suggested that the complexities of the autho-
rizing act, when women write about other women, reflect the problems
inherent in the mother-daughter relationship:

> *Women writing about women, I am persuaded, are*
> *likely to move toward a subject that symbolically re-*
> *flects their internalized relations with their mothers*
> *and that offers them an opportunity to recreate those*
> *relations. Whether our foremothers are famous and*
> *their histories distorted, or unknown and their histo-*
> *ries neglected, the act of daughters writing about them*
> *is likely to be, on some level, an act of retrieval that*
> *is experienced as rescue. When the work is most in-*
> *tensely experienced as rescue, the fantasy of reciprocal*
> *reparations is likely to become an underlying impulse*
> *in it. That is, in the rescue—the reparative interpre-*
> *tation and re-creation—of a woman who was ne-*
> *glected or misunderstood, we may be seeking indi-*
> *rectly the reparative rescue of ourselves, in the sense*
> *of coming to understand and accept ourselves better.*
> *In writing about our foremothers, we can be prepared*
> *to experience the specific nature for each of us of the*
> *mother-daughter dynamic, but we cannot be fully*
> *forearmed.*
> (375 – 376)

The biographer, says Chevigny, must be prepared to experience the empathy, identification, and ultimately the separation from her subject that makes possible the release of fantasies and the autonomous act of self-authorization. It may be that Mistral suffered the effects of incomplete separation from her mother, whose re-creation in her writing only served to distort her own self-image.

Almost twenty years after writing this essay, Mistral wrote a literary portrait of Victoria Ocampo. Although they first met in Madrid in 1930, it was in 1937 that they became close friends during an extended visit Gabriela made to Victoria's summer home in Mar del Plata. Curiously enough, these two women shared the same birthday, April 7, although Gabriela was a year older; this coincidence heightened their sense of sororal identification, already strengthened by shared interests:

> *On the surface, Victoria's cosmopolitan refinement*
> *contrasted sharply with her Chilean friend's rural*
> *simplicity. In the days they spent together, however,*
> *they were drawn to one another by their common*

> *Basque heritage, their shared admiration of Tagore's*
> *poetry, their love of nature, children, the sea, letter-*
> *writing, and the enormous concern they both felt for*
> *the future of South America as a free continent. At*
> *heart, they were both humanists and crusaders for jus-*
> *tice, though Mistral preferred to focus on the problems*
> *of racism and the Indians of her native Valley of*
> *Elqui, whereas Victoria was more preoccupied with*
> *the cause of women's rights.*
> (MEYER 160 – 161)

Mistral's essay, "Victoria Ocampo," one of the most perceptive ever written about Ocampo, focuses on the dilemma of her development as a writer: the reluctance that plagued her until middle age to write in her native language due to an early cultural bias toward French, inculcated by her upbringing and social environment. Her "linguistic bigamy," says Mistral, led Ocampo to betray her "completely and unexpectedly Argentine" (49) nature, which comes out in person-to-person conversations. Acknowledging a popular "black legend" that paints Ocampo one-dimensionally as Eurocentric, Mistral testifies to another side that surfaces "as soon as she tosses away the mirror in which she contemplates and disfigures herself at will" (49). She understands that Ocampo's problem as an author is fundamentally a lack of confidence in Spanish compounded by an excessive reverence for male writers in whose works she cannot find the reflection of her female, Argentine self. She is, ironically, as Ocampo herself once put it, an outsider in her own culture as well as in Europe, "the owner of a soul without a passport" ("Quiromancia" 147). The Bakhtinian concept of double-voiced discourse, adapted by Elaine Showalter to explain women's authorial dilemma, takes on added layers of significance in this South American context.

Ocampo's second volume of *Testimonios*, containing several essays on women writers including Virginia Woolf and Emily Brontë, led Gabriela Mistral to praise the organic authenticity Victoria had managed to achieve in her writing about other women. In the Brontë essay in particular, Mistral found the "Victoria Ocampo, of fertile body and so rich in potential, full of nutrients like the *ceibo* or the *araucaria*, the Victoria of violent impulse and character as clearcut as the *cordillera* peaks, the Victoria of open opinions and familiar expressions" ("Victoria Ocampo" 55). This was a Victoria with whom Gabriela, the ur-American, could identify. Yet she made a revealing confession in a personal letter: "your language, your own personal one, . . . is better than mine in its *freshness and warmth*, and in its plasticity and *movement*," adding that Victoria's "literary exigence" intimidated her and made writing about her difficult (Meyer 162).[4] The fact that Mistral took up that challenge and succeeded so eloquently is evidence of her own verbal skills as well as her commitment to deconstruct the biased legend that portrayed Victoria simply as a "foreignizer."

Mistral herself had written an essay on Emily Brontë in 1930, and she and Victoria more than likely discussed their mutual fascination with the Brontë family during their conversations in Mar del Plata in 1937. Comparing their approaches to this English writer who had authorial dilemmas of a different magnitude, one sees that both Ocampo and Mistral highlight the influence on Brontë of the austere Yorkshire countryside, the spartan parsonage, and the puritan father who ignored his daughters' talents in favor of a single, wastrel son. Where Mistral's portrait of Emily Brontë captures vividly and poetically the morbid aspects of the motherless environment in which the six Brontë children were raised, Ocampo's essay—much longer, more detailed, and punctuated by autobiographical comments—evokes the drama within Emily herself in a world that denied her a public voice. Reading Victoria Ocampo's essay one feels her identification with the Englishwoman's metaphysical appetites and earthly passions, so amply reflected in her fictional protagonists, Catherine and Heathcliffe. Gabriela Mistral's essay is a sensitive but more dispassionate re-creation of Brontë family life on the Scottish heath, emphasizing the inhuman treatment the girls endured from an unfeeling father and a drunkard brother.

At the end of Ocampo's essay, the reader encounters a theory she frequently repeated regarding two types of writers: those whose work is primarily "compensatory" and those whose work is primarily "complementary" ("Emily Brontë" 154–155). Emily Brontë, she says, is of the latter type whose writing is a reflection of their lives. It could be said that Ocampo herself was also that kind of writer, whereas Mistral might better fit the category of those whose work tends to compensate for what might have been. However one reads the reciprocal reflections in these essays, they form patterns of "aesthetic knowledge," personal configurations of truth en-gendered by the intersections of literary portraiture possible only when both parties are women. If the reader too is female and maybe also Spanish American, more layers of mirroring may occur as ego boundaries are transcended by the bonds of gender and cultural identification.

According to Mikhail Bakhtin's "Author and Hero in Aesthetic Activity," written in the early 1920s, the mirror metaphor is actually insufficient to describe the "sympathetic understanding" that makes possible the aesthetic act of biography (103). Bakhtin attributes the unique vision needed to author another's life as an "excess of seeing" (166), the individual perspective from which one can see what the subject itself cannot; indeed, self and other are mutually dependent for achieving a dialogic totality of being. Virginia Woolf took this concept one step further when she recognized in *A Room of One's Own* that "it is one of the good offices that sex can discharge for sex—to describe that spot the size of a shilling at the back of the head" (94). If women can testify to undocumented aspects of men's lives without succumbing to the self-aggrandizement of "looking-glass vision" (36), they can also "catch those unrecorded gestures, those unsaid or half-said words, which form themselves, no more palpably than the shadows of moths on the ceiling, when women are alone, unlit by the capricious and colored light of the other sex" (88).

One such portrait was written by Victoria Ocampo in Mar del Plata shortly after she received news of Woolf's suicide half a world away, in war-torn Europe. Entitled "Virginia Woolf en mi recuerdo" (Virginia Woolf in My Memory), it is the most lyrical of her various essays on Woolf, an elegy in musical tonalities to a female hero, composed in a woman's tongue and with a woman's eye. Rather than laud Woolf's enduring accomplishments as a writer, Ocampo recalls the transitory gestures of the woman herself (the "shadows of moths on the ceiling"): the seemingly banal conversation of their last visit together, the way she loved flowers, the austere beauty of her unpainted face, her petulance at being photographed.

But memory, like music, resonates with echoes that transcend time and space; it seeks aesthetic patterns that blend and connect across the boundaries between lived and imagined life. Similarly, Ocampo's essay emphasizes the triadic relationship between author, character, and reader by blending Woolf's personal torment into the anguish of Clarissa Dalloway trying to cope with ordinary life the day she learns of Septimus Warren Smith's suicide, along with moments of Ocampo's own pain on the day she learns of Woolf's death. The specular discourse in this essay places the South American woman's experience on par with the European's—alike but different. Even more important, the testimony that only Ocampo can give about Woolf adds a unique perspective to the larger portrait women can collectively draw for one another.

Like Woolf and her "moments of being," Ocampo understands that memory, in Bakhtinian terms, can give aesthetic wholeness to a life defined as much by imagined fantasy as by lived reality. Ultimately, her essay is a meditation on death and its power to communicate the meaning of life. But it is not just about Virginia's death; it is about death as Victoria, the survivor, has experienced it. Echoes of her own mother's death reverberate in her feelings of loss, and the contemplation of suicide as resistance to the ideologies of authoritarianism builds a bridge of understanding between herself, Clarissa, and Virginia:

> *Those to whom the memory of a gesture of a hand*
> *we have loved says nothing by itself carry with them,*
> *perhaps, the memory of other hands whose gestures*
> *move them with equal tenderness. . . . Perhaps they*
> *may read their memories in ours. When Narcissus*
> *looks at himself in the river, the river looks at itself in*
> *the eyes of Narcissus. We're all made of the same sub-*
> *stance. So close to one another without knowing it,*
> *without on occasion accepting it. United by our com-*
> *mon human condition.*
> ("CARTA A VIRGINIA WOOLF" 419)

Ocampo "reads" Woolf through the matrix of her life and her fiction while simultaneously discovering truths about herself. By foregrounding her own voice while also quoting Virginia and Clarissa, she creates a chorus of women's voices that transcend the boundaries of history, literature, and geography. This relational, dialogic, intersubjective approach to reading/writing is one of the strengths women bring to literature (Schweickart 48). It also encourages the self-authorizing venture through the connectedness the female self finds in another woman's example.

In a recent study of autobiographical writing in Spanish America, Sylvia Molloy notes that Ocampo's essays are "vehicles for oblique self-figuration," "mini-performances" in which "the process is the same—the appropriation of texts and voices of others" (72–73).[5] Initially arguing that Ocampo's reliance on the male-authored canon is evidence of her dependency, Molloy concedes that this may have been the only recourse for a woman reader in her time and circumstance. Essentially she faults Ocampo for a "lack of writerly *authority*," which she attributes not so much to her gender as to her anxieties of "literary competence and social standing" (71). I would suggest, however, that this sense of writerly authority—which I assume to mean a combination of self-confidence and self-identity as Molloy describes it—is not the voice Ocampo was seeking, nor is it a voice with which many women writers are comfortable.[6] If the impression of authority is not found in her essays, it may be because her stated objective as early as 1934 was to write "like a woman" because "a woman cannot unburden herself of her thoughts and feelings in a man's style, just as she cannot speak with a man's voice" ("Carta a Virginia Woolf" 12). Ocampo's rhetorical strategies reflect her need to interact dialogically with both texts and readers, not a desire to achieve authoritative control over them. As Sidonie Smith has suggested, women writing from the margins of discourse are challenging the traditional hegemonic discourse and destabilizing conventional literary values, among them the notion of unitary "authority" as a sine qua non for gaining respect as a writer (59).

Women's voices are heard much more clearly today than when Mistral and Ocampo were writing, not to mention Sor Juana, thanks in large measure to the resonances and reflections of specular discourse. Rosario Castellanos' seminal collection of essays, *Mujer que sabe latín . . .* (Woman Who Knows Latin . . . , 1973), is one example of this ongoing intellectual tradition, as is Rosario Ferré's *Sitio a Eros* (Eros Besieged, 1980). The fact that women writers continue to write about their female predecessors, however, indicates that the self-authorizing venture is still considered a perilous one in Spanish America. Women writers now acknowledge that reciprocal reflections can promote a feeling of solidarity and empower both authors and readers, as Elena Poniatowska concluded in her 1985 portrait of Rosario Castellanos: "What I would like is for Rosario Castellanos' life to be the best argument to convince all women who have any creative vocation to carry on and believe in themselves" (132). Gradually, in the spirit of these efforts, the cultural hall of mirrors in Spanish America is being adjusted to reflect authentic images of women of yesterday and today.

NOTES

1. Rosario Ferré has written an excellent study, "Los misterios de los retratos de Sor Juana" (The Mysteries of Sor Juana's Portraits), analyzing Sor Juana's verse portraits of women as affirmations of her constant search for knowledge from a woman's perspective.

2. Jean Franco has pointed out that, during Mistral's stay in Mexico, where she wrote this text for the Ministry of Education under José Vasconcelos, she subscribed to his "Messianic vision" of the role of women in the postrevolution-

ary state. The highest calling for an unmarried woman was to be a teacher in the literacy campaign; for the married woman, her supreme mission was to be a nurturing mother (103).

3. Sara Castro-Klaren has written about this essay from a feminist linguistic perspective and included a somewhat abbreviated translation of it by Rosario Ferré in the anthology *Women's Writing in Latin America* (9, 27–29). For an interesting comparative study of another daughter's elegy to her mother, see Mexican author Nellie Campobello's *Las manos de mamá (My Mother's Hands,* 1938).

4. When I wrote the biography of Ocampo, I knew of the existence of Mistral's essay about her from letters Gabriela wrote to Victoria, but I did not locate it until after my book went to press. In my book I quote from the personal correspondence between them, which Victoria and Doris Dana kindly made available to me.

5. Molloy and Castro-Klaren point out the importance of specular discourse in Spanish American women's writing in their introductions to *Women's Writing in Latin America.* Castro-Klaren stresses the search for ideological affinities in women writing about other women writers, and Molloy points to the "sororal solicitude" and the female endeavor to breach a "representational gap" in androcentric literature by contemplating one's own image in the familiar image of another (6–7, 115, 123).

6. The issue of "authority" is problematic for a woman author who speaks from "otherness." According to Diane Price Herndl, "A feminine language lives on the boundary. A feminine text overthrows the hierarchies. . . . Like the voices Bakhtin hears in the novel's carnival, the female voice laughs in the face of authority" (11).

WORKS CITED

A Woman of Genius: The Intellectual Autobiography of Sor Juana Inés de la Cruz. Trans. and intro. Margaret Sayers Peden. Salisbury, Conn.: Lime Rock Press, 1982.

Bakhtin, M. M. "Author and Hero in Aesthetic Activity." In *Art and Answerability: Early Philosophical Essays by M. M. Bakhtin,* 4–256. Ed. Michael Holquist and Vadim Liapunov. Austin: University of Texas Press, 1990.

Behler, Ernst. *Irony and the Discourse of Modernity.* Seattle: University of Washington Press, 1990.

Campobello, Nellie. *Cartucho and My Mother's Hands.* Trans. Doris Meyer and Irene Matthews. Intro. Elena Poniatowska. Austin: University of Texas Press, 1988.

Castro-Klaren, Sara, Sylvia Molloy, and Beatriz Sarlo, eds. *Women's Writing in Latin America: An Anthology.* Boulder: Westview, 1991.

Chevigny, Bell Gale. "Daughters Writing: Toward a Theory of Women's Biography." In *Between Women*, 357–379. Ed. Carol Ascher, Louise DeSalvo, and Sara Ruddick. Boston: Beacon, 1984.

Ferré, Rosario. "Los misterios de los retratos de Sor Juana." In *El árbol y sus sombras*, 17–44. Mexico City: Fondo de Cultura Económica, 1989.

Franco, Jean. *Plotting Women: Gender and Representation in Mexico*. New York: Columbia University Press, 1989.

Godoy Alcayaga, Lucila [Gabriela Mistral], "Emilia Brontë: La familia del reverendo Brontë." In *Gabriela piensa en . . .* , 25–36. Ed. Roque Esteban Scarpa. Santiago, Chile: Editorial Andrés Bello, 1978.

———. "Gabriela piensa en la madre ausente." In *Gabriela piensa en . . .* , 17–20. Santiago, Chile: Editorial Andrés Bello, 1978.

———. "Victoria Ocampo." In *Gabriela piensa en . . .* , 49–56. Santiago, Chile: Editorial Andrés Bello, 1978.

Good, Graham. *The Observing Self: Rediscovering the Essay*. London: Routledge, 1988.

Herndl, Diane Price. "The Dilemmas of a Feminine Dialogic." In *Feminism, Bakhtin, and the Dialogic*, 7–24. Ed. Dale M. Bauer and S. Jaret McKinstry. Albany: State University of New York, 1991.

Ludmer, Josefina. "Tricks of the Weak." In *Feminist Perspectives on Sor Juana Inés de la Cruz*, 86–93. Ed. Stephanie Merrim. Detroit: Wayne State University Press, 1991.

McLeod, Glenda. *Virtue and Venom: Catalogs of Women from Antiquity to the Renaissance*. Ann Arbor: University of Michigan Press, 1991.

Meyer, Doris. *Victoria Ocampo: Against the Wind and the Tide*. 2d ed. Austin: University of Texas Press, 1990.

Molloy, Sylvia. *At Face Value: Autobiographical Writing in Spanish America*. Cambridge: Cambridge University Press, 1991.

Ocampo, Victoria. "Carta a Virginia Woolf." In *Testimonios*, 7–17. Madrid: Revista de Occidente, 1935.

———. "Emily Brontë (Terra incognita)." In *Testimonios*, 2a. serie, 95–165. Buenos Aires: Ediciones Sur, 1941.

———. "Quiromancia de la pampa." In *Testimonios*, 143–155. Madrid: Revista de Occidente, 1935.

———. "Virginia Woolf en mi recuerdo." In *Testimonios*, 2a. serie. 415–428. Buenos Aires: Ediciones Sur, 1941.

Poniatowska, Elena. "Rosario Castellanos: ¡Vida, nada te debo!" In *¡Ay vida, no me mereces!*, 43–132. Mexico City: Joaquín Mortiz, 1985.

Schweickart, Patrocinio P. "Reading Ourselves: Toward a Feminist Theory of Reading." In *Gender and Reading: Essays on Readers, Texts, and Contexts*, 31–62. Ed. Elizabeth A. Flynn and Patrocinio P. Schweickart. Baltimore: Johns Hopkins University Press, 1986.

Showalter, Elaine. "Feminist Criticism in the Wilderness." *Critical Inquiry* 8 (Winter 1981), 179–204.

Smith, Sidonie. *A Poetics of Women's Autobiography: Marginality and the Fictions of Self-Representation*. Bloomington: Indiana University Press, 1987.

Woolf, Virginia. *A Room of One's Own*. 1929. New York: Harcourt, Brace & World, 1957.

Richard Rosa and

Doris Sommer

TERESA DE
LA PARRA
AMERICA'S
WOMANLY SOUL

Invited to talk about herself, Teresa de la Parra (1889–1936), in a series of lectures written for Bogotá and rehearsed in Havana, preferred to talk about her venerable lineage of intensely verbal and efficacious women. Rather than tokenize her female self, Parra located her accomplishments in a long line of accomplished women, all Spanish American women, in fact, from the Conquest on. "Influencia de la mujer en la formación del alma americana" (The Influence of Women in the Formation of the American Soul) is the general title for her three lectures of 1930 (*Obra* 471–528). They are Parra's only production of anything like formal essays, perhaps because her life was short and so strained, in the last decade, by fatal tuberculosis. The talks were apparently an enormous success, with crowds spilling over the balconies and into hallways and with enthusiastic coverage from the press. Enormously entertaining to read, they must have been even more delightful to hear, given Parra's personal charm and her lament—through the narrator of *Las memorias de Mamá Blanca* (*Mama Blanca's Memoirs*, 1929)—that the written word kills the musical spirit of language.

Evocations of doña Marina's (Malinche's) flair for negotiations and forgiveness during the Conquest of Mexico, the genre of oral epistles that includes, for example, Sor Juana's occasional sonnets to the vicereine, long quotes from anonymous "Amarilis" who represents so many unpublished and unknown colonial women poets screened from view and from the corrupting heat of the tropics, are all memorable, thanks to Parra's delivery. But one wonders if the crowds came away with any substantive information or result that was not already announced by the apparently benign title of the lectures. Perhaps these performances were merely occasions for dwelling on loving detail, a talent that Parra's fans knew how to appreciate when they invited her to speak.

This harmless hearing will, however, miss a radically female, if not feminist, departure from standard essays and histories. It will miss the provocation in the very title of the talks. Women's "influence" for Teresa de la Parra is no meek intervention; it is definitive in the history of the Americas. Influence here carries something of Harold Bloom's meaning, so strong that it provokes unconquerable anxiety. Quoting Oscar Wilde on the problem, Bloom worries about it: "Because to influence a person is to give him one's own soul. . . . He becomes an echo of someone else's music, an actor of a part that has not been written for him" (6). In their charming, apparently frivolous and inoffensive review of Latin America's history from the Conquest to independence, Parra's essays in fact perform an outrageous occlusion of the men who have been giving themselves credit for forging history. Parra leaves them behind as she foregrounds female fashioners. History's men occupy the same laughably dignified space that the authoritarian but ineffectual father inhabits in *Las memorias de Mamá Blanca*: "the thankless role of God." The presumed superiority of Cortés over doña Marina, for example, or of Lope de Vega over the "Amarilis" who sent him pseudonymous poetry, is chastened in Parra's rereadings. And the pattern of reducing male presumption in the face of female agency repeats so consistently throughout the lectures that by the last one, when Simón Bolívar himself turns out to be the product of female creativity and the beneficiary of female valor, the reader has been trained to wink at the text with more complicity than skepticism.

Probably one of doña Marina's earliest apologists,[1] Teresa de la Parra credits her with the most difficult and crucial maneuvers accomplished during the Mexican campaign. She mediated, mitigated the conflict, and set the tone for a truly catholic conciliation, figured by the scene of her own forgiving conciliation with the mother who sold her into slavery.

> *There is no mission that she fails to perform, no peace proposals that she does not preside at along with Cortés. She goes about sweetening the bitterness as she translates everyone's discourse. This faith in her intervention, as if it were a secret Providence, guides us continuously through the countless crises that Bernal Díaz narrates.*
> (482)

If only she had been in his story of "la noche triste" (a major defeat by the Aztecs), Parra's ideal reader might lament, that night would have been less calamitous. But her very real presence in Díaz's book is what Parra finds most noteworthy. As a simple man attentive to detail and to surprise, unlike the official historian Gómara whose writing was more prescribed by bureaucratic form, Bernal Díaz writes in a popular vein that Parra identifies with her own. Being "so full of trivial detail!," his book never hesitates to dwell on Marina in the midst of heroic history. "She will be the polestar of his story, which is not really a history but something loftier and more beautiful: a prose ballad" (484).

Marina's epoch-making words are reported, not recorded. This is true also for El Inca Garcilaso's mother, and for the numberless passionate patriots who fueled independence in their kitchens, bedrooms, and sometimes in unconquerable movement from one liberated point to another. It is as if women's work, performed consistently, efficaciously, quietly, had no need of self-glorifying signatures, a sure sign of (male) insecurity. Garcilaso signs his own name to his mother's stories, "the highest pinnacle," in Parra's estimation, of his *Comentarios reales*.

> *Memoirs of his childhood, memories of memories*
> *that others told him, converge there and unite*
> *through love the two main currents that will form*
> *the future American nation. . . . It is the echo*
> *of the maternal voice, which, under the stars at*
> *night, used to tell him the legends of the Incan*
> *tradition.*
> (489)

By recording them in Spanish, Garcilaso evidently appropriates Incan lore into his Spanish (patriarchal) code. But underneath the legal language, Parra points out, lies the organizing rhythm and music of a mother's world.

That unaffected musicality, and the patient repetition of narrative lines, sets the tone for the entire colonial period, according to Teresa de la Parra. It is a quintessentially feminine period that drew time in reassuring circles. For her, the colony transpires in the chronotope we associate with traditional, anonymous fiction; it is a matrix of stories without a particular subject or signature. Anonymity is the decisive sign here. To refuse to identify oneself as a singular subject leaves the discursive space open, accommodating, ironically democratic. Said otherwise, history is beside the point in colonial life: "Naive and happy, like peoples who have no history, the Colony closes itself off entirely behind the Church, the home, and the convent" (490).

And yet anonymity itself, even the cloistered life of convent and kitchen, would—by a paradox of male politics—marshal colonial women for history. When Spain expelled the Jesuits from America in 1767 in an effort to police partisans for independence, it simultaneously closed America's women off from their repetitive, cloistered lives and produced more local patriots than it imagined. Unhappy, but also unfettered, women would wonder about the future. On the one hand, since the Crown had shown that it held nothing to be holy, the Crown could not presume any legitimate authority. On the other hand, with their "spiritual dictators" gone, women met the "emotional catastrophe" by adjusting Catholicism to the tropics, feminizing it, which amounted to paganizing Christianity (512). Once they reduced mortal sin to a vague abstraction, and once the terrible God of the Inquisition began to look more and more like the lord of a plantation whose paternalism extended to financing and presiding over African dances, the vacancy left by old authority would welcome such revolutionaries as Voltaire and Rousseau. For Teresa de la Parra, it was not the famous men, celebrated in histories, who really won independence; instead, political freedom was an anonymous and collective confection of their more modest mates (513).

The most dramatic example of official overestimation, as already mentioned, was Simón Bolívar himself. He was not merely influenced by women, even in the strong sense Parra intends here; he was practically created by them. Bolívar appears on Parra's pages as a blank figure on whom others—mostly women—inscribe their desire, their fiction. His mentor, Simón Rodríguez, is another mercurial figure whose significance comes from presiding over those women. Rodríguez is one of those men, Parra taunts, who have "gotten too close to genius without ever reaching it, and go mad." In one of his transports, he cast Bolívar in the role of Rousseau's Emile. But it was Bolívar's cousin in Paris, Fany de Villars, who would bring the role to life on the stage of her elegant salon. Influence, here (remembering Wilde's worry), is literally giving "an actor . . . a part that has not been written for him." "Fany sized him up with one glance and decided to open up the doors of success to him" (522). But in translating Rodríguez's enlightened desire to Fany's feminine fantasy, the featured actor of American freedom will have changed from educable Emile to Chateaubriand's romantic René. Fany is the one who anoints Bolívar's brow, like the Old Testament prophet who turned goatherd into king, before she launched the liberator's fateful journey home. Like Cortés' Marina and Garcilaso's mother, Bolívar's cousin is the voice that conditions American history.

The point in all three essays seems to be consistent, and almost predicts the fashion for social history that would develop alongside contemporary feminism: women make history just as (or because) they make homes. But beyond affirming the decisive and salutary influence of women, the essays show a marked indifference to coherent argumentation, unless, of course, the argument is simply that women have been making the decisive differences in history. Whether those differences seem restrictive or revolutionary from the perspective of official history, Parra's point is that women's work is always a balm and a blessing. Like Walt Whitman, that other defender of Americanism in its multifarious forms, Parra might have responded to criticism of ideological inconsistency with, "Do I contradict myself? Very well, I contradict myself." (It is tempting to speculate that their same-sex eroticism freed both writers, in some measure, from simple hierarchies and defensive preferences.) Still, there seems to be no contradiction at the meta-ideological level of theme: women have civilized the continent through the virtues of unconditional love and self-sacrifice, the very virtues that Catholicism worships in a feminized God and in his virginal mother.

> *I had begun to prepare, in these three lectures, a kind of historical overview of feminine abnegation in our countries, that is, of the hidden but happy influence that women have exercised during the Conquest, the Colonization, and Independence. . . . I have kept, then, to my selfless women. Frankly speaking, I will tell you that down deep in my heart I prefer them: they have the charm of the past and the infinite poetry of voluntary and sincere sacrifice.*
> (474 – 475)

Here the reader will notice that Parra is *reinscribing* or reaffirming the theme, admitting that second thoughts intervened between the formulation and the conclusion. In fact, on the previous page of this first lecture, two minutes earlier for the listening public, she had said, "The crisis that today's women are confronting cannot be resolved by preaching submission, submission and more submission, as was the practice during the time when a quiet life could be confined entirely behind doors" (473).

Rather than noting what might be—and no doubt has been—taken as woman's generic failure to be consistent, we may choose to read the contradiction as Parra herself thematizes it. She offers two reasons for simultaneously praising and resisting female self-sacrifice. One is the chronological and developmental differences that separate modern women from their foremothers of the Conquest through independence.

> *My affection for the Colony will never bring me to say, as some do in lyrical moments, that I would have wanted to be born then. No. I feel very well in my own time and I admire it. As far as it concerns me, I should say that almost all of my childhood was colonial and that the need to react against it, at a moment in which we are all revolutionaries—as much because of a spirit that demands justice as because of a spirit that practices petulance—that need was the cause that made me into a writer.*
> (490)

The self-attribution of petulance, then, allows Parra the irony of traveling alone in short skirts and stylish hats to celebrate female confinement, whether in the nunnery ("Inside the peaceful cell, intelligence was cultivated harmoniously along with virtue, those two closed and neighboring gardens" [496]) or the equally cloistered home where Amarilis wrote unrequitable love poems to Lope de Vega. A year after Teresa de la Parra's amorous outing with Lydia Cabrera to Italy, the cosmopolitan and fiercely independent woman reflects on the splendid spiritual flights of women who found freedom from prohibitions only with their imagination.

The other reason for contradiction coyly justifies those who expect women to be confused. In Parra's version, though, the confusion is purposeful, peaceloving, perhaps prescient of feminist and deconstructive moves away from antagonistic polar oppositions. It is the loving "irresponsibility" that characterized Mamá Blanca's "disorderly soul" and resonates with her forebears:

> *I believe that as long as politicians, military men, journalists, and historians spend their lives putting*

> *antagonistic labels on things, the job for young*
> *people, simple people, and above all women, since we*
> *are many and quite disorderly, is to shuffle the labels*
> *in order to reestablish cordial confusion.*
> (477)

The labels do not disappear for Parra, but they no longer distinguish between correct and incorrect, mine and yours. For example, she reviews the struggles for independence through two equally admirable, literally familial, foremothers: Great-Grandmother Panchita, a stubborn royalist, and Great-Aunt Teresa Soublette, a passionate patriot. Nevertheless, Parra's preference for peace and for the privilege her family enjoyed during "indolent" times (as if no one really slaved on plantations) amounts to preferring colonial continuity over revolutionary change. Revolution brought intolerance; "When a fight to the death came, it finished off anyone in the middle" (505). In any case, Great-Aunt Teresa's dedication to independence had more to do with love for an illustrious father (general and president) than with love of country. Parra repeats her critique of revolution in letters from her tuberculosis sanatorium, letters to Lydia Cabrera about plans to write a novel about Bolívar: "I am now convinced," Parra writes in 1932, "that with Bolívar in control of that poor Caracas of one hundred thirty years ago, with its forty thousand inhabitants, the city left the Colony behind, along with all the enchantments, virtues, and graces that any city in history might have had. That's why I'm not anti-Spanish, Cabra" (Hiriart 152).

Fans of Teresa de la Parra will find downright embarrassing other expressions of privileged conservatism in both her essays and the letters. Black slaves are commended for their loyalty (one would never guess at the history of rebellions throughout the Americas), and Spaniards fomented revolutionary resentment by strategically favoring *pardos*, or mulattoes, who were the "natural enemies" of the white criollos (510). Miscegenation is evidently at the root of political confusion, as are the peevish complaints of students in Machado's contemporary Cuba and Gómez's dictatorial Venezuela. "I say, just as Goethe used to say, that 'I prefer to suffer the injustice of tyranny over the injustice of disorder.' That's why I'm a Gómez supporter, to a certain point, and I would have been for Machado too, if only to oppose the false apostles" (Hiriart 155).

The panegyric to long-suffering maternal mitigators of conflict in the third essay comes as no surprise, given this preference for stability, any stability, which amounts to a horror of politics. It underlines the general

moral about female fostering announced in the title of these talks and
repeated throughout.

> *During more than three centuries they had worked in*
> *the shadow, like bees; without leaving a name, they*
> *left us their creation of wax and honey. They wove,*
> *with their abnegation, the patriarchal spirit of the*
> *criollo family. And by caressing the language with*
> *their voices, they worked into its fabric all the ca-*
> *dences and sweetness of their daydreams.*
> (513)

What may be surprising, though, are the final pages of accolades for
the gutsy woman who thrived precisely on social and military conflict,
Manuelita Sáenz, "La Libertadora." Like other commentators, Parra
remembers her for saving Bolívar's life in 1828, and for her progressively more military and provocative outfits. But she also remembers
Manuelita for blasting the very conventions that made other women so
admirably submissive: "Manuelita is interesting in the extreme, for more
than just her picturesque flair. She also represents, if one considers the
case well, a violent protest against woman's traditional servitude, and
against a future that promised only the not-always-open door of marriage" (524).

Where in this conclusion is the praise of mitigation, of a bias toward
conserving and tolerating apolitical neutrality? Men do us the favor,
Parra had said in the first essay, of soiling their hands in politics so that
we can remain true angels of our national and continental houses. Military service, suffragism, and public debate were all thankfully beyond
the protective limits of domestic spirituality (474). And yet the essays end
in a defiant and sustained embrace of military and combative Manuelita.
Is this because the female "liberator" prepares a future in which woman
and wife are no longer synonymous in Spanish, a future that Teresa
de la Parra can freely inhabit, intimately with Lydia Cabrera, for example? To this loving friend, forty-three-year-old ailing Parra would
complain that her own traditional mother and sister threatened to infan-
talize her.

> *A plan to reduce me again to a minor, under an iron*
> *tutelage where they would have the deciding voices.*
> *I'm about ready for such a plan! Although I under-*

*stand that I'm being ill mannered, and that I should
be grateful for their efficiency, the business about ar-
ranging the house has made me furious. . . . I'd be
more likely to kill myself doing foolish things, given
my contradictory nature, and make them see that they
can't dominate me.*
(HIRIART 147)

Of course it is possible that Teresa de la Parra's liberating embrace of
Manuelita is neither proleptic nor programmatic of rebelliousness. It may
be simply another, outlying example of Parra's inclusive gesture in these
essays about women. She includes them all, whether it takes nostalgia or
utopian projections to do so. Meek Amarilis merits inclusion for her
meekness, proud Panchita for her pride, and manly Manuelita for her
transgressive *vir*-tues. The point is that everything fits into a woman's
soul, and by extension into the feminized soul of America celebrated in
Parra's essays. Like *Las memorias de Mamá Blanca*, the essays are structured like a fan, opening a new fold with each page. Reading them becomes an unfamiliar but deliciously dizzying exercise in following the
folds as they zigzag in and out of apparent contradictions. The folds
would ideally add up to a conflicted but inclusive history. And even
where some wrinkles are evidently stuck, as in the forgotten or purpose-
fully excluded heroines of ethnic struggles (since Catholic Hispanism
here is universal by definition), the gift of Parra's accommodating form
is that it has the potential to fan out more fully in other hands.

NOTES

1. See more recent revisions of la Malinche, for example the work by Enrí-
quez and Mirande.

WORKS CITED

Bloom, Harold. *The Anxiety of Influence*. Oxford: Oxford University Press,
1973.
Enriquez, Evangelia, and Alfredo Mirande. "Liberation, Chicana Style: Colonial
Roots of Feministas Chicanas." *De Colores* 4:3 (1978), 7–21.

Hiriart, Rosario. *Cartas a Lydia Cabrera: Correspondencia inédita de Gabriela Mistral y Teresa de la Parra*. Madrid: Ediciones Torremozas, 1988.

Parra, Teresa de la. *Obra: Narrativa, ensayos, cartas*. Selección y estudio de Velia Bosch. Caracas: Biblioteca Ayacucho, 1982.

María Cristina
Arambel Guiñazú

"BABEL" AND
DE FRANCESCA
A BEATRICE

TWO FOUNDING ESSAYS
BY VICTORIA OCAMPO

Victoria Ocampo's literary vocation finds its expression in the essay, a form she cultivates throughout her life. Through this genre she fulfills her need for self-examination while also bearing witness to the changes and experiences of her time. These characteristics give coherence to the otherwise diverse content of the ten volumes of her essays, titled *Testimonios* (Testimonies). This study will focus on the first essays written by Ocampo, "Babel" (1920) and *De Francesca a Beatrice* (From Francesca to Beatrice, 1924), considered here as prologues to her later work.

Ocampo has recognized her debt to the *Essais* of Michel de Montaigne, which combine the thorough and logical examination of a given subject with a very personal point of view. The strong presence of the narrative "I" and the progression from hypothesis to conclusion allow Ocampo, in these first essays, to frame questions that subvert traditional ideas based on authority and to open up a space for her own writing. The two essays under consideration differ from those of Montaigne in that they conceal a very intimate search for balance under the form of literary criticism.

Ocampo's first article appeared in *La Nación* in 1920, in French, under the title "Babel." Out of the mythical confusion of tongues arises a new language whose authority finds its origin in the distant biblical text. From its beginning the essay proposes a new version of the well-known text:

> *Jehovah did not alter the words of Noah's children,*
> *but rather he changed the perception that each of*

their brains had of those words. The words continued
being externally as they had been until then but in-
ternally they became different for each man. The
words, then, continued, sounding like they always
had but their resonance was distinct in each ear.
(*TESTIMONIOS* I : 33) [1]

In her own version, Ocampo offers a theory of textual interpretation. Jehovah must not have created a multiplicity of languages but instead have altered the power of individual perception. The value of a language as a system of communicaton becomes subordinate, then, to the use that each person makes of it. The point of view that influences the understanding of a message differs according to the individual. In Saussurean terminology, *parole* takes precedence over *langue* and *langage*. Without universality, meaning remains in a state of readiness that permits it to be mobile and variable. Each word, however well known, proposes an enigma to be elucidated by the hearer or reader who, converted into translator and intrepreter, receives the message he or she is capable of understanding. A common language is subject to as many variations of interpretation as there are instances of communication. In other words, the diversity of understanding has as its result the creation of multiple interpretations and languages, which depend on each individual's personal "translation"; this operation destroys the hermeneutic that aspires to find a true and unique message, and replaces it with the acceptance of a great variety of ideas, each partially valid.

The theory she expounds authorizes Ocampo to write her own version of the facts. The interpretation expounded in "Babel" not only puts the original text into question but also allows the author to cast judgment on the Supreme Authority: "Perhaps Jehovah himself was unaware of the dreadful repercussion it would have on future generations" (34). Imagining a perverse divinity without responsibility for the effects of his actions does away with the idea of perfection and gives freedom of action to human beings. Ocampo fills the vacuum that authority leaves, transforming herself into an author. Given an originary confusion, she feels justified in adopting a subversive attitude and replacing texts attributed to the First Author. That is, in her first article Ocampo seizes the power traditionally attributed to the voice of the Bible, relativizing its value and legitimizing numerous interpretations.

Her own discourse is in this way inserted into the long tradition of texts that comprise Western culture, the whole constituted by interpretations of interpretations, all of them original. In the autobiography that she writes years later, Ocampo deems her first essay a "stammer" and says that she wrote it in the margin of a copy of the *Divina Commedia*. Designating it as the appendix of another, greater, text, the author decenters her first text and tries to take away some of its value. The original and proper text is imperfect, fragmentary, and incomplete, but remaining situated outside the orbit of power grants even more relevance to its unsettling task.

The purpose of "Babel" consists of discussing, in order to refute, the meaning of the word "equality" as it was applied in the time of the French Revolution. Not only does it designate according to Ocampo an unattainable utopia, but, were such a utopia possible, it would be the equivalent of injustice. Her argument rests on the fact that nature favors creatures in diverse ways. Denying the possibility of utopian equality Ocampo affirms her difference from the rest of society, at the same time that she determines for herself the right to contradict traditionally accepted opinions.

The consequences derived from this first essay are several. To begin with, Ocampo's "I" presents itself from the very beginning as marginal and eccentric, and, further, her writing belongs in the realm of the improper, of metaphors that multiply meanings. In such a sense, it is significant that the essay takes as its point of departure the myth of Babel, which aims to explain the origin of the various languages starting from the division between two epochs: the first, unknown to and impossible for humanity, in which only proper language, unequivocal and without metaphor, exists; and the second, the only one of which we have experience, in which difference, the improper, and translation reign. As an heir of Babel, Ocampo suspends all judgments about veracity; her interpretation inscribes itself in the realm of multiple possibilities, and there exists the possibility of dialogue among them all.

In the text emerge two poles that to a certain extent oppose each other: against the liberty that supposes the idea of the multiplicity of meaning there arises a personal, dominant interpretation that her public labor initiates. The tension between the recognized polysemy of language and the message she wants to transmit does not, however, lead to a dead end. The conversational tone, characteristic of the genre, incites the reader to meditate and even to respond; the essayist does not present her opinions as absolute but rather as the result of an interpretation, subject to variations. In support of the variability of opinions, the author declares at the beginning of "Babel" that she has discussed the topic often, always in a different way, putting down on paper only one of her reflections. Furthermore, in this way Ocampo does not impose her interpretation on the reader, limiting her authority to giving one possible version among many. This condition of subjectivity paradoxically makes Babel, symbol of the fall into Jehovah's disfavor and the sentencing to a permanent mutual incomprehension, turn out to be the introduction of Ocampo as a writer. The impossibility of a monological language and the subjective character of the essay grant to the writer the right to elaborate her point of view in a language that, belonging to nobody, can be altered at her pleasure.

The colloquial tone of the essay is established from the question that begins it, "Have you ever reflected on the humiliating failure of the masons of Babel?," and invites the reader to participate in the discussion. The dialogue, although led by the essayist based on her personal experiences, seems not to conclude. Ocampo's answer asserts happiness in difference but it does not exclude other, different answers.

The discussion on the topic of equality is of great importance precisely because it makes room for the introduction of a new authority. The argument is simple: if we are all unequal and all have different opinions, then we all also have the right to express them. Ocampo exercises her right in order to express ideas that are outside of the canons and for which she makes herself answerable. That is, by relativizing opinions and breaking with the idea of objectivity she creates a space for her work. With this action she challenges the customs of her age and the milieu in which she lives. In the Buenos Aires of 1920 one did not look with favor on a woman of the haute bourgeoisie taking up her pen and making her opinions known on topics that were considered philosophical. These first essays, written as general commentaries, at no point allude to the particular situation of woman; had they done so, their publication would have been impossible. But it is under this general discourse, apparently innocuous, that the woman author defends her personal interpretation.

To better understand the importance of these essays it is necessary to refer to the circumstances in which Ocampo wrote them. She began her literary career at a moment in which her private life was in full ferment. Matrimonial failure, the beginning of the most important emotional relationship of her life, the silence in which she hid from her family the reality of her situation: all coincided with the writing of her first published texts. Her break with her husband and her adultery were symptomatic of her rebellion against the rules that directed the behavior of the haute bourgeoisie. On the one hand, society granted her a place of importance, but on the other, it denied her the power to express herself as she pleased. The illegality of the situation in which she lived served as a bridge for carrying the rebellion over to the written word, which offered her one more opportunity for defiance. The triangular relationship of adultery replaced the two-termed matrimonial one; with this change, traditional power relations were altered. Ocampo stopped being a wife subject to well-structured rules, to become a coparticipant in a couple in which both members were equally outside the law. In her autobiography she explains the importance of the displacements necessary to fulfill her role and their influence on the image she constructs of herself. Alternating the proper place, the family house situated in the center of the city, with a space that was improper and unknown to her in the suburbs, along with exchanging the roles she played, made her feel "other." She lived in imposture and experienced her situation as if she herself were metaphor, writing; in each space she adopted a different mask, fully aware that both simulated something extra. The dissimulation that she practiced in her daily life was translated into her writings, which appear as veiled confessions.

Thanks to the condemnation to silence society had imposed on her, Ocampo wrote in 1924 the essay *De Francesca a Beatrice*. Pretending to be a reader's guide to the *Divina Commedia*, it disguises her personal love story. The essay, which, following the plan of the original, takes as a point of departure the Inferno and culminates in Paradise after having labored through Purgatory, concentrates its interest in the love of Francesca and Paolo, which it places in counterpoint to the platonic love of Beatrice and Dante. Ocampo as reader understands the sin of adultery of the couple condemned to hell and, as she writes about it, comments on her own situation. If indeed the reading of the happiness of Beatrice and Dante in the empyrean extorts from her some phrases of admiration, that state has nothing to do with her own. Beatrice is a divine messenger, transmitter of the message of unique value, and, as such, she belongs to the pre-Babelic order, while Francesca preserves an enigma always open to interpretation. She comments thus on the behavior of Beatrice: "Beatrice responds to Dante's entreaty not with her mouth and eyes but with her smile and glance: soul of the mouth, soul of the eyes, whose material possession is impossible" (*De Francesca a Beatrice* 86). Beatrice belongs to the divine realm, of truth, of language before the fall of Babel. Her corporeality disappears in exchange for the unity of God, just as her messages, her "smile" and "glance," transmit pure spirituality.

The torment of Francesca and Paolo, in contrast, consists of their not being able to escape the realm of the senses; they are limited by their bodies. And to say "body" means "language." Ocampo's identification with Francesca explains her vocation, her choosing the word and literature. To choose this model over that of Beatrice is to recognize the domination of difference, of the multiple diversification literature offers, as Ocampo had already announced in "Babel."

With the commentary on the fifth canto of the Inferno, Ocampo interprets Francesca and interprets herself. In her writing, both characters proclaim their lives in unison, without repentance or denial. If Dante's text formulates the condemnation of the sin, Ocampo's text redeems her guilt in the affirmation of the action. Literary commentary challenges legal discourse. Both women gain atonement through suffering and becoming tragic heroines. Rereading the essay, Ocampo comments in her autobiography,

> *Passion-love is that of Paolo and Francesca, that is, the Circle of torment where Dante places them. . . . Passion-love is a tremendous hunger and not only from the body, not only from the heart but from something within us that escapes all classification and analysis, and all precise designation. Its nature is such that it only satiates itself by going beyond to another level. . . . From the cliffs of passion-love, the uncertainty of being at the edge of something tremendous invades us. We are at the threshold of a mystery that we grope at with a blind man's hand. It is as if we were discovering the existence of an exit toward eternity.*
> (*AUTOBIOGRAFÍA* 3 : 32 – 33. NOTICE OCAMPO'S USE OF THE FIRST PERSON PLURAL, INDICATING HER IDENTIFICATION WITH FRANCESCA.)

The particulars mentioned so far explain Ocampo's choice of the essay as her literary form, since it is the form best suited for the expression of a personality. The double register she utilizes in "Babel" and in *De Francesca a Beatrice* compensates for the silence of her daily life, and literary criticism is the means for relating the personal. Thus Ocampo premeditatedly uses the instruments that the masons of Babel have bequeathed to her. And so it is that her essays, even if they deal with a great variety of topics, always translate either rebellion, sympathy, or rejection, all expressions of a self, an "I," that permanently examines itself. It is not surprising, then, that the volumes of her essays serve her toward the midpoint of her career as notes for her autobiography.

The two essays here studied, as well as the majority of those that Ocampo wrote afterwards, have for their purpose literary criticism. Even "Babel," a meditation upon the idea of equality, is based on Canto XV of the *Purgatorio*. José Clemente, in a study of the essay in Argentina, distinguishes between the essay and literary criticism. The first supposedly develops abstract themes while the second occupies itself with the concrete (10). This difference has no relevance in the case of Ocampo since the criticism practiced by her reveals the reader and her reading. Her method therefore is of great importance: Ocampo repeatedly affirms that her readings are those of an enthusiast because her person prolongs itself in them. The agreements and rejections facing the texts she reads always depend on her capacity for identification: in Dante she says that she finds "vital nutriment," and she adds in her autobiography: "I wonder if that great poem has ever been read that way, with that need to find in it a fraternal echo of our anguish and the hope of finding some answer" (*Autobiografía* 3:44).

Some similarity can be seen between this type of reading and the type that Rachel Brownstein observes in young girls who seek through the lives of their heroines to try out more interesting and important roles than their own (xxiv). The great difference between both readings lies in the fact that for Ocampo, reading—practiced all her life—is the equivalent of a sustenance without which she cannot live; what is read is incorporated directly into the reader. This vital activity, practiced thus since childhood, finds support in her adulthood in Virginia Woolf's concept of the "common reader," which she mentions repeatedly. Ocampo wants to liberate herself from the rules directing literary criticism. Therefore she rebels against erudite criticism that does not encourage reading among the general public and that limits itself to opening arid discussions among a narrow circle of specialists. Interpretations derived from these readings close the texts within antagonistic theses that prove their own uselessness. Ocampo encourages a personal reading, allowing the reader self-understanding and blurring the notion of fiction: no trench exists to separate the life of books from daily life; between both there are ramifications that annul the distinction. Readers are characters in the books they read, and what they find in them is applicable to their experience.

That interaction grants a great freedom to the act of reading; anyone is capable of elaborating interpretations, all of them being equally valid. A metaphor widely used by Ocampo in relation to the texts she reads speaks eloquently on this matter. She considers them "spaces" in which she "penetrates," in which the lines "came out as she passed by," expressing a close acquaintance (*De Francesca a Beatrice* 9–10). The reading proposed by Ocampo supposes a mutual relationship between reader and text in which both attract each other and establish an almost physical intimacy.

Reading as personal labor and the practice of the essay as a literary form favor the flourishing of an "I," explaining why Ocampo figures so preponderantly in her work. One may appropriate Montaigne's phrase, "Je suis moi-même la matière de mon livre" (I myself am the subject of my book); essays, like an autobiography, form a whole that responds to Ocampo's double purpose of knowing herself and publishing images about herself. By means of this search Ocampo constructs a very complex vision of herself, one that encompasses many readings. The readings are incorporated into her text but also into her "I," her sense of self. In this way, adultery serves as the metaphor of her writing: the self as narrator who emerges from the collection of essays is constituted by a great variety of texts and masks. Her work is double: on the one hand, she offers different points of view that argue with established viewpoints, and on the other, she gives birth to a plural "I" that debates with itself. To read Francesca, established as the model of a woman sinner, and grant her a heroic role is tantamount to questioning the classifications that assure society's thought; at the same time, it is to see herself as a new Francesca.

The central figuration of a self who adheres to practices like these that threaten patriarchal order unleashes the reproaches of critics. Symptomatic of this is that the judgments of these men redound not upon the essays but upon the author. When Ocampo submits *De Francesca a Beatrice* to the critical judgment of Angel Estrada and Paul Groussac, two authorities on the subject, both suggest, for opposite reasons, that she abandon her undertaking. The former considers her writing too personal while the latter accuses her of pedantry and recommends that she choose impersonal topics (*Autobiografía* 3:105–109). Converted into society's spokesmen, they want to rein in her publications. Facing the clarity—however much they contradict each other—of the critics, Ocampo in contrast champions ambiguity. That Ocampo is trying with these essays to make a space for her writing does not pass unnoticed by these critics. In fact, what bothers them most seems to be the fact that the person who writes in this way is a woman. Although Ortega, Ocampo's personal friend, was the one who published her *De Francesca a Beatrice* in his *Revista de Occidente*, he also expressed reservations. The critic added an epilogue that, although it claims to flatter the author, ends up being notably ambiguous. Even though he alludes to Ocampo's essay, Ortega takes advantage of the occasion to explain his ideas about women and the role they should play in society. Following an essentialist line of thought, he fixes women in passivity and suffering. One can see his thought summarized in one of his aphorisms: "The task of woman, when she is nothing but woman, is to be the concrete ideal ('charm,' 'illusion') of the male. Nothing more. But nothing less" (*De Francesca a Beatrice* 103). The Spanish critic obviously thinks that Ocampo is breaking barriers and is entering into areas where she does not belong. His epilogue is added to the reproaches of Estrada and Groussac and forms part of the network of discourses that restrict the action of an "authority" that proclaims itself beyond the norm.

Ocampo, who in these first essays did not mention the fact of being a woman nor make references to feminist positions, understood the motives of these attacks. In her autobiography she described what it meant for a woman to write for the public:

> It was scandalous, as much as driving a car through the streets of Buenos Aires was. For that I received a copious rain of insults. And what passersby shouted when they saw me pass by, sitting in the car with the steering wheel in my hand, others thought when they read my articles. But the readership of La Nación was not as spontaneous as the pedestrians. Their opinions were, nevertheless, the same.
> (*AUTOBIOGRAFÍA* 3 : 103)

The author felt censured and pushed to the margins, both of literature and of society. It is no surprise, then, that the self arising from the essays should suffer from insecurity and seek support for its opinions in the texts it read. The advantage that the literary-critical essay offered Ocampo is that the narrative voice can lean on the prestige of a recognized authority. The integration into the text of fragments belonging to others, a characteristic present in Ocampo's entire production, displays the subject as a compound that therefore is ambivalent. If she clearly identifies the patriarchal system as the promoter of injustice, she also shows great respect for many of the figures who represent it. The self that emerges from Ocampo through her oeuvre is a textual composite that does not eliminate its contradictions. Blas Matamoro has observed the admiration that the essays express for a great majority of male authors. One must nevertheless avoid generalization; many women are admired by Ocampo as well: Emily Brontë, Woolf, Gabriela Mistral, Anne de Noailles, María de Maeztu, and Susan Sontag. Nor should one forget the alterations that model texts undergo in Ocampo's reading: her interpretations always offer original points of view. The idea of a "common reader" characterizes Ocampo as reader, and, in her writing, dialogues between subject and society, between subject and reader, and dialogues within the subject herself all proliferate. Seldom or never do we hear a monologue.

NOTES

1. Victoria Ocampo, "Babel." The text, cited for its greater availability, is from *Testimonios*, Primera serie, 1920–1934 (Buenos Aires: Ediciones Fundación Sur, 1981). Further quotations from this text will appear followed by the page number from this edition.

WORKS CITED

Brownstein, Rachel M. *Becoming a Heroine*. New York: Viking, 1982.
Clemente, José E. *El ensayo*. Buenos Aires: Ediciones Culturales Argentinas, 1961.
Matamoro, Blas. *Genio y figura de Victoria Ocampo*. Buenos Aires: Editorial Universitaria de Buenos Aires, 1986.
Montaigne, Michel de. *Essais*. Paris: Société des Belles Lettres, 1973.
Ocampo, Victoria. *Autobiografía*. 6 vols. Buenos Aires: Ediciones Revista Sur, 1982–1984.
———. "Babel." In *Testimonios*, 1a. serie, 1920–1934, 33–39. Buenos Aires: Ediciones Fundación Sur, 1981.
———. *De Francesca a Beatrice*. Buenos Aires: Ediciones Fundación Sur, 1983.
Ortega y Gasset, José. "Epílogo." In *De Francesca a Beatrice* by Victoria Ocampo, 91–119. Buenos Aires: Ediciones Fundación Sur, 1983.

Gwen Kirkpatrick ALFONSINA STORNI
AS "TAO LAO"
JOURNALISM'S ROVING
EYE AND POETRY'S
CONFESSIONAL "I"

One of the disparaging criticisms lev-
eled at women's writing has been its personal nature in contrast to more
universalist topics. In the same way that women artists such as Frida
Kahlo have been seen as self-obsessed and limited in thematics, these
women have been judged as limited by the scope of their sources, their
own lives. Our question then is, how do women in certain epochs transform the public space allotted to them? Why do female writers turn to
their own lives, or stylized versions of them, for so much of their creative
material? As many observers of women's writing have noted, there is a
strong attraction to personal forms of expression such as letters, diaries,
and journals. As Susan Gubar states, "[T]he mythic lives of women artists from Emily Dickinson . . . to Isadora Duncan . . . also reveal the
close identification between the artist and her art" (1). Alfonsina Storni's
life (1892–1938) provides a striking case of this identification, surely
crafted in part for public reception. From the beginning of the twentieth
century, sentimentalism and melodrama had been assigned to the wom-
en's corner, with tragedy and realism winning out as the most esteemed
modes in stage and film. Storni's move to position herself in the melodramatic or confessional vein with ironic commentary shows her possi-
bly conscious choice of a perspective from which to write and from
which to succeed.

The popularity of Storni's best-known poetry stands in direct contrast
to the negative reaction it provoked from her critics. Most attacked by
many of her contemporaries were the "confessional" nature of her poetry
and its "impure" aesthetics. Storni, obviously aware of these criticisms,
apparently made sure to continue her practices up until the later stages of

her career. As her prose work points out, she was aware of the criticism yet continued in the explicitly confessional vein, with the poem "You Want Me White" being the clearest expression of her defiant poetic stance. By comparing her with other well-known poets of her time, one can see the clear dynamics of her confessional poetry as a contestatory poetics. It responds to many of the vanguardist experiments, and perhaps just as important, it establishes Storni's awareness of the *popular* nature of her work.

By now, Storni's life is well known and "Alfonsina" has acquired the aura of legend. She was a child of Swiss-Italian immigrants in provincial Argentina, had a teacher-training school education, was an unwed mother, moved to the big city of Buenos Aires in 1912, had a series of jobs in offices and factories and an early entry into journalism and teaching, and most importantly, occupied a very visible spot as a young writer and poet in certain literary circles.[1] Her early fame won her a constant and fairly consistent "middlebrow" public. Her name rarely appeared in the well-known vanguardist publications of her day, directed by writers such as Borges, Güiraldes, Girondo, and others, except for the occasional caricature or disparaging remark.[2] Yet she did occupy a steady spotlight as a contributor in the pages of the major newspaper *La Nación*, traditional literary journals such as *Nosotros*, and widely distributed publications of a more popular nature for which she wrote numerous essays throughout her adult life.[3]

Storni as poet is as much a creation of the journalistic mode as she is a participant in journalism herself. Melodrama and sentimentalism are dominant elements in her essays as well as in her poetry, overshadowing to a large extent more explicit investigations of social movements or customs. Yet she often adopts the conventions of melodrama and sentimentalism, largely unexplored in serious literary history, in the service of social exposé and denunciation. The immediacy of melodrama and sentimentalism and their acceptability as conventions for women's readings gave Storni the vehicle to express her ideas about a wide range of topics. Topics that might have been unappetizing for popular periodicals, such as family upheaval due to women's work outside the home or the pitfalls of the city awaiting young women from the country, could be recast as sentimental melodrama. Surely influenced by the increasing popularity of the cinema and its spotlight on new heroines and "stars," Storni found a way to incorporate the conventions of melodrama into her journalistic critiques. For example, in the vanguardist writings of the period, elements of the "modern," such as the lower-middle-class suburbs, the streetcar, the subway, and the working woman, are often celebrated. Storni, although working with some of the same materials, sometimes "romanticizes" such scenes by the introduction of stock characters such as the poor, the elderly, the fashionable and arrogant, and small children, and "deromanticizes" them by scenes of physical and emotional abandonment. Thus, while she models her journalistic essays on the popular conventions of the period, she subtly responds to the practices and topics of the vanguard and clearly shows the underside and details of life of such "modern" elements through sentimentality and melodrama. With these practices she complies with the conventions of the "Women's Page" of newspapers and journals in her chatty, informative style about the latest fashions of the city streets, especially in her articles signed with the pseudonym "Tao Lao" in *La Nación*, which regularly appeared in the section "Feminine Sketches."[4] Yet even such a seemingly innocuous setting gives her opportunity to dismantle appearances and zero in on telltale marks of social class and economic status.

Storni's journalistic production shows a sharp eye for details that reveal social status, the style of dress or bearing that belies provincial origin, the conventions of fashion, sentimentalism, and an uncanny perception of the changes undergone in an urban sphere rapidly transformed by immigration, industrialization, and the push and shove of the realignment of social patterns.[5] We might remember that her best-known poetic work, i.e., the poetry published between 1916 and 1930, was produced in the same years as Vallejo's first two books, *The Black Heralds* and *Trilce*, Neruda's *Twenty Love Poems and a Song of Despair*, Borges' *San Martin Notebook* and *Moon across the Street*, and Gabriela Mistral's early poetry, and that it corresponds with the end of the Mexican Revolution and certainly the impact of the First World War and the Russian Revolution. Her first book of poetry, *The Restlessness of the Rosebush* (1916) was published only two years after Delmira Agustini's death at an early age and in the same year as Rubén Darío's death. Situating her thus within Latin American literary history may give us some way to examine her construction of the unmistakable "I" of her poetry. If other poets are experimenting with the dissolution of the subject, the escape of the "I," the fanning out of multiple perspectives, or the capture of the instantaneous image, Storni reasserts a kind of unitary subject as full bodied as that of the Romantics. Autobiography is mixed with social commentary, and each perspective is claimed as one personally experienced by "Alfonsina."

We might also position her in another way, within the changes that occurred in Buenos Aires itself from her arrival there until 1930, a perspective best viewed from her essayistic production. What did Storni encounter when she arrived in Buenos Aires in 1912? What did she see during the next decades that she recorded in her writing? We find some indications of cultural norms in the poetry itself, in the impact of the sentimental novel, in the popular theatre, and most of all in the rapid expansion of the movies as a cultural force in that period. On other levels, her essays reveal the radical dislocations in gender and familial roles in a rapidly urbanizing environment, where foreign and internal immigration was accelerating the massive social and cultural changes that came with the First World War and with the particularities of South America's most populous city.

What was life like in the Buenos Aires she moved to from the provinces? Argentina, especially Buenos Aires, showed the results of a prosperous and expansive economy, fueled by agricultural exports and massive numbers of European immigrants. The public school system was managing to incorporate massive new arrivals, and in 1914 over 65 percent of the population of Buenos Aires was considered functionally literate, a strikingly high index when compared with almost any other nation.[6] In the same year the census showed that two-thirds of Buenos Aires' inhabitants were foreign born, and among males and the working class this figure was much higher. In 1914 there were also three hundred brothels registered by the government in Buenos Aires, with surely many more unregistered ones, keeping alive the city's fame as a capital of white slavery.

Education and journalism were the two occupations that first gave women access to professional status outside the home. Obviously, the growth of industrialization had moved women outside the home and into factories, and the expansion of commerce had created jobs for female office workers and salesclerks in early twentieth-century Buenos Aires.[7] The beginnings of Storni's career in Buenos Aires coincided with World War I, an event that was to transform Argentina even though the country was not directly involved. It shook Argentina's export-based economy, leading to a period of unemployment and a shift in production patterns. In addition, and more importantly for our purposes, World War I marked a major change in the public roles and perceptions of women. Women in Europe and the United States were pushed into roles outside the home in the years of the war crisis, propelling changes in their work status and in the public perception of the role of women. Even though Argentina did not receive the brunt of the war experience, it did receive, through films, magazines, and other media, striking images of the "New Woman." Short hair and short skirts, public flaunting of Victorian modes of propriety, smoking in public—these were some of the images that attracted or repelled moviegoers and magazine and newspaper readers. Universal (male) suffrage had been granted by the Sáenz Peña Law of 1912, and apparently Argentina was on the road to increased democratization and prosperity. Women's suffrage groups had lobbied for the vote for women, but much more progress had been made in the areas of health and labor legislation for women and children than in female suffrage.

Much of the city's earlier (pre–World War I) economic growth had occurred in the service sectors, since most of the population was still centered in the capital. The majority of the working class was composed of recent immigrants, while the largest sectors of a growing middle class were from immigrant backgrounds, often first generation. The rapidly expanding service sector, from working class to more middle-class groups such as teachers and journalists, made room for women to enter the working force outside the home. Storni's article "The Perfect Typist" for *La Nación* (9 May 1920) sketches in a few sentences the "recipe" for molding the new class of women service workers:

> *Select a young woman from eighteen to twenty-one years old who lives in an apartment building in any distant neighborhood. Discreetly paint her eyes. Bleach her hair. File her nails. Tailor her a fashionable little suit, quite short. Flatten her stomach. . . . Put a bird inside her head (preferably a blue one). Send her to a commercial academy for two or three months. (Up to five pesos a month.) Then keep her waiting on commercial ads for one, two, or three years. Hire her for very little.*

The sketch highlights the dream-building process involved in the recruitment of women for service work, and ironizes the less glamorous and precarious realities of this new class.

As Francesca Miller explains in her study of women's education in Latin America, during the twenties "the first generation of urban, literate women appeared—in Buenos Aires, in São Paulo and Rio de Janeiro, in Santiago, Montevideo, Mexico City, and Havana. In the early decades of the twentieth century the expansion of female education meshed with the drive to modernize and the perceived need for an educated citizenry" (59). This occurred in countries that had developed a sizable middle class, a phenomenon closely linked with expanded education, for males as well as for females. Argentina's striking growth, fueled by immigration since the late nineteenth century, helped to make education an important element of the creation of citizens, a concept that had been promoted by Sarmiento in the latter decades of the nineteenth century.

The growth of the economy, slowed down by the First World War, rebounded after 1918. Buenos Aires was the hub of the government and the heart of the banking and finance sectors and a newly emerging publishing industry.[8] This rapidly expanding industry gives us a key to the formation of writers of the period. Matching the expansion of the population and the growth of a reading public, newspapers, magazines, novels by installment, and other publications flourished, with products for each sector of the reading public, from the barely literate to the university educated.

By the twenties, driven by the high literacy and relative prosperity of Buenos Aires' two million inhabitants, there were two dozen newspapers published in the capital (including those in foreign languages) as well as magazines of every kind, including Conde Nast's new *porteño* edition of *Vogue*.[9] The very popular and long-lived *Caras y Caretas*, begun in the early years of the century, would include Storni's works, as would the influential literary magazine *Nosotros*, founded in 1907 and lasting thirty-six years. At the same time that vanguardist literati of the "Florida" group were engaging in polemics and iconoclast writings in literary journals such as *Martín Fierro, Proa*, and the mural journal *Prisma*, other writers of a more political bent were concentrated around the group known as the "Boedo" writers. Most of the attention to the journalism of the period has centered on these two groups, so important in the formation of literature throughout the Spanish-speaking world.[10]

It is not surprising that many short-lived publications directed toward the middle class, produced by persons whose names are no longer remembered, are neglected in most studies. Yet precisely because this was the type of publication that so often employed women in their roles as writers, sometimes as anonymous scribes, we must look here for keys to the formation of women as professional writers. Storni is one of the very few women whose name appears as a contributor to literary magazines, rivaled only in frequency by her very different compatriot, Norah Lange.[11] In more popular publications, women's names appear more frequently, perhaps in part to serve a reading public that included growing numbers of women.

A review of the contributors to both popular and literary journals of the second and third decades of the twentieth century finds Storni's name listed in many of them, including *La Nota* (1915–1920, established specifically to support the Allied cause during the war), *Babel* (1921–1929), *Ediciones Selectas Americanas* (1919–1922), *Myriam* (an illustrated magazine, 1915–1919), *Atenea* (1918–1919), *Hebe* (1918–1920), *Tribuna Libre* (1918–1920?), *Revista Nacional* (1918–1920), *Nervio* (1931–1934), *La Revista del Mundo* (1919), *Poesía* (1933), *Atlántida* (1911–1914), and of course her long-term contributions (beginning in 1920) to *La Nación* as well as to the daily *La Prensa*.[12] These contributions are of varying types, including poems, short stories (usually very abbreviated for the exigencies of magazine format), epistolary short stories, serious essays, "sketches" of fashion or customs, and sometimes even epigrammatic entries on varied topics, tied together by the column format. While popular periodicals might focus on movie stars and debutantes, Storni managed to include vignettes of a burgeoning low-salaried group of female workers. A brief review of a few of her titles from *La Nación*, such as the previously cited "The Perfect Typist" (9 May 1920), "Why Do So Few Teachers Marry?" (13 March 1921), "Women as Women's Enemy" (22 May 1921), "Buenos Aires Dancers" (16 May 1920), and "The Woman Emigrant" (1 August 1920), shows that her columns were designed to attract a wide readership on the page devoted to "Women's Sketches." Increasingly, newspapers served as the print marketplace, advertising and showcasing new products, fashions, even lifestyles. In a major daily such as *La Nación*, Storni's column's placement among fashion and cosmetic advertisements, recipes, and society notes obviously lent some constraints to her essays. At the same time, however, the juxtaposition of the bazaar of consumer goods with Storni's social commentary saves her the task of always drawing her essays to a conclusion. A subtly satirical article on "The Bride" amidst engagement announcements or advertisements for bridal gowns lets the female reader draw her own conclusions.

Storni depended on her journalistic essays for income, as well as for exposing her poetry to the public. She obviously tailored her essays to the demands of the particular periodical, and could range from intimate chatter to harsh denunciations of social ills. The women's pages of *La Nación* are not the forum for those of Storni's essays more critical of

society—the Church's attitude toward women ("Letter to the Eternal Father," *La Nota* 27 June 1919) or women's civil rights, especially those of
single mothers and illegitimate children ("Women's Civil Rights," *La
Nota* 22 August 1919, or "Against Charity," *La Nota* 14 November
1919). Storni possessed a distinctive voice, but she knew how to modu-
late it depending on her public and editors. She was mindful of her role
as the rebellious, transgressive woman, which obviously gave her wider
berth than would have been granted to other writers. She did assume the
role of the champion of women, but her favorite roles to defend were
those that most closely reflected her own background, working-class to
lower-middle-class women who were achieving some social mobility
through education and journalism.

Storni is not, however, always the champion of all women or of the
working classes. For example, her own experience in an immigrant
family does not necessarily make her sympathize with the urban immigrant experience. She is clearly ambivalent about the effects of immigration and the burgeoning commercialism of Buenos Aires. In line with
many social theorists of her time, she speaks of the "evolution" of certain
national groups, treating her country as an organism undergoing growing pains. An immigrant herself who came to Argentina as a young
child, she appears to identify more with the citizen from the provinces
than with the immigrant from foreign shores. Her own upbringing in
the provinces appears to have led her to identify with the "native" or
criollo Argentine, another important category of "immigrant" in the
fast-growing Argentine capital. In "Concerning Ourselves" (*La Nota* 26
May 1917) she complains, "Why are the Buenos Aires masses so rude,
and why do women in this lovely city suffer such clumsy lack of cour-
tesy? This capital features a kindness that is morally killing it: its port."
Buenos Aires' lack of a common history, its "bizarre and Babylonian"
collectivity, lacks the long-term development that would correct its
"natural, imported negligence." Storni reconstitutes an "ourselves" that
cannot accommodate all comers, an idea heightened during the period
by the formation of the Argentine Patriotic League. Storni, while not
involved in the league itself, perhaps reflects some of its unease over the
new and changing mixtures of the city. Its "youth" here is not a sign of
vigor but a mark of immaturity, especially in regard to the treatment of
women "whenever they are outside the home or the salon." Storni's
remedy is her most frequently cited one, the family, as "primary collective institution, the base and foundation of the race."

Storni claims a special spiritual development for women and believes in a special feminine spiritual constitution, an inherent character that must be nurtured by education and home training. Women do need the protection of men, a protection nonetheless often lacking. In 1927 she explains in *Nosotros* (no. 215, 48–55) the reasons for the failure of her recently produced dramatic works. Describing her own situation, she explains,

> But launched on life's current to win one's daily
> bread, like most women in modern cities, longing for
> the masculine protection that deserts; because in the
> rough fight for money that characterizes the century,
> one scarcely has energy to protect oneself, I must de-
> mand interest on the experience: this interest . . . is
> the explanation of our lives and others' lives, an ex-
> planation that may or may not be transformed in art.
> (54)

The explanation she finds for the differences between the sexes is somewhat softened from her poetic positioning in poems such as "You Want Me White," but men seek pleasure and women, security: "I found men and women in fighting positions; the men, to obtain sweets of plea-sure, and the women to find someone to feed them." She repeats tradi-tional stereotypes of women's nature, even though she suggests that women as a group are evolving toward a higher morality: "I could see that if men are more selfish than women, women are more dishonest, in general terms, since they must fight with the weapons of the oppressed: feigning, astuteness, calculation" (55). The scene she outlines might serve as part of the plot for a movie of the period. The woman, forced to de-pend on her wiles and her cunning for survival, must learn to manage less complicated but more self-centered men, although it is only tough circumstance that forces her to hide her better nature. Yet independence appears to be linked to masculinity. Despite her claims for the inherent nurturing nature of females, Storni examines the concept of masculinity as a social construction. Feminine "complexity" itself is a product more of social status than of gender itself:

> The woman who is financially independent acquires
> many masculine traits. Her fundamental independence
> makes her not need men; and her ideas, before men's,
> are freer and clearer. More in control of her inner

> *truth, as she is closer to liberty, her purposes will not*
> *revolve exclusively around masculine conquest. But*
> *for the woman with no more dowry than her own*
> *self, her condition of economic oppression also in-*
> *creases her complexity. . . . Servants, whatever their*
> *sex, usually have feminine idiosyncrasies.*
> (47)

In her *La Nación* column on "The Male" (12 June 1921) she points out that the male of legend has lost his status in modern society: "Minuscule men have replaced the great men of legend. In families of the modern cities one sees the male, stripped of his attributes, happily napping, while sisters and mothers are hard at work in the shadow so their men can seem to be men" (5). As in a play, women are busy in the shadows, pulling strings and moving props so onlookers can believe in the illusion that individuals are still secure within a strong patriarchal structure.

In her journalistic essays, especially in her contributions to *La Nación*, Storni combines the roving eye of the passerby—"As I was walking through the streets of Buenos Aires"—with the unmistakable "I" of Alfonsina, the confessional poet of her first books of poetry. While her topics range from "Wedding Gifts" to "Women's Emancipation," and even though many essays show signs of the rush to meet deadlines or perhaps an editorial cut that leaves the reader suspended, Alfonsina Storni's remarkable writing career is unique, and at the same time exemplary of a generation. Like so many of her time and class, she entered the literary ranks through any means available. Often the only woman in a list of contributors or at a meeting of literati, she adopted the modes available to women, such as the newspapers' women's pages, and put her own stamp on them. Some of the essays listed above were written during periods of great upheaval and change in Argentine political life. On these particulars, with the exception of suffrage and legislation regarding the civil status of women and children, she comments very little. She does write of the world war and of women's importance to the Allies, but of specific political movements she reveals little in print. In her published work, her world is formed mainly by things in her immediate path of vision or within her inner life. The social structures she most often examines are those created by familial and gender roles, and she often views institutions outside this range, such as government and religion, as shaped by family and gender structures.

Storni is a sharp-eyed witness to her time and place. Like many women around her, she was moving into a workforce outside the home as technology and social realignments made enormous shifts in society. Unlike many women, however, she had the courage, the economic need, and the personal ambition to move into areas where few women had gone before. She fashioned an essayistic roving "I" that traveled the streets of Buenos Aires, allowing the confessional "I" so well known from her poetry to color the current daily events she chose to narrate. In a move parallel to the direction of the growing movie industry of her day, she knew how to capture the heightened gestures of melodrama and to stage her own street scenes within similar frameworks. Storni's personalized vision of her milieu was directed toward a specific audience, one eager for the newly minted myths of urban modernity but all too aware of the fissures daily reality made in those myths. She used the rapidly expanding journalistic medium to give us vignettes of her place and time, snapshots that sometimes mixed uneasily with the advertising emporium of the women's pages. Her own self-fashioning within the public eye as "Alfonsina," impassioned poet who had herself known anonymity and struggle on those city streets, gave her a vantage point from which to look back at the crowd.

NOTES

1. Rachel Phillips gives an excellent overview in English of Storni's career in *Alfonsina Storni: From Poetess to Poet*. A selection of translations of her poems can be found in the collection edited by Marion Freeman.

2. In the vanguardist magazine *Martín Fierro* Storni was satirized for her overt eroticism and her adherence to the poetic conventions of rhyme and meter. For example, in a selection called "Mentiras criollas" (Creole Lies) from issue 24, 14 November 1925, there is a mocking reference to Storni's personal life as well as to her writing: "Este nuevo hijo de la fecunda poetisa (refiriéndose al último libro de Alfonsina Storni)" (This new son of the fertile poetess [referring to Alfonsina Storni's latest book]). Quoted in *Martín Fierro (1927–1928): Antología y prólogo*, ed. Beatriz Sarlo Sabajanes (Buenos Aires: Carlos Pérez Editor, 1969), p. 119.

3. A complete listing of Storni's works may be found in Marta Baralis, *Bibliografía argentina de artes y letras*.

4. Storni wrote for *La Nación* until the end of her life, although not always as "Tao Lao." I have not learned why she chose this pseudonym, although its odd rhyme and "foreign" nature perhaps were chosen to give some latitude for eccentricity and humor in her writings. It is quite possible that Storni used other pseudonyms such as bylines like "La Niña Boba" (Silly Girl) in *La Nota*.

5. I have examined previously some of these writings in "The Journalism of Alfonsina Storni: A New Approach to Women's History in Argentina" (1990).

6. For information related to Argentina during this period, see David Rock.

7. For an overview of similar changes in other parts of the world, see E. J. Hobsbawm, "The Arts Transformed" (*The Age of Empire* 219–242), and Elaine Showalter, "New Woman" (*Sexual Anarchy* 38–58).

8. According to Jorge Rivera (344), Buenos Aires did not have its own publishing industry until around 1914. Until that time, most books were published by individual agreements with printers, not through editorial houses.

9. Christopher Leland (xvii). Leland's introductory chapters offer an exceptional synthesis of the cultural dynamics of the twenties in Argentina.

10. Beatriz Sarlo in *El imperio de los sentimientos* explored a different publishing world, the popular novel, often sold by installments, in its heyday in the second decade of the century. Her *Una modernidad periférica: Buenos Aires* imaginatively reconstructs the cultural life of Buenos Aires in part by its periodical literature.

11. Sarlo contrasted Lange and Storni as two sides of the same coin, decorum/ transgression, in *Una modernidad periférica: Buenos Aires*: "Confronting the social morality that imposed the effacements I pointed out in Norah Lange, Alfonsina preferred to exalt, or even carnivalize her difference . . . and to accept her 'derailed' marginality" (84).

12. The compilation by Lafleur, Provenzano, and Alonso is invaluable for a review of literary periodicals in Argentina. For a comprehensive review of women's periodicals in Latin America over two centuries, see Janet Greenberg's listings in *Women, Culture and Politics in Latin America* (1990).

WORKS CITED

Baralis, Marta. *Bibliografía argentina de artes y letras.* Vol 18. Buenos Aires: Fondo Nacional de las Artes, 1964.

Feijóo, María del Carmen. "Las feministas." In *La vida de nuestro pueblo,* vol. 9. Buenos Aires: Centro Editor de América Latina, 1982.

Freeman, Marion, ed. *Alfonsina Storni: Selected Poems.* Trans. M. Freeman et al. Fredonia, N.Y.: White Pine Press, 1987.

Greenberg, Janet. "Toward a History of Women's Periodicals in Latin America: A Working Bibliography." In *Women, Culture and Politics in Latin America,* 182–231. Berkeley and Los Angeles: University of California Press, 1990.

Gubar, Susan. "'The Blank Page' and Female Creativity." *Critical Inquiry* 8 (Winter 1981), 243–263.

Hobsbawm, E. J. *The Age of Empire: 1875–1914.* New York: Vintage Books, 1989.

Kirkpatrick, Gwen. "The Journalism of Alfonsina Storni: A New Approach to

Women's History in Argentina." In *Women, Culture and Politics in Latin America*, 105–129. Berkeley and Los Angeles: University of California Press, 1990.

Lafleur, Hector Rene, with Sergio D. Provenzano and Fernando P. Alonso. *Las revistas literarias argentinas, 1893–1967*. Buenos Aires: Centro Editor de América Latina, 1968.

Leland, Christopher. *The Last Happy Men: The Generation of 1922, Fiction, and the Argentine Reality*. Syracuse, N.Y.: Syracuse University Press, 1986.

Mangone, Carlos. "La República Radical: Entre *Crítica* y *El Mundo*." In *Historia social de la literatura argentina*, 75–103. Ed. David Viñas. Buenos Aires: Editorial Contrapunto, 1989.

Miller, Francesca. *Latin American Women and the Search for Social Justice*. Hanover, N.H.: University Press of New England, 1991.

Phillips, Rachel. *Alfonsina Storni: From Poetess to Poet*. London: Tamesis, 1975.

Rivera, Jorge B. "La forja del escritor profesional (1900–1930): Los escritores y los nuevos medios masivos." In *Capítulos: Historia de la literatura argentina*, 3:337–384. Buenos Aires: CELA, 1980.

Rock, David. "Argentina from the First World War to the Revolution of 1930." In *Cambridge History of Latin America*, 5:419–452. Ed. Leslie Bethell. Cambridge: Cambridge University Press, 1986.

———. "Argentina in 1914: The Pampas, the Interior, Buenos Aires." In *Cambridge History of Latin America*, 5:398–418. Cambridge: Cambridge University Press, 1986.

Sarlo, Beatriz. *El imperio de los sentimientos*. Buenos Aires: Catálogos, 1985.

———. *Una modernidad periférica: Buenos Aires 1920 y 1930*. Buenos Aires: Ediciones Nueva Vision, 1988.

Sarlo, Beatriz, ed. *Martín Fierro (1924–1927): Antología y prólogo*. Buenos Aires: Carlos Pérez, 1969.

Seminar on Feminism and Culture in Latin America. *Women, Culture and Politics in Latin America*. Berkeley and Los Angeles: University of California Press, 1990.

Showalter, Elaine. *Sexual Anarchy: Gender and Culture at the Fin de Siècle*. New York: Penguin Group, 1990.

Storni, Alfonsina. "La perfecta dactilógrafa." *La Nación* (May 9, 1920), 1.

———. "Sobre nosotros." *La Nota* (May 26, 1917), 1865–1866.

———. "El varón." *La Nación* (June 12, 1921), 5–6.

Melvin S.
Arrington, Jr.

MAGDA PORTAL, VANGUARD CRITIC

It has been clearly established that the European vanguard movements of the first half of the twentieth century exerted a profound influence on literature and politics in Spanish America. The aim of the literary vanguard was to promote originality and newness through experimentation, to recreate in a new mold, to dare to go beyond established limits.[1] This program called for drastic renovation of the existing modes of expression and resulted in the uprooting of old, outmoded forms and formulations about literature. The movement was characterized by an aggressive, iconoclastic spirit, a combativeness that in reality encompassed nothing less than a desire for total liberation, aesthetically and politically. While the political movements of that era were defining themselves in terms of "-isms"—anarchism, socialism, communism, fascism—the radical new ideas infiltrating the arts came to be designated in similar fashion: futurism, ultraism, dadaism, and surrealism, to name only a few. For the purposes of this discussion all of these terms relating to the new artistic manifestations will be grouped under the broad umbrella of vanguardism.[2]

The vanguard movements developed two separate and philosophically distinct branches, one emphasizing the aesthetics of "pure art" and the other advocating a literature of commitment and protest in order to effect radical changes in social and political institutions. The works of two of the leading poets of this century, Vicente Huidobro and Pablo Neruda, both Chileans, aptly define these two diametrically opposed approaches, aestheticism (Huidobro) versus political commitment (Neruda). It is to the latter branch that the subject of this study, Peruvian writer, political activist, and feminist Magda Portal (1903–1989), belongs.[3] Without apology, Portal used literature, particularly her essays, as a vehicle for advancing her political and social agendas.

Magda Portal was just one of many young writers who became caught up in the whirlwind of intellectual activity of the post–World War I era. At a young age she began to work for the causes she held dear—equal rights for women and social justice for all—goals to which she remained dedicated throughout her life. In the political arena Portal worked closely with the leading Peruvian intellectual figure of the day, José Carlos Mariátegui, and she soon became one of the major players in the Peruvian APRA or Aprista Party.[4] She traveled widely throughout Spanish America promoting her political ideas, in particular her goal of seeing Peruvian women take their rightful places in the life of the country. Persecuted for her activities in the Aprista movement, she was at various times imprisoned and deported.[5]

In the field of literature, Portal achieved recognition as a poet, short-story writer, novelist, essayist, and director of the politically oriented journal *Trampolín* (Lima, 1926–1927), a publication that underwent several name changes, becoming successively *Hangar, Rascacielos,* and *Timonel.* She produced several volumes of poetry, among them *Una esperanza i el mar* (One Hope and the Sea, 1927), in which she employed sea imagery and dealt with themes of love, solitude, and anguish. As a fiction writer she collaborated with her companion, Serafín Delmar (pseudonym of Reynaldo Bolaños), on the volume of short stories *El derecho de matar* (The Right to Kill, 1926) and later solo-authored the novel *La trampa* (The Trap, 1956). Portal's essays were often doctrinaire pieces in which she passionately set forth her political views, as in *Hacia la mujer nueva* (Toward the New Woman, 1933), which ends with the propagandistic slogan "SOLO EL APRISMO SALVARA AL PERU" (Only Aprismo will save Peru). In a little-known but significant essay entitled *El nuevo poema i su orientación hacia una estética económica* (The New Poetry and Its Aesthetic of Social and Political Commitment, 1928), she examines the new trends in Spanish American poetry, illustrating her observations with a sampling of the works of representative poets writing in the new style.[6]

In order to understand fully the context and premise of *El nuevo poema* it will be necessary to exhume an earlier piece, "Andamios de vida" (Platforms of Life, 1927), a brief article that lay buried for many years among the pages of Mariátegui's journal, *Amauta.*[7] In "Andamios" Portal began to erect an intellectual foundation to justify the appearance on the literary scene of what she termed "the new art." Her rationale in support of this phenomenon encapsulated the revolutionary literary theories she would apply the following year in her survey of the new poetry.

The most obvious aspect of Portal's writings, the feature that was to become her trademark, was what Daniel Reedy has referred to as "the inseparability of the aesthetics of her works from her political commitment" ("Magda Portal" 491). The bond between politics and art and the desirability of employing the latter in the service of the former comprised the basic tenets of this new aesthetic doctrine. Although social protest played an important role in her poetry, it was through the essay that she had the most success in communicating these ideas. In "Andamios" she repeatedly refers to vanguard literature as "the new art," equating it with the "new aesthetic manifestations." The new writing was, in her judgment, an art form that perfectly complemented the triumph of "the new ideological creeds which signal the dawning of a new day for the brotherhood of humankind" (206).

In "Andamios" she discusses "the new art" as an inevitable result of the First World War, the Russian Revolution, scientific advances of the age, and the new philosophy. According to her description, it requires commitment rather than complacency: "the new art always sings of the reality of action" (207). Art has always been an outgrowth of sociological and philosophical tendencies, that is, a by-product of society, with close ties to the social reality—not divorced from that reality. It is "a kind of mirror that reveals what society will become" (207). This "new art" emerged in response to the aftermath of World War I, that bloody conflict that put an end to sterile decadence by injecting life and humanity into literary expression. Therefore, she expresses her disdain for "the worthless pomp and circumstance of Darío's poetry" by proclaiming that beauty for its own sake is sterile.[8] Art should be a creative force, rooted in life:

> *Before the war art was decadent, totally sterile and*
> *lifeless, an enervating and degenerative blight on all*
> *life except the world of artificial paradises. The war*
> *with its gashes of blood added more humanity and a*
> *greater feeling of life to artistic manifestations, and,*
> *as in every chaotic age, art endured its own chaos to*
> *escape from literary decadence, finally arriving at*
> *the broad, sun-drenched steppes of liberty, which sig-*
> *nify the new art, an art not bound to any particular*
> *school, an art fraternally linked in thoughts and ac-*

*tion to the Social Revolution whose seeds bear fruit in
the real world.*
(207)

In "Andamios" Portal views the task of the artist as one of aesthetic
and ideological renovation, a function Mariátegui's visionary vanguard
journal *Amauta* has courageously undertaken. In the article's opening
sentence, however, she qualifies her definition of art: *"Amauta's* view of
art is eclectic; it subscribes to all of art's credos so long as Beauty is allowed to illuminate the patches of darkness that emanate from deep below
the surface" (206). Here, with the phrase "subterranean mines," which
connotes a place of exploitation and calls to mind specific victims (the
miners), she begins her own "undermining" of the system responsible
for the exploitation. For Portal, the literary aesthetic has its limits; essentially, it denotes committed literature enlisted in the struggle against injustice. In short, this seemingly inconsequential three-page article underscores Portal's belief in the humanization of art and in the coming social
revolution, in which she will actively participate. These ideas would become the guiding principle of *El nuevo poema*, which appeared the following year, 1928.

Since Portal was a published poet, she was well qualified to evaluate
the "new poetry" of the 1920s. Her observations in *El nuevo poema* offer
a unique perspective on the evolving Spanish American literature of that
period and signal a shift in the focus of criticism. Clearly, her approach
is symptomatic of a new trend, a movement away from an emphasis on
the purely artistic aspects of a literary text to a primary concern for extraliterary considerations.

In *El nuevo poema* Portal expresses her belief that the political and economic subjugation of the masses from colonial times to the twentieth
century had resulted in cultural and artistic stagnation. Long after losing
its colonies, Spain continued to exert its cultural domination, effectively
stifling any genuine artistic expression in America. Even though the pre-
ceding generation of writers, the *modernistas*, had reawakened the creative impulse, they were for the most part out of touch with the emerging culture. A socially and politically committed poet with a Marxist
orientation, Magda Portal had little regard for the aristocratic tastes and
ivory-tower mentality of that earlier generation. Interestingly, even Portal engaged in a form of aesthetic experimentation, in her case with punc-
tuation and spelling. Thus she, too, was guilty of indulging in stylistic
strokes bordering on the whimsical, a charge she often leveled at the

advocates of "pure art." With classic vanguard iconoclasm she filled her writings with dashes, sometimes employing them in place of the more traditional commas. These rapid, slashing strokes graphically convey the feeling of movement and energy that epitomized the new age. In a similarly rebellious vein she routinely wrote the Spanish word for "and" as *i* instead of the standard *y*.

Like many of her contemporaries, Portal recognized Yankee imperialism as a threat. She predicted that economic colonization would be followed by cultural colonization, a move that would signal the end of indigenous culture. The new vanguard poetry, however, had much to offer, especially with regard to its innovative imagery depicting the sights and sounds of the industrial age (machines, factories, airplanes). Along with the new "-isms" came new literary techniques. Suddenly, the *modernistas* were no longer modern. Although she had high praise for the new poets, she was quick to identify the ones who lacked a well-defined political ideology, the implication being that this was a weakness that somehow devalued those writers' artistic achievements.

Following these preliminary observations, Portal begins a survey of vanguard poetry in which she introduces the poets and offers selections from their work. More than just a catalog of names, however, *El nuevo poema* serves as a miniature anthology of the "new writing" of that day. Appropriately, the volume is international rather than regional in coverage, a reflection of how widely the vanguard aesthetic had spread throughout the Americas. The first poet presented is Juan Parra del Riego, whom she calls the greatest personality of her generation. She praises him for reviving polyrhythm and for his "beautiful sporty poems, agile and vibrant" (10). Ultimately, Portal allows extraliterary factors to outweigh the intrinsic value of his poetry. Since Parra del Riego is considered an advocate of middle-class values (which she considers anathema), her overall evaluation must, therefore, be negative.

Next, she comments on the writings of the Chilean Juan Marín and credits him with revolutionizing the technique and content of poetry. Marín's works exalt modern urban life as seen in his poem "Superavión" (Superplane), a fragment of which is reproduced in this section of the essay. She labels Marín "an intensely modern poet" (11) and, in the same breath, tempers her enthusiasm by pointing out that he lacks a clearly defined ideology. Without stating specific examples, she criticizes Neruda's early poetry, his "pure poetry, highly metaphorical and based on emotions" (11) produced under the influence of Huidobro as typical of those of her generation who have yet to discover "an Americanist consciousness," not to mention a class consciousness. Obviously, the same statement could not have been made of Pablo Neruda a decade later.

Several poets are included as examples of "-isms." In Mexico she singles out the creator of *estridentismo* (stridentism), Manuel Maples Arce, as an example of "the new artistic/ideological modality" (12). Maples Arce redirects poetry along the uncharted roads of the new aesthetic, instilling in his verse an awarenesss of social issues. She praises him as the first Mexican poet to understand beauty in its proletarian sense, the beauty of the anonymous masses. Portal includes two selections— "Urbe" (Metropolis), dedicated to the workers of Mexico, and "Revolución,"—calling the latter a daring work of "penetrating beauty" (13).

Although she criticizes Huidobro, the father of *creacionismo*, for distancing art from social reality, she nevertheless identifies him with the vanguard struggle for liberation in Latin America. Also a part of this struggle is the Guatemalan Cardoza y Aragón, who merits consideration for advocating the new concept that individual liberty is limited by "the freedom of the masses" (15). She also introduces her readers to Alberto Hidalgo, the originator of *simplismo*, who has among his noteworthy "pure poetry" two or three works that are ideologically leftist. Of these Portal selects "Biografía de la palabra Revolución" (Biography of the Word *Revolution*) for inclusion in her "anthology."

Several literary figures are mentioned in passing. She identifies Alvaro Yunke and Nicolás Olivari as poets with a proletarian soul and also finds Uruguayans Juan M. Filartigas and Emilio Frugoni and the deceased Chilean poet Gómez Rojas worthy of attention. Among Cubans she recognizes the talents of Mariblanca Sabas Alomá and includes one of her poems. Next, she discusses Serafín Delmar (mentioned above), to whom she devotes almost three pages, the most coverage given to any poet in the essay with the exception of Maples Arce. This is not surprising considering Portal's romantic involvement with Delmar and their previous joint effort on *El derecho de matar*. She praises him for promoting "an aesthetic system structured on economic and political considerations" (17) and calls him a son of the earth whose voice has not been tainted by corrupt bourgeois society. As examples of his work she reproduces "Frente al mundo" (Facing the World) and "Himno a la Tierra" (Hymn to the Earth) from his book *Radiogramas del Pacífico* (Radio Messages from the Pacific).

Following her discussion of Delmar, Portal presents two more Mexican writers. The first of these is the *estridentista* Germán List Arzubide, whose work she considers ideologically correct even though his poetry is classified as "pure art." From his book *Plebe* (The Common People) she takes the selection "La siega" (The Harvest). She also recognizes Carlos Gutiérrez Cruz, a Mexican poet closely identified with the masses, and makes reference to his book *Sangre roja* (Red Blood), from which she selects the poem "Al minero" (To the Miner).

At this juncture Portal begins another international catalog of poets associated with the new literary tendencies, limiting herself to those most clearly defined as revolutionary and calling them "militant soldiers in the ranks of the social struggle" (22). Among Bolivians she names Oscar Cerruto and Omar Estrella. Also singled out for praise is the Uruguayan Blanca Luz Brum. The list continues with Delahoza and Masikes in Cuba; Dromundo and Muñoz Cota in Mexico; and Julián Petrovick, Nicanor de la Fuente, César Miró Quesada, and Esteban Pavletich in Peru, the latter a writer who published his revolutionary poetry in wall-poster format. The anthology portion of *El nuevo poema* concludes with a brief mention of two indigenous poets, both of whom hail from the area around Lake Titicaca, the heartland of South America: Alejandro Peralta, upon whom she bestows the title "foremost indigenous poet" (24), and Gamaliel Churata, who has made major contributions to the popular indigenous theatre of the region.

Following this overview of poets and their work, Portal summarizes the essay with a general discussion of the vanguard aesthetic. The world war and the revolution gave birth to a new ideology, which in turn produced the new art, a profoundly human art to go hand in hand with the transformation of society. This modern mode of artistic expression is no longer bound by the aristocratic, ivory-tower decadence of the past. No longer does it cater to the mission of pure poetry, which was to delight, to give pleasure to the reader. The idea of simply being aesthetically pleasing is a dehumanizing aspect that fails to take into account the cries of the masses, whose voices can be heard emanating from the mines, the factories, and the countryside. In her conclusion to *El nuevo poema*, Portal welcomes the new aesthetic with its message that Beauty, once a symbol of the privileged classes, is now, according to Marxist interpretation, fulfilling its social mission by becoming a tool of the disadvantaged masses in their struggle for justice.

At the heart of the essay is her personal view of how one should read modern literature. Certain key phrases, such as "the interpretation of sociological phenomena in terms of beauty" (10), encapsulate her definition of art. And in case there are any doubts about her meaning of the word *beauty*, she spells it out with the clarifying phrase "the proletarian meaning of beauty" (15). This type of solidarity with the masses can never be fully comprehended by the privileged classes, whose vision is obscured by their bourgeois mentality. Portal laments that poets waste their efforts on "pure art," a type of writing she conflates with the idle pursuits of the aristocracy, diametrically opposed to her own aesthetics and the social causes she champions. While the masses, to whom a university education is but a dream, have not yet produced widely recognized poets, they do nonetheless create their own poetry. Unlike bourgeois art, their compositions, which normally take the form of popular songs, serve a useful purpose by giving voice to collective concerns. Thus, she optimistically heralds the coming of the poet of the masses.

In *El nuevo poema* Portal establishes a direct link between history and culture, with the former always determining the way the latter manifests itself. In her role as critic in this essay she redefines beauty in literature as an extension of her own political and social views. The new criticism that she envisions, one in which politics and aesthetics converge, is in total harmony with the new writing. This approach to Spanish American literature has become so commonplace today that it is often taken for granted. In the 1920s, however, with *modernismo* still holding sway in many areas, these radical ideas placed her in the forefront of literary criticism. In assessing vanguard poetry Portal took up her position along the same front lines where she had always stationed herself as a political activist. Since in her mind politics and poetry were inextricably linked, there was no reason to do otherwise.

NOTES

1. The title of Magda Portal's essay, *El nuevo poema i su orientación hacia una estética económica*, reflects the emphasis placed on all things new. This interest in newness was likewise manifested in the title of political writings, for example, Portal's *Hacia la mujer nueva*.

2. See Forster, *Tradition and Renewal*, for a thorough discussion of the various "-isms" of vanguard literature. For a country-by-country survey of vanguardism see Forster and Jackson.

3. Among Peruvian authors of the vanguard era, the most recognizable name and the best example of a committed writer was the poet César Vallejo (1892–1938).

4. APRA, the Alianza Popular Revolucionaria Americana, was the political party founded by Víctor Raúl Haya de la Torre.

5. For a more detailed account of Portal's life and political activity see Daniel

Reedy, "Aspects." For a brief description of the content of Portal's poetry collections and selected other writings see Marting (1987).

6. Daniel Reedy, "Magda Portal," examines Portal's major literary themes and provides a survey of criticism of her work.

7. "Andamios de vida" and many other key texts that help to explain this period of literary history are now easily accessible in Nelson Osorio's one-volume collection *Manifiestos, proclamas y polémicas de la vanguardia literaria hispanoamericana* (see Portal, "Andamios").

8. Nicaraguan poet Rubén Darío (1867–1916) was the self-proclaimed leader of the *modernistas*. This international movement, which roughly spanned the two decades between 1890 and 1910, embraced writers who sought refuge from the disappointments and tedium of everyday reality by escaping into pure art. They espoused an aestheticism best exemplified by the creed "art for art's sake."

WORKS CITED

Forster, Merlin H. "Latin American Vanguardismo: Chronology and Terminology." In *Tradition and Renewal: Essays on Twentieth-Century Latin American Literature and Culture*, 11–50. Ed. Merlin H. Forster. Urbana: University of Illinois Press, 1975.

Forster, Merlin H., and K. David Jackson, comps. *Vanguardism in Latin American Literature: An Annotated Bibliographical Guide*. New York: Greenwood, 1990.

Marting, Diane E., ed. *Women Writers of Spanish America: An Annotated Bio-Bibliographical Guide*. New York: Greenwood, 1987.

Portal, Magda. "Andamios de vida." In *Manifiestos, proclamas y polémicas de la vanguardia literaria hispanoamericana*, 206–208. Ed. Nelson Osorio T. Caracas: Biblioteca Ayacucho, 1988.

―――. *Una esperanza i el mar*. Lima: Minerva, 1927.

―――. *Hacia la mujer nueva*. Lima: Cooperativa Aprista Atahualpa, [1933].

―――. *El nuevo poema i su orientación hacia una estética económica*. Mexico City: Ediciones Apra, 1928.

―――. *La trampa*. Lima: Andimar Peruana, 1956.

Portal, Magda, and Serafín Delmar. *El derecho de matar*. La Paz: n.p., 1926.

Reedy, Daniel R. "Aspects of the Feminist Movement in Peruvian Letters and Politics." In *The Place of Literature in Interdisciplinary Approaches*, 53–64. Ed. Eugene R. Huck. Annals of the Southeastern Conference on Latin American Studies 6 (March 1975). Carrollton, Ga.: Thomasson Printing, 1975.

―――. "Magda Portal." In *Spanish American Women Writers: A Bio-Bibliographical Source Book*, 483–492. Ed. Diane E. Marting. New York: Greenwood, 1990.

Janet N. Gold

YOLANDA OREAMUNO

THE ART OF

PASSIONATE

ENGAGEMENT

"**S**peaking of literature, I confess that personally I am FED UP, in capital letters, with folklore" ("Protesta" 96).[1] With these words, in no uncertain terms, Yolanda Oreamuno challenged Costa Rican writers to look beyond what she disparagingly called "folklore" to create a literature more reflective of their country's reality.

According to most accounts of Costa Rican letters, certain styles, themes, and preoccupations dominated the literary landscape for given periods of time, with more or less proficient practitioners of these genres coming and going in groups fraternally referred to as "generations." But one school stands out for its longevity: *costumbrismo*, or narratives of rural manners and customs—what Oreamuno chose to call folklore.

Abelardo Bonilla, don of Costa Rican letters and the country's preeminent literary historian, has observed that *costumbrismo* is the literary theme and style that has been the seed and centerpiece of Costa Rican narrative since the nineteenth century as well as the inspiration for subsequent bifurcations into various types of realism.[2] In the costumbrist realism of Joaquín García Monge, who first attempted to reproduce the spoken language of his rural subjects, or the social realism of the so-called Generation of '40, who collectively denounced imperialism and the suffering of the working class (particularly on the banana plantations of the United Fruit Company), the rural landscape, peasants, and farm workers were almost universally accepted in Costa Rica as what narrative was all about. Bonilla goes so far as to say that in fact it was impossible in the early decades of the twentieth century to write a work of fiction in any theme or style that was not regionalist, given the political and economic panorama of the country (135).[3] Nonetheless, Yolanda Orea-

muno, undaunted by the hegemonic monolith of tradition, decided it
was time to write the urban novel.

In his more recent interpretation of Costa Rican literary history, Jorge
Valdeperas presents an even more homogenized picture when he concludes that the Generation of '40 developed a single theme (social injustice) in a single genre (the novel), based on a shared proletarian and socialist worldview. Recognizing that in fact there are some Costa Rican
authors who do not fit this pattern, he calls them exceptions that prove
the rule. Faced with the enigma of Yolanda Oreamuno—usually included in the Generation of '40 and most often tacked to the end of the
list of generational members because of her identity as a woman writer
or an innovator whose texts do not follow the generational pattern—
faced with this woman who can neither be ignored nor squeezed into a
totalizing tale of literary history, he calls her an "island" in Costa Rican
letters because she railed against *costumbrismo* and subscribed neither to
the socially committed novel of the majority of her contemporaries nor
to the art-for-art's-sake ideology of the only other notable writer of that
time, José Marín Cañas (55).[4]

Writer and literary historian Sergio Ramírez took Oreamuno beyond
the national boundaries of Costa Rica by positioning her not only as an
innovator and precursor but, in somewhat of an exaggeration, as high
priestess of the contemporary narrative in Central America, propagator
of an attitude that sought to rescue Central American literature from the
limitations of regionalism (10).

Victoria Urbano recognizes that the parameters of generation and geography are not inclusive enough to describe Oreamuno's work. Rather,
she locates her in literary currents that were evolving in Europe and the
United States as well as in Latin America, what Oreamuno herself called
"the modern American movement" ("Protesta" 97), which included experiments in psychological realism, stream of consciousness, and interior
monologue (Urbano 49–57).

Oreamuno's classification as an "island" may be explained in part by
the fact that her writing was innovative and in part by the fact that she
was a woman exercising a profession still predominantly male. But it is
also illuminating to posit a different way of understanding Oreamuno's
practice of her profession, a way that highlights the categories of gender,
nationality, and literary movement but that allows for her particular
brand of difference and attempts to stand beside her in her isolation/
marginality and view her writing from its own center and authenticity
rather than as peripheral, insular, or somehow ahead of its time, as the

terms *precursor* and *forerunner* suggest. The following discussion of her essays and fiction is an invitation to read her as a woman who fights back, talks back, and looks for new and different ways to locate herself (rather than be located) in literary history through a practice characterized by passionate engagement with her subject and with herself.

While some critics have gone to great lengths to exhume and analyze the Proustian influence in her work, thereby proving her modernity and establishing her position in the narrative vanguard of Central America, her own thoughts on the subject of influence highlight her aggressively independent stance.[5] "Proust's magic lives in me because he is the only author capable of inspiring emotion in me, and ideas, ideas genuinely mine, not Proustian ideas."[6] She was clearly sensitive to the undesirability of copying models and profoundly attracted to the idea of her unique and individual self. This self-centeredness produced a high level of subjectivity in her writing, a characteristic that Manuel Picado Gómez has interpreted as a shortcoming (61), while Luz Ivette Martínez sees it as typical of women's texts and not to be considered necessarily a fault (78). Urbano goes so far as to declare that there is one central theme in all of Oreamuno's texts: YO/Yolanda Oreamuno. But if we reverse the equation we see not that her texts are subjective but that her subjectivity is a text, that her obsession with self is her way of engaging dynamically with her writing. She enters her texts in a very real way: she characteristically locates herself in every essay, inserting the first person singular pronoun with grace and authority. And there is no mistaking who is in charge in her household.

As Francine Masiello discovered in her study of Latin American women writing in the 1920s and 1930s, the prevailing literary movements were male centered and left "little space for women" (36). Faced with images of women with which they were unwilling to identify, writers such as María Luisa Bombal and Teresa de la Parra "subverted patriarchal discourse and the ruling logic of traditional writing" (37). In a strikingly parallel fashion, Yolanda Oreamuno, in the 1940s in Central America, refused to enter the literary mainstream, presenting a challenge to what had been almost exclusively a men's club. Oreamuno was virtually alone among Central American women in confronting the literary establishment via her essays and fiction, although other women were in a direct and combative way attacking the prevailing aesthetic order through other genres.[7]

Yolanda Oreamuno was a strong-willed and intelligent woman; she was precocious, arrogant, sensual, physically beautiful, opinionated, and analytical.[8] Born in San José in 1916, she died in Mexico City a brief but intense forty years later. She started publishing in 1936, and by age twenty-three had already established herself as an original and provocative critic of Costa Rican life and letters. Most of her pieces were published in the *Repertorio Americano*. Founded in 1919 by Joaquín García Monge, the *Repertorio* appeared weekly or biweekly until his death in 1959. One of the most respected and long-lived literary publications of Latin America in the twentieth century, it carried selections from the Spanish and Latin American press as well as translations of U.S. and European authors. Essays by Gabriela Mistral, Amanda Labarca, and Magda Portal could be read as well as the thoughts of Costa Rican women such as activist and writer Carmen Lyra and educator Emma Gamboa. Oreamuno's contributions to the *Repertorio* were unique for a Costa Rican woman, and difficult to classify.[9] Some are readily recognizable as essays in that they argue a point or present an idea that is developed and supported with argument and analysis. In this category are her most controversial ideas, the ones that affronted the Costa Rican self-image and provoked the most negative reactions. Others are highly personalized and poetic travel narratives, or descriptive meditations on the sensual relationship between one's inner and outer reality.

One of her earliest essays is also one of her clearest and most coherent. "¿Qué hora es?" (What Time Is It?) was her submission for a competition at her alma mater, the Colegio Superior de Señoritas, to address the topic "Ways you suggest for the school to liberate Costa Rican women from the frivolity of their environment." After acknowledging the different problems faced in school by young women of different social classes due to their respective economic conditions and future economic prospects, she criticizes parents for not giving their daughters opportunities to think for themselves and make their own decisions, thereby developing a sense of self-worth. She faults patriarchal society for creating women who have no ambitions of their own beyond living through their husbands. She calls for a public education that would help form what she calls a "genuine feminine personality" (52): a sense of rights and responsibilities, a healthy ambition, noble preoccupations, and a knowledge of one's self. And she insists that the problem is complex: reforming the schools without addressing the education received at home, the inequities produced by the distribution of wealth, and the social and psychological dependence of women created by male/female relationships cannot bring about integral change. Her prose is lucid, her thoughts are enlightened,

and her tone is committed and impassioned. (One cannot help but wonder why she received only second prize.)

In 1939 the *Repertorio* carried her scathing indictment of the Costa
Rican national character, "El ambiente tico y los mitos tropicales" (Trop-
ical Myths and the Costa Rican Environment). Assuming the role of self-
appointed cultural critic, of intellectual conscience of her time and place,
she mocks what she sees as the passive spirit of her people: a fear of the
grand and a corresponding taste for the insignificant. She seems to be
sensing the limits of her own literary future in Costa Rica when she complains that this powerful and hateful environment muddies the best intentions, distorts vocations, and aborts large ideas before they can even be
conceived (16). While recognizing that blaming some nebulous ambiance
is a collective self-deception, that indeed the atmosphere of a nation is
formed from the inside out, she also admits that the reasons for this
spiritual mediocrity have historical roots. Her tone is petulant, angry,
and impatient. She is clearly trying to start a fight, to engage her readers
in a spirited intellectual exchange. But there are already hints that she is
becoming disillusioned with the polemical essay as a way of making
waves:

> *If you write a strongly worded article today and shock*
> *the critics, and are foolish enough to maintain this*
> *tone in the next article; if it appeared yesterday in the*
> *newspapers with bold headlines, tomorrow it will*
> *appear delicately placed on the literary page, the day*
> *after tomorrow in the sports section, and if you con-*
> *tinue it will end up on the society page. . . . Quickly,*
> *without a fight or a fuss, you are silenced. We don't*
> *even like sensationalism.*
> (19 – 20)

Oreamuno was an elitist in a way that only a woman could be. Had
she been a man engaged in verbal assaults and counterattacks in the press
she would have fit into a long and not dishonorable literary tradition in
Latin America. Had she been a woman participating in literary life as a
poet of exalted emotion, muse to the male literati, or even as a feminist
or social activist, she would have fit into one or another of the prevailing
literary currents. But to be a woman and an individualist, to be unwilling
to accept, negotiate, conciliate, or keep silent, was a decision that both

marginalized and glamorized her, and one that she seems to have made with full awareness of the consequences, indeed enjoying her notoriety.

Her last and probably best-known attack on the Costa Rican literary establishment was "Protesta contra el folklore" (Protest against Folklore), at once an obituary for what she perceived to be a literary mode and thematic that should be put to rest, and a call to Costa Rican writers to rise to the challenge of modernity. Published in the *Repertorio* in 1943, her essay praises the well-written regionalist and costumbrist novels of the past, but insists that the times have changed and that the challenge facing writers now is to portray the realities of urbanization, industrialization, and alienation. She calls the national propensity to typify and romanticize the rural dweller servile, catering to a foreign taste for the exotic that produces "folklore," a term she uses pejoratively to imply false local color palatable to the tourist.

As mentioned earlier, Sergio Ramírez has singled out Oreamuno as leading the way for the Central American novel to enter the mainstream of modern trends, pointing to "Protesta contra el folklore" as a kind of declaration of independence from the regionalist narrative. Her understanding of the limitations of geography and nationality led her to the conclusion that she must find a new language with which to express the universal realities alive within characters and situations bound in time and place to their own particularities. In a letter to Costa Rican writer Joaquín Gutiérrez, referring to his novel *Puerto Limón*, she writes:

> *I don't believe in the American book, when "American" refers only to being geographically located in a specific place, and encompasses only certain problems. What makes your book great is in no way its Costa Rican quality, nor its constant reference to problems of an economic nature. It is, without question, your ability to transform a momentary problem into a permanent one and to endow your characters and scenes with such vitality that they seem to belong to everyone.*
> (258)

Although there are rumors of other, unedited manuscripts, Oreamuno's one published novel, *La ruta de su evasión* (The Route of Her Evasion), which won the "15 de septiembre de 1948" prize for the Central American novel, awarded in Guatemala, is a faithful experiment in the ideas she espoused in her essays and correspondence. The text, a complex and tortuous introspection carried out by the moribund Teresa and members of her family, has been described as a series of small, concentric novels within a novel (Urbano 142). Located in no particular time or place, it explores, rather, the inner landscapes and clocks of its characters through the interweaving of interior monologues, autobiographical narratives, dialogue, and narratorial intrusion.[10]

The idea of the environment or the essence of a physical space or landscape that Oreamuno intellectualized in "¿Qué hora es?" and "El ambiente tico y los mitos tropicales" continued to intrigue her throughout her life, this interest manifesting itself in unique prose pieces that might best be described as sensual meditations on the notion of place. Increasingly bored and restive in Costa Rica, she traveled frequently. The act of moving through unfamiliar landscapes and the attempt to articulate her response to nature and climate motivated "40° sobre cero" (40° Centigrade), for example, written while she was in Panama and published in 1937.

Oreamuno begins the text with a question that she never resolves: "Inspiration (I call it desire to write): is it a situation that goes from inside out, that comes to one because of a need to exteriorize oneself, or is it a situation imposed by the landscape, a process of the environment?" (137). She postulates the existence of certain things so subtly and evocatively powerful that they are capable of awakening the imagination, even under conditions as adverse to creativity as the heavy, steamy heat of a Panama afternoon. As she drives through the countryside she comes upon the ruins of a church and describes a moment of sublime beauty as she experiences "[t]he triumph of the landscape over the imagination. Reality as I see it is better, purer, than reality as my mind can pervert it" (141). Because she ultimately ignores her initial question, which one assumes to be the purpose of the text, one has the sense that the rational mode has been superimposed on the poetry of the experience, and that in fact the need to answer the question has been erased by the senses.

In 1944 in Bogotá she wrote "Apología del limón dulce y el paisaje" (Apology for the Sweet Lemon and the Landscape) while sitting in a garden at twilight, peeling and eating a sweet lemon as her creative imagination found a moment in the landscape, a lapse in the treetops where body and spirit arrived at a truce. No questions were asked or conclusions drawn. The meditative moment is lush with description: the senses come alive as if for the express purpose of shedding the weight of physicality. The thinker and the thought become one.

This identification with the environment is dramatized in "Valle alto" (High Valley), a short story written two years later that combines Oreamuno's fascination with nature's sensuality and her vision of the universalization of narrative place. A man and a woman, anonymous unnamed strangers, find themselves stranded, miles from any city, at the mercy of an impending storm. In a flight of erotic fantasy the two make love in perfect rhythm with the storm that also ends the dry season and revives nature. The following morning the woman wakes up alone with only a vague memory of what happened. No narrator intrudes to explain, and the woman simply returns to her thoughts. The ambiguity between inner and outer realities is allowed to remain in a state of grace. A sentence from "Apología del limón dulce y el paisaje" explains perfectly this narrative moment: "At this point in the landscape, neither so high as to be impossible, nor so low as I, delineation is lost, reality becomes opaque, there is a living and narrow margin for fantasy" (157).

In her ongoing argument with Costa Rica and Costa Rican literature, Oreamuno problematized her identification with her birth nation and consequently remained open to the possibility of other kinds of citizenship. She became a Guatemalan citizen in the late 1940s and spent her last years in Mexico. Not surprisingly, solitude is a recurrent theme in her correspondence as well as in her fiction, and friends and critics often comment on the sad irony of the fact that she was buried in Mexico City in a numbered grave without even a headstone bearing her name, until her remains were brought to Costa Rica five years later. But one can imagine that solitude was also her muse, that it came to represent for her the strength of her individuality and the challenge to define herself. In 1944 she wrote "México es mío" (Mexico Is Mine), a text describing Mexico City—its evenings and nights, its streets, parks, and markets, its people's industriousness and poverty. With each succeeding passage she identifies more passionately with Mexico, taking on spiritual citizenship in this country where she feels more urgently inspired to participate than she ever did in her own homeland. Even in her anonymity, perhaps because of it, she appropriates the nation.

A story published a few years later, "Un regalo" (A Gift), is about a man who lives alone. The first section of the text is an essaylike dissertation on loneliness that characterizes the solitary individual as one who flees from contact with other human beings because "the antidote to solitude is not company: it is the word" (177). Yolanda Oreamuno, like her lonely characters, defined herself alone, confronting and engaging solitude with the written word. In her essays, she creates herself as the self-contained, independent-minded observer, analyst, critic. She inhabits her texts, claiming citizenship in the realm of intelligence and imagination. In her calculated attacks on mediocrity, she implicitly suggests her own superiority.

The trenches she dug in her battles against her time and place separated her from the mainstream, but we should not mourn her isolation as a condition imposed by an uncomprehending generation of fellow writers. What we should instead appreciate is the fact that with the passage of time the Generation of '40 in Costa Rica forms a comfortable blur remembered admiringly but with little curiosity, while the iconoclastic and passionate Yolanda Oreamuno continues to engage the intellects and emotions of her readers.

NOTES

1. This quotation from "Protesta contra el folklore" and other essays cited in this paper are collected in *A lo largo del corto camino* (1961).

2. Margarita Castro Rawson also demonstrated the exclusivity enjoyed by this genre in *El costumbrismo en Costa Rica*.

3. Other literary historians who concur with Bonilla's thematic and generational outlines are Virginia Sandoval de Fonseca and Seymour Menton. Even those scholars who differ with Bonilla for ideological or methodological reasons, such as Picado Gómez and Valdeperas, tend to accept the generational focus.

4. Valdeperas of course is not alone in his reluctance to analyze her isolation. Elizabeth Portuguez de Bolaños, Seymour Menton, and Luz Ivette Martínez Santiago all describe her work but do not attempt to explain it.

5. See, for example, Rima de Vallbona's article on *La ruta de su evasión*.

6. In a letter to Lilia Ramos, reproduced in Lilia Ramos, "Yolanda Oreamuno en mi recuerdo eviterno," *A lo largo del corto camino* (335).

7. Clementina Suárez (Honduras) and Eunice Odio (Costa Rica), for example, challenged poetic discourse with their aggressively woman-centered poetry.

8. Oreamuno's uncompromising personality and intellect, along with her physical beauty and choice of lifestyle, inspired numerous poems, character sketches, and critical appraisals of her life and work during her lifetime as well as at her death. A selection of these, as well as excerpts from her correspondence, all of which provide insights into her character and personality, can be found in *A lo largo del corto camino*.

9. From her examination of Costa Rican women's essays, Leonor Garnier concludes that most of these writers have preferred historical and biographical topics or those dealing with education.

10. Victoria Urbano has outlined the various types of monologue in the novel in *Una escritora costarricense*, 167–175.

WORKS CITED

Bonilla, Abelardo. *Historia de la literatura costarricense*. San José: Editorial Universitaria, 1957.

Castro Rawson, Margarita. *El costumbrismo en Costa Rica*. San José: Lehmann, 1966.

Garnier, Leonor. *Antología femenina del ensayo costarricense*. San José: Ministerio de Cultura, Juventud y Deportes, 1976.

Martínez Santiago, Luz Ivette. *Carmen Naranjo y la narrativa femenina en Costa Rica*. San José: EDUCA, 1987.

Masiello, Francine. "Women, State and Family in Latin American Literature of the 1920s." In *Women, Culture and Politics in Latin America*, 27–47. Berkeley and Los Angeles: University of California Press, 1990.

Menton, Seymour. *El cuento costarricense*. Lawrence: University Press of Kansas, 1964.

Oreamuno, Yolanda. *A lo largo del corto camino*. San José: Editorial Costa Rica, 1961.

———. *La ruta de su evasión*. San José: EDUCA, 1984.

Picado Gómez, Manuel. *"La ruta de su evasión" de Yolanda Oreamuno*. San José: Editorial Universidad, 1979.

Portuguez de Bolaños, Elizabeth. *El cuento en Costa Rica*. San José: Lehmann, 1964.

Ramírez, Sergio. *La narrativa centroamericana*. San Salvador: Editorial Universitaria, n.d.

Sandoval de Fonseca, Virginia. *Resumen de la literatura costarricense*. San José: Editorial Costa Rica, 1978.

Urbano, Victoria. *Una escritora costarricense: Yolanda Oreamuno*. Madrid: Ediciones Castilla de Oro, 1968.

Valdeperas, Jorge. *Para una nueva interpretación de la literatura costarricense*. San José: Editorial Costa Rica, 1979.

Vallbona, Rima de. *"La ruta de su evasión* de Yolanda Oreamuno: Escritura proustiana suplementada." *Revista Iberoamericana* 53 (January–June 1987): 193–218.

Martha

LaFollette

Miller

THE AMBIVALENCE
OF POWER
SELF-DISPARAGEMENT IN THE
NEWSPAPER EDITORIALS OF
ROSARIO CASTELLANOS

Rosario Castellanos (1925–1974) has won prominence as one of Latin America's most important women writers. Though her work has not always evoked unqualified admiration, she has nevertheless managed to break through the barrier separating women writers as such from the more august number of writers in general. Thus she appears as the only representative of her sex in Dauster's 1987 book on five contemporary Mexican poets, *The Double Strand*, and, similarly, joins Fuentes and Rulfo as one of three writers treated in depth in Poniatowska's *¡Ay vida, no me mereces!* (Ah Life, You Don't Deserve Me!).

Poniatowska's study reveals how successfully Castellanos had established herself in Mexico before her untimely death at age forty–nine. In addition to publishing feverishly, producing twenty-three books in twenty-six years, she had forged close connections with Mexico's first family. As ambassador to Israel, she had earned the admiration not only of academic circles but of Golda Meir and fellow diplomats as well. When she died, suggests Poniatowska, her star was still rising. She was Mexico's most important woman, and further political positions were likely (129–130).

Contrary to what we might expect, the recognition Castellanos enjoyed did not translate into an air of confidence and satisfaction in her writing. There is a curious incongruity between her actual accomplishments and the negative and self-derisive way she characterized herself, both in person and in print. Poniatowska notes her extreme self-mockery (71).

Castellanos' self-derision is particularly evident on the editorial pages of *Excélsior*, where she published regularly during the height of her success. Her articles often reveal the apparent ambivalence with which she faced her achievements, an attitude that seemed to grow along with her power and influence. Not infrequently, she acknowledges her success but then, as if overtaken by anxiety about her role, undermines any impression of competence by disclaimers and self-ridicule. Or she paints herself in a domestic light, dwelling on reassuringly feminine aspects of her life—home and hearth, motherhood, primping, links with the child within her—even as she speaks of attending state dinners with the world's most prominent figures. The irony she aims at discriminatory views of women is often undercut by her ingratiatingly "feminine" way of presenting herself.

"Autorretrato con maxifalda" (Self-Portrait in a Maxiskirt) amply illustrates Castellanos' ambivalent self-depiction.[1] Its point of departure is an earlier *Excélsior* article by Abel Quezada, in which he names Castellanos as a likely candidate for president of Mexico's national university. In response, she draws attention to his suggestion by publicly restating it, then rejects his idea while portraying herself half jokingly as fearful and inept.

Throughout the article, Castellanos depicts herself ambivalently, wavering between power (which she gives masculine overtones) and powerlessness (which she gives feminine ones). The conflicting self-references that dominate her opening paragraphs capture her ambivalence. Using the proverbial image of women as defective and less than whole, she describes herself on the one hand as "the chaste woman, at home with a broken leg" (226). On the other, she proudly quotes Quezada's depiction of her as better supplied with a wardrobe of pants than are many men. After ridiculing her vain response to his article by comparing herself to a prototypically silly female animal, a hen with fluffed feathers, she proceeds seemingly to prove but actually to disprove his masculinizing characterization of her. She ironically exaggerates her bravery: yes, she can light a match from time to time, she occasionally ventures out despite her terror of dogs, and she has even been known to ride horseback!

But by referring to horses, Castellanos undermines her ironic self-derision. Undercutting the description of her impotence in controlling her mount is the allusion to one of her serious past endeavors, one that forms part of an arsenal of credentials (or a wardrobe of *pantalones*) that indeed qualify her for a responsible post: her experiences in Chiapas with educational projects involving the indigenous population. In her twelfth paragraph, furthermore, she briefly touches on other areas of real accomplishment. In doing so she compares herself to a powerful male (the Aztec chieftain Cuauhtémoc) and uses terms—*batalla* and *aventura*—often reserved for masculine endeavors (229). Yet even in describing her bravery she strikes a note of self-disparagement; her valor entails forging ahead in situations for which her preparation is deficient. As examples, she cites holding administrative positions outside her area of specialization, traveling in countries whose traditions are different from hers, and teaching in universities where the language spoken is one in which she is totally inept (229).

Castellanos closes the essay with an anecdote that affirms her openness to challenges yet undercuts her daring by portraying her in a ridiculous light. She describes her first trip to Acapulco, when on the calmest beach there, she had jumped bravely into a wave on a dare, only to end up on the sand, sputtering and writhing with her eyes closed, making a spectacle of herself. Putting Quezada's suggestion into the context of this childhood humiliation, she seems to shudder at the thought of similar results. She thus responds to the dare of taking on the university presidency with a decisive no (230).

This article can be understood, on the one hand, as Castellanos' rejection of Quezada's defeminizing portrait of her as wearing pants (hence her self-portrayal in a maxiskirt). But on the other hand, the work is an acknowledgment of her successes in male-dominated arenas. Like the waves on the beach at Caletilla, her self-derision and her assertions of power are almost inseparable, succeeding each other relentlessly.

Many of the articles Castellanos wrote for *Excélsior* while ambassador to Israel similarly combine overt references to her authority and achievements with undercutting techniques of appeasement. In "Génesis de una embajadora" (The Making of an Ambassador), she portrays herself not as one who earned her diplomatic post but as the heroine of a fairy tale who undergoes several symbolic births before her final rebirth as ambassador to Israel. She describes awakening to poetry as a child, when she sought to win through talent the attention she had not been given for her intrinsic worth. She then refers to her later incarnation as a female trying desperately to attract a mate in order to propagate the species. She concludes, "I was reincarnated as a literature teacher abroad and then in Mexico. At first, I was off the mark, but I finally got it right. Then all of a sudden, wham! I'm appointed ambassador. . . . I accepted because . . . I have confidence, not so much in my own abilities, but in the generosity

of others" (250). Her fairy-tale approach to her own history attributes
her success solely to luck, to circumstances beyond her effort and talent,
and to the indulgence of other people.

Castellanos seems reluctant to speak matter-of-factly about even small
triumphs. Perhaps fearing marginalization in a society where women
presumably work only if lacking men to take care of them (Poniatowska
102), she instead uses what Poniatowska describes as a "feminine language" that is always begging someone's pardon (82).[2] The coy, apolo-
getic tone with which she opens "El escritor, ese absurdo dinosaurio"
(The Writer, That Absurd Dinosaur) would be hard to imagine in a male
writer of similar stature: "I don't like to brag, but as a truthful journalist
I must report my election as president of Commission 1 of the Third
Latin American Conference of Writers" (328).[3]

And in "A pesar de proponérselo" (Despite One's Intentions), Castellanos' reference to an invitation she received to dine with Nixon and
Kissinger—two of the world's most powerful men at the time—is accompanied by the reassuringly feminine image of her applying her
makeup and by a self-derisive little joke: "(I'm not at all conceited, am
I?)" (306). The rest of the essay treats humorously her difficulty in being
recognized in Israel until a newspaper published a Mexican recipe alongside her picture. Ironically, though this article could be read as a protest
against society's resistance to acknowledging women in anything other
than traditionally female roles, Castellanos' insistent references to feminine accoutrements and her refusal to portray her professional role totally
seriously seem to evince a fear that without some effort at appeasement,
her ambassadorial image could threaten her acceptability as a woman.

In many other articles Castellanos balances her professional incursions
into male territory with propitiatory gestures of feminine weakness. In
an essay she contributed to *Los narradores ante el público* (Narrators before
the Public), a volume in which she was included precisely because of her
accomplishments as a writer, she describes herself as inept in her studies, stating that at the university she was only allowed to associate with
more talented students through fortuitous personal connections. In the
same essay, she refers to her early writings with her customary disdain
(93–95). In "Memorias de una radioescucha" (Memoirs of a Radio Lis-
tener), she again portrays herself as having stumbled passively onto her
successes (275). In two essays, "La liberación de la mujer, aquí" (Wom-
en's Liberation, Here) and "Monstruo de su laberinto" (Monster of Its
Labyrinth), she employs the derogatory term "hysterical," often used
against women, to describe herself (67, 224). As in "Autorretrato con

maxifalda," furthermore, she depicts herself with some frequency as dependent or childlike. In "Hora de la verdad" (The Moment of Truth) she laments her impotence at finding herself in a hotel room with no one to zip up her dress. She becomes "a totally helpless creature," "orphaned and divorced" (295).

Significantly, too, the columns Castellanos wrote from her diplomatic post in Tel Aviv tend to focus less on political topics than on personal ones. She especially favors domestic and maternal themes, writing about such matters as her Mexican housekeeper's adjustment problems in Israel (282, 297) and her experiences as a parent (287).[4]

The arresting incongruity between the image Castellanos projects in her essays and her actual achievements, as well as between her reputed personal charm (Poniatowska 51–52, 58) and the clumsiness with which she endows herself on paper, may be related to an aspect of her writings that Dauster has seen as fundamental: the search for an authorial stance (134).[5] What comes across in her editorials, as well as in her other works, as a contradictory and self-undercutting *persona* no doubt can be explained in many ways. To cite the dearth of models for both her literary and political roles would be in line with a large body of feminist thought. Early childhood psychological factors—her parents' seeming preference for her brother and their neglect of her upon his death, for example— may partly explain her negative self-portrayal and ambivalence about power. Yet in the case of her newspaper writings, her discourse is shaped not only by her past but by her audience's needs and expectations as well. Though written for *Excélsior*'s editorial pages, and thus for a male-dominated public forum emphasizing male-dominated national affairs and geopolitics, her articles create a public *persona* clearly differentiated from masculine models. The ambivalence and self-disparagement characteristic of these articles suggest a struggle between the desire to interact freely as a woman in intellectual arenas and the fear of loss of femininity (and masculine approval) if she does so.[6] This struggle can be understood as a manifestation of fundamental patterns of gender identity in contemporary capitalist societies as elucidated by the theorists Nancy Chodorow and Judith Kegan Gardiner. Their writings, based on a variety of psychoanalytic theories, help to explain how gender-related issues in Mexican society may have contributed to Castellanos' ambivalent self-portrayal, to her integration into, but simultaneous differentiation from, a masculine-dominated context.

According to the theories discussed by Chodorow, though both boys and girls start life identifying with their mother, males later must acquire an identity based on differentiation from their first caretaker. Males feel masculine to the extent that they are not connected to and similar to women. They shift their identification to their fathers, but because fathers are generally not present in the way mothers are, this identification ends up being a "positional" one rather than a personal one; that is, the boy identifies with "cultural images of masculinity" rather than with his father as a person. Boys learn their role, Chodorow states, not through relating to men but through denying their "affective relationship to their mothers" (177). And in contrast to women, males learn what is masculine through observing men's nonfamilial roles. Because of the aura that the absent father assumes in the family, masculinity becomes something more prized but less accessible than the femininity of the more available mother. The fact that masculinity is problematic results in a devaluation of the feminine. Separate masculine social activities are defined as superior, and women are thought incapable of "socially important" action: "It becomes important to think that women's economic and social contribution cannot equal men's" (182).

Judith Kegan Gardiner, considering the implications of Chodorow's discussion of female development, observes that a girl's development does not require the distancing from the mother that a boy's development demands, for she "forms her gender identity positively, in becoming like the mother with whom she begins life in a symbiotic merger" (182). Yet the Oedipal process is not easily resolved by the female, since she maintains "an oscillating triangular relationship" between herself, her mother, and her father (183). Her "[e]go and body boundaries," moreover, "remain flexible" (182), allowing a return to earlier stages when required to nurture children. Thus, for Gardiner female identity is "typically less fixed, less unitary, and more flexible than male individuality" (183). And whereas a male resolves his Oedipal conflict cleanly by identifying with his father, and then assumes an occupational role in society and a separate role as husband and father, for the woman these two spheres are traditionally conflated, with both occupational and personal identity dependent on her status as wife and mother. The female may identify personally with her mother but reject the "'positional identification' with the mother as victim" (186).

The differences in identity acquisition between contemporary males and females brought up in a traditional manner have important consequences. The male (because of the need to separate from the mother) is more likely than a woman to have difficulty maintaining gender identity. But the female may suffer from a troubled self-concept (due to rejection of her mother's role) or from problems maintaining her separateness from others, since her identity, being less fixed, remains in process.

The self-image Castellanos projects in her newspaper articles can be interpreted as deriving, in a variety of ways, from the basic psychosocial development of males and females in contemporary Western society. The inordinate self-disparagement she exhibits, bordering on self-hatred, may be a product of unresolved Oedipal hostility, which according to Chodorow can lead to self-depreciation (182). Castellanos indeed did reject her mother "positionally." She describes extreme revulsion at seeing her mother, dying of cancer, playing the martyr and caring for her ungrateful father when he was ill with a simple cold (Poniatowska 116). Her attitude toward her parents in this passage (first pitying her mother, then wanting to kill her and pitying her father) reveals the oscillation between parents Chodorow attributes to the little girl's development. (Similarly, in *Balún Canán*, Castellanos exhibits more sympathy for males caught in unfair situations than for females.)

Yet the abnegation that Castellanos abhors in her mother is a characteristic that she identifies in herself (*El uso de la palabra* 222). And the female dependence on marriage for a secure self-image, which she decries in "Costumbres mexicanas" (Mexican Customs) and elsewhere, is an attitude that she herself, according to Poniatowska, strongly exhibited (61).

Not only Castellanos' ambivalent self-portrayal but other traits as well may stem from the basic psychosocial patterns Gardiner and Chodorow describe. The female writer's difficulty in establishing her identity may result in the blurring of the public and the private, which explains Poniatowska's charge that Castellanos washed her dirty laundry in public (58). Gardiner's theory that women writers tend to shift in their perspectives regarding characters, producing ambivalence in their readers, may further explain the incongruities of Castellanos' self-portrayal. Yet Castellanos' negative attitude toward herself may also result from the psychological requirements of her audience, which, in the case of her newspaper articles, included educated Mexican males. Her self-depreciation may be a response both to her growing successes and to her male audience's need for differentiation from the feminine.

Chodorow suggests that male identity acquisition involves warding off closeness to the mother, rejecting and devaluing the feminine, and maintaining distinctions between the sexes. Female identity does not depend on these processes. But influenced by their flexible ego boundaries, women may respond to male audiences by providing the differentiation that this audience needs from them. As Castellanos operated ever more successfully in male spheres (of which the editorial pages of *Excélsior* are a notable example), she may have unconsciously shaped her discourse to avoid posing a threat to her audience's sense of masculinity. For Gardiner, such sensitivity to societal expectations is typical of women, who may modify "dress, speech, and behavior" to match social views of "what women should be" (184, 190).

If we accept the theories of Chodorow and Gardiner, we can conclude that, simply because Castellanos is a sensitive woman and not because of any abnormality on her part, writing becomes a problem for her in a way that it would not for a male in Mexican society. For a man, writing (publication) means identification with a male model that reinforces identity. The competition writing entails (and even the process of appropriation and differentiation described by Harold Bloom as an Oedipal struggle, a version of Freud's family romance [8, 10]) in a sense creates similarity as writers assert their masculinity and their symbolic readiness to take over the female. For a woman, in contrast, competing publicly with the male means symbolically destroying the possibility of love for herself (she becomes a "castrating woman"). Her being free, and thus like a man, can also pose a threat to her son's acquisition of identity through identification with his father. Thus, Castellanos appeases through her self-depreciation, her image of helplessness, her emphasis on her domestic roles, and a certain coy concealment of worldly knowledge (as when, describing her need for someone to zip up her dress, she emphasizes both sexuality and chastity at the same time). Castellanos indeed seems to have been quite sensitive to "rules" governing appropriate female behavior toward males.[7]

The effort Castellanos put into differentiating herself from men may seem extreme. Yet in her article "Herencia de una madre: El rencor vivo" (A Mother's Inheritance: Rancor Personified) she identifies aspects of Mexican family life that by making masculine identity more difficult to acquire may have exacerbated the need for male differentiation from the female, leading also to the intense *machismo* described in "Costumbres mexicanas." In "Herencia de una madre" she uses Rulfo's *Pedro Páramo* to discuss the Mexican male's abandonment of the female and their son's subsequent humiliating quest for his father. She bolsters her view with Santiago Ramírez's notion of the Mexican family as exhibiting an excess of maternal affection and a "total absence of the father" and with Octavio Paz's statement of the Mexican problem of "the search for filiation." The Mexican male's difficulty in finding his identity may have led to an even stronger masculine need to devalue and differentiate from the feminine in Mexico than in other countries. That despite such resistance Castellanos forged ahead toward her many successes is admirable and her attempts at appeasement and ingratiation understandable.

NOTES

This work was supported in part by funds from the Foundation of the University of North Carolina at Charlotte and from the state of North Carolina.

1. Unless appearing separately in the list of works cited, all essays are from *El uso de la palabra*.

2. For Poniatowska, Castellanos had internalized the cliché that intellectual women lose femininity (87). Castellanos, says Poniatowska, disregarded her intellectual assets to judge herself only on her success or failure in love (61). Poniatowska views Castellanos' self-derision, her tendency to downplay her success, and her emphasis on personal rather than political or social issues as attempts to avoid marginalization (57–58, 82).

3. Poniatowska considers such self-justification endemic in female writers from Sor Juana on (101).

4. Compare Castellanos with Neruda, who served as Chile's ambassador to France. Though he considered himself an *arriviste* with few credentials for the post, he nevertheless emphasizes the political context of his position in his memoirs (a genre that could easily allow the personal to predominate). Yet Castellanos, writing specifically for those pages in *Excélsior* devoted to international politics, maintains a homey, personal image.

5. Dauster detects Castellanos' awareness of the pressure of collective societal messages (162). For further views on her apparent ambivalence about herself, see Palley and Salgado.

6. Poniatowska sees contradiction in Castellanos: "[S]he wants to save all women and fears going crazy if she loses the man" (126).

7. In "Cartas," she recalls preserving the pride of the Indians she worked with through her own ineptitude at horseback riding.

WORKS CITED

Bloom, Harold. *The Anxiety of Influence: A Theory of Poetry*. New York: Oxford University Press, 1973.

Castellanos, Rosario. "Cartas a Elías Nandino." *Revista de Bellas Artes* 18 (November–December 1974), 20–23.

———. "Herencia de una madre: El rencor vivo." *Excélsior* (13 October 1972), A6, A8.

————. "La participación de la mujer mexicana en la educación formal." In *Mujer que sabe latín . . . .* Mexico City: SepSetentas, 1973.

————. "Rosario Castellanos." In *Confrontaciones: Los narradores ante el público*, 89–98. Mexico City: Joaquín Mortiz, 1966.

————. *El uso de la palabra: Una mirada a la realidad.* Mexico City: Editores Mexicanos Unidos, 1982.

Chodorow, Nancy. *The Reproduction of Mothering.* Berkeley: University of California Press, 1978.

Dauster, Frank. *The Double Strand: Five Contemporary Mexican Poets.* Lexington: University of Kentucky Press, 1987.

Gardiner, Judith Kegan. "On Female Identity and Writing by Women." In *Writing and Sexual Difference*, 177–191. Ed. Elizabeth Abel. Chicago: University of Chicago Press, 1982.

Palley, Julian. "Introducción." In *Meditación en el umbral: Antología poética* by Rosario Castellanos, 37–41. Mexico City: Fondo de Cultura Económica, 1985.

Poniatowska, Elena. *¡Ay vida, no me mereces!* Mexico City: Joaquín Mortiz, 1985.

Salgado, María. "El 'Autorretrato' de Rosario Castellanos: Reflexiones sobre la feminidad y el arte de retratarse en México." *Letras Femeninas* 14:1–2 (1988), 64–72.

Ardis L. Nelson CARMEN
NARANJO AND
COSTA RICAN
CULTURE

Carmen Naranjo (b. 1930) is an impor-
tant figure in Costa Rican letters and culture.[1] Since 1962 she has published seven volumes of poetry, four books of short stories, seven novels,
and four books of essays. She has held cultural and political posts that
have given her a public voice, and she has been instrumental in the ad-
vancement of women's rights in Costa Rica. The wide range of experience and expression articulated in Naranjo's literary and professional ca-
reers has provided a model of female leadership and creativity. As a
successful writer committed to the eradication of apathy and hypocrisy,
she has provided insightful criticism of the human situation in an ongoing dialogue with Costa Rican society. Since her essays are not as
well known as her fiction and poetry, this paper will begin to correct the
imbalance, providing an overview of her major works in this genre.

Analyzing Naranjo's writing makes it clear that she is what we might
call a cultural activist. As an essayist her goal has been to demonstrate
the importance of culture in Latin America, especially through her book
Cultura (Culture, 1978), written for UNESCO and distributed throughout Central America, Mexico, and Colombia. She writes on a wide range
of topics and for different audiences, but even those essays that are decidedly technical in nature focus on issues of human interaction and
concern. Her book written for ICAP (Instituto Centroamericano de Administración Pública), *Las relaciones públicas en las instituciones de seguridad social* (Public Relations in Social Security Institutions, 1977), for
example, is part of a series on *Aspectos humanos de la administración* (Human Aspects of Administration). The topics of books and pamphlets
written for UNICEF, UNESCO, and the Ministry of Culture, Youth,

and Sports between 1969 and 1988 range from issues for rural and working women to alcoholism, child rearing, education, and the distribution of books. Naranjo's journalistic articles, which number over two hundred, present a wide diversity of knowledge and interests: literature, art, theatre, women's issues, humor, mass communications, tourism, and social, economic, and political problems.

For the purposes of this paper, however, we will examine Naranjo's four major essay collections within the context of the unique history of Costa Rica and the political forces of the 1970s. From the time of its independence in 1821, Costa Rica has been characterized by a superior valuation of peace, democracy, and education. In 1823 the governing body declared that "the provision of education is the essential foundation of individual happiness and the prosperity of all" (Rovinski 9). But Costa Rica did more than pay lip service to these principles. The 1869 constitution declared that education would be "universal, free, and the responsibility of the State." In 1887 education was made compulsory and secular. As of 1977 education comprised 35 percent of the national budget, an impressive statistic due largely to the fact that there is no military budget.

Costa Rica is known for its antimilitarism, especially since the abolition of the army in 1948 when national hero José Figueres Ferrer handed over the keys to the barracks and instructed one of his ministers to turn the Fortress Bella Vista into a school. Today the fortress houses the National Museum. In 1987 President Oscar Arias Sánchez received the Nobel Peace Prize for the Arias Plan for Central America.

Before the Ministry of Culture was established in 1970, Costa Rica's priorities lay in pragmatic issues to the exclusion of artistic and even scientific development. Under the government of Figueres (1970–1974), however, a Ministry of Culture, Youth, and Sports was created for the first time, providing the power and financial resources to manage cultural affairs separately from education. This was a revolutionary effort meant to unite the educated and the illiterate in a process of cultural training. At that time one-third of the population was comprised of students, yet the country still had an illiteracy rate of 14 percent (Rovinski 14–21).

As Minister of Culture during the subsequent administration of Daniel Oduber Quirós (1974–1978), Carmen Naranjo was directly responsible for initiating and establishing many cultural institutions, including the Department of Cinema, the National Theatre Company, the National Symphonic Orchestra, the Publishing House of Costa Rica, and the College of Costa Rica. As Naranjo recalls expressing, "I want Costa Rica to grow culturally by one millimeter, but it must be the *whole* country" ("Premio" 8).

Cultura is a book dedicated to clarifying the concept of culture and the multifarious ways in which it can be manifested in everyday life. Indeed, Naranjo serves as a spokesperson for the democratization of the cultural heritage, which she sees as a dynamic entity that gives meaning and sustenance to the people. *Cultura* forms a conceptual base for her other essays, four of which will be discussed in terms of their elaboration of the major components of her definition of culture: ". . . all that which contributes to the heritage of a people and manifests itself as communication, tradition, national identity, beliefs, and artistic expression, whether popular or individual. Culture includes such important factors for all peoples as *language, customs,* the expression of *religious belief* that transcends reality, and the wealth of *creativity* that enriches a people's heritage" (*Cultura* 4–5, emphasis added).

Although *Cultura* is a generic book in the sense that it was written for several Latin American countries under the UNESCO umbrella, it provides a model for establishing an infrastructure for cultural development on the administrative level. It is a treatise of sorts that serves as a guide to developing nations in the areas of art, literature, and science. Naranjo's views on culture are formulated within the Costa Rican experience of placing importance on education and are a reflection of the work actually done in Costa Rica. Seen in the perspective of its original function as a UNESCO publication, the purpose for its direct, straightforward style becomes clear. Naranjo has distilled the essence of the Costa Rican policy to produce a cultural manifesto.

Cultura first discusses cultural action, defined as all labor that foments culture, keeping in mind two primordial principles: (a) the enrichment of a people resides in the growth of its culture, and (b) cultural heritage does not belong to a particular group but rather must be shared by all members of the society (7–8). In order to maintain contact with their culture, people need to be reminded of its value, shown how to recognize and respect it, and discover their own identity through a responsible interaction with it, either confirming or negating its traditions (12). A cultural policy would foster an education that would stimulate the desire to think and discover, give and receive, change and grow in ways that would contribute to society and help maintain its integrity and vitality (11–16). For Naranjo, the cultural heritage of a country is more important than economic concerns, for on this heritage are based real independence and quality of life. Being involved with it brings to the people an awareness, a connectedness, and a commitment (28).

When Naranjo recommends a cultural policy she is referring to a government policy, such as the one instigated under Figueres, that takes into account all sectors of society, raises an awareness of the cultural heritage, and encourages its extension and enrichment. While a mandated approach may not sound viable to us, Rovinski points out that the creation of a centralizing agency for Costa Rican activities was not the result of a totalitarian conception of culture but rather of the persistence of writers, poets, artists, musicians, and scientists who, in a combined effort, informed the public of their works and sought to inspire creativity (Rovinski 15–16). Naranjo recognizes that cultural action cannot be dictated, but rather it needs a climate of freedom in which all can participate. A cultural policy establishes norms, principles, and regulations to protect responsible freedom in creating and recreating cultural values (*Cultura* 17–20).

An unregulated mass media was seen as one of the greatest threats to this climate of creative participation in the 1970s epoch of enthusiasm and innovation. The quality of mass communication media was researched by the Ministry of Culture, concerned about the fact that radio and television were privately owned except for three radio stations: one owned by the university and two by religious groups. Only 1.29 percent of television programming was devoted to cultural films, largely financed by the government (Rovinski 46). Naranjo addresses this issue by describing the effects of commercial television as anticulture, a negation of traditional values, and a depersonalization and placation of the populace.

Since most television programming is received from the United States, including dubbed commercials, Naranjo's stance may sound anti-American, yet the complaints she voices have also been articulated in the United States. The fact that many people spend far too many hours passively absorbing whatever appears on the screen tends to produce a hypnotized society. This, plus the way language is used on commercially sponsored radio and TV, can have devastating effects on the public. Naranjo's beliefs led her to propose in 1974 the unsuccessful Radio and Television Bill; two years after that she resigned from the Ministry of Culture. In her resignation speech, she lamented the lack of support for some of her projects. The fact is that she had been called subversive for exposing Costa Rican society to the ills of their country through film programs on deforestation, malnutrition, poverty, and alcoholism (Martínez Santiago 126–27).

Naranjo's concern with authentic communication brings us to language, as one of the four points in her definition of culture. Whereas in *Cultura* Naranjo generalizes from the Costa Rican experience to a universalized program for Latin America, in *Cinco temas en busca de un pensador* (Five Themes in Search of a Thinker, 1967) she studies five typical Costa Rican expressions, most of which are common to all Spanish-speaking countries, and critiques them as symbolic of the Costa Rican mentality. This small volume attests to Naranjo's critical acumen and her early disillusionment with the sociopolitical apathy of her compatriots.

Her reaction to some everyday expressions that may seem perfectly harmless often verges on the extreme, but, as we know, language is not an innocent tool. It has been used for centuries as an instrument of empires to dominate conquered peoples and of patriarchal societies to maintain control over women and minorities. In *Cinco temas* Naranjo offers a microscopic examination of the nuances of these expressions "to see if I can agitate people and get them to change for the better,"[2] although she admits her pessimism in the book's conclusion. Naranjo lashes out against the weaknesses of the Costa Rican's value system, suggesting that the country suffers from a lack of character. Her hope is that what she perceives as negative and escapist attitudes may be overcome through education and a new sense of social responsibility. As Minister of Culture seven years later she would have the opportunity to influence change in a more auspicious manner.

The sayings of *Cinco temas*, still in vogue today, are seen as signs of a decadence in verbal communication. The most popular one discussed by Naranjo is "Porta a mí" (What do I care?), a contraction of the original "A mí ¿qué me importa?" The expression conveys apathy and indifference to whatever does not affect the speaker directly and is often followed by the reiterative "de por sí" (anyway) ("Vivito" 14). Another is the common retort "Ahí vamos pasando" (We're doing OK). In this expression Naranjo detects fundamental insecurity lurking behind a facade of conformity and anonimity. On top of this, when the Costa Rican shrugs his shoulders and replies, "¿Qué le vamos a hacer?" (What can we do about it?), he progresses from conformity to resignation and fatalism.

"Idiay" (So what), the one expression unique to Costa Rica, has several meanings depending on the situation and tone of voice of the speaker. As an interrogative it can mean "Get to the point," "What about me?" or "What else could I do?" Without the interrogative and spoken from a defensive stance, "idiay" can mean "What do you want from me?" In each case Naranjo's interpretation is perspicacious, as she continually urges honesty over escapism.

Naranjo's harshness in *Cinco temas* softens considerably in her later writing as she gains more compassion for her fellow Costa Ricans. Her essayistic work on religion is based mostly on the investigation and observation of another culture, although some comparisons are made with Costa Rica. *Por Israel y por las páginas de la Biblia* (Passing through Israel and the Pages of the Bible, 1976) is a collection of some fifty essays written by Naranjo while serving as Costa Rican ambassador to Israel (1972–1974). She sent them to San José, where they appeared in *La Nación* and *La República* and were later published as a book by the Jewish community of San José. The section relating to Israel is comprised of well-researched essays on Israeli history and traditions in which Naranjo's tendency to didacticism is glimpsed, as, for example, when she lauds the Israelis for their sobriety in contrast with the Latin American's social drinking.

For the most part, however, *Por Israel* is informative, humorous at times, and interesting for its cultural contrasts. One such comparison deals with *el mal de ojo* (the evil eye), which in Jewish tradition invokes a punishment from God, whereas in Catholic Caribbean cultures it is a curse put on one person by another. Another example is the insult. In Spanish-speaking countries an insult to one's mother is very grave due to the exalted position of the Virgin Mary, symbol and prototype of motherhood. In Hebrew there is no vocabulary for insults, so people resort to derogatory comments in Arabic, or they pronounce a malediction invoking God's participation (19–20).

In the section "Por las páginas de la Biblia" we find interpretive essays on biblical themes. Naranjo's treatment of Adam and Eve is of special interest. A variation on this essay was presented in 1977 as a part of "Mitos culturales de la mujer" (Cultural Myths about Women)[3] at the First Mexican–Central American Symposium on Research on Women in Mexico, later included in *Mujer y cultura* (Women and Culture, 1989). This later version is strongly feminist, contrasting with the conservative tone of the original essay, thus showing a transition in Naranjo's thought that leads us to consider the way in which women are viewed in Costa Rica.

The first version of this essay was written in Israel in 1973 and was entitled "Adán y Eva: La primera pareja" (Adam and Eve: The First Couple). Essentially a traditional reading of the biblical passage, Naranjo adds only an optimistic assertion as to the couple's companionship and unity even as they faced the hardships of exile from Paradise. In the later version, called "El mito de Eva" (The Myth of Eve), a different focus is perceived. Besides the suppression of several paragraphs on Adam, a full two pages of the approximately five-page essay have been added, all of which emphasizes a feminist interpretation of Eve. The added material begins thus: "The conception of the woman as a being derived from another has substantially aggravated human relationships" (*Mujer* 14). Naranjo writes favorably about Eve's inquisitive nature but points out that her spontaneity is considered dangerous by society: "In addition to revealing, the myth also warns. Not only does it place woman within the most absolute subordination, . . . it also announces the dangers of a rebellion, of an independent act" (17). This version was published after Naranjo had served as Minister of Culture of Costa Rica.

The 1970s gave rise to a significant global awakening about women's issues. In several hallmark proclamations made by the United Nations, such as The Decade for Women: Equality, Development and Peace (1976–1985) or the resolution passed in 1979 by the General Assembly on The Elimination of All Forms of Discrimination against Women, recognition was given to the fact that women were being discriminated against. The resolution was ratified in Costa Rica in 1984, effectively giving the principles of the convention a priority status over the national laws since the Political Constitution of Costa Rica grants a superior value to international treaties. Nonetheless, the statutes of this convention are not applied in actuality, particularly with respect to affirmative action, as was shown in the debate on the draft of the Law for Social Equality of Women, a controversial law written by Carmen Naranjo and passed in 1989 (United Nations 7).

Although statistics on Costa Rica bode well for women in many respects from life expectancy to literacy,[4] attitudes often lag far behind when it comes to real change. Costa Rica is a predominantly Catholic country where *machismo* is strong and women's liberation is seen by many as a threat to the established order. The fact that poverty affects a full third of Costa Rican homes (as of 1988) aggravates an already oppressive environment for women. For the 30 percent of active women who work, for example, it often translates to suffering not only a double day but also the disapproval of family and spouse.

Naranjo has used every possible outlet at her disposition to educate the Costa Rican public and to work for change in laws, customs, and destructive attitudes toward women. In the volume *Mujer y cultura*, she consolidates approximately forty brief essays, published previously as separate pieces in magazines and journals, into a coherent grouping of "Cultural Myths about Women," "Women and Circumstance," "Famous Women," and "Feminism and Liberation."

In "Cultural Myths" Naranjo analyzes mythological and literary figures that reflect Western values, critiquing customs that propagate the subservience and exploitation of women. According to Naranjo, the negative myth of the liberated woman has led many Costa Rican women to reject the path of liberation for fear of losing what little security they have. Her quite basic approach to a topic that has become commonplace in the United States is perfectly justified for a Costa Rican audience. From a number of studies it is clear that many Costa Ricans are far from understanding that the goal of liberation is for both men and women to have the right and opportunity to develop to their potential as human beings. One such study of sixty Costa Rican women factory-workers confirms that women's perspective of themselves and other women is entirely different from their perspective of men. Since a woman is ordinarily in the home, raising a family, they accept that "instead of being educated, she is protected" (González Suárez 106).

"Women and Circumstance" speaks directly to women to encourage them to appreciate themselves and their capabilities. Naranjo considers a variety of situations encountered by women in their daily lives, from health, housing, family, and work to issues such as beauty contests, old age, and domestic violence, and she suggests coping attitudes and actions. These journalistic essays are written for a population of women who have had little or no support on the path toward self-realization.

In "Famous Women" Naranjo presents a series of vignettes of the lives of Spanish American women poets, novelists, painters, musicians, and heroines as models of what some women have been able to achieve in the cultural arena. She concludes that change takes place in two stages: knowledge and understanding are followed by creative participation. She hopes that *Mujer y cultura* may serve as a first step toward this understanding (37–40).

"Feminism and Liberation" is comprised of four essays that provide a clear definition of feminism and outline some of the movement's basic issues and their development in Costa Rica. Following the model of Ida Magli, who equates women with language, Naranjo asserts that women, as alphabet, form the basis of our culture's symbolisms and that they must appropriate their own language. Naranjo defines feminism as a consciousness-raising and humanistic endeavor, emphasizing the eradication of inequality and discrimination for all people. An awareness of woman's real value as "sustainer of life, peace, and justice" (196) must replace the perception of her as pure, weak, incapable, a secondary being whose value is measured by her capacity to serve. To liberate women is to free them from traditional roles and attitudes and charge them with "liberties, hopes, decisions, and happiness" (205).

It is interesting to note that in her acceptance speech to the Costa Rican Academy of Language, "Los Quijotes modernos" (Modern Quixotes, 1990), Naranjo addresses the problem of idealism in today's society and, in so doing, touches emphatically on creativity, the fourth component in her definition of culture. Referring to Cervantes' well-known protagonist, she points out how he follows the path of creativity by daring to be different. In his search for authenticity, don Quixote abandons traditional comforts and responsibilities to pursue his dream even though he is faced with alienation and ridicule from others who mock his eccentricity. But, asks Naranjo, does his existence as the prototypical ridiculous idealist in our contemporary imagination now inhibit us from following the same path? Naranjo asks that we imagine a Quixote-less world:

> And here we are at the dawn of the twenty-first century, somewhat at a loss when it comes to bravery, and thus we barely dare to exist. There's no reason for avoiding it, for not being Quixotes, because don Quixote never existed. Nor is there one for becoming Sanchos, because we are surrounded by Sanchos without profiles, by those who don't know how to grow and transform themselves into heroes.
> (290)

Without Cervantes' masterpiece, Naranjo suggests, our language would be impoverished but our creative impulses might be freer. This provocative essay ironically underscores the quixotic role Naranjo herself has assumed as cultural activist in a Central American society threatened with poverty and complacency.

The major themes of Naranjo's essays, then, focus on the broad cultural issues of language, religion, customs, and creativity as she urges her fellow citizens toward transformative authenticity. Probably more than any woman in Costa Rica, Naranjo has used her political influence to promote gender equality and social liberation through her writing and her cultural involvement. The direct and uncomplicated style she uses in her essays, in contrast to her fictional writing, puts her in contact with a wide public, one that Naranjo loves to surprise and incite to action. Her reader inevitably engages with a woman who participates fully in the cultural dynamics of her country and inspires others to do the same.[5]

NOTES

Research for this paper was supported in part by a grant from the Florida State University.

1. Upon graduating from the University of Costa Rica Naranjo served as a public official in a series of positions in Costa Rica and abroad, including Assistant Administrative Director of the Bureau of Social Security; Ambassador to Israel; Minister of Culture, Youth, and Sports; United Nations Delegate for Children's Affairs in Mexico; UNICEF Representative in Guatemala; Director of EDUCA [Central American University Press]; and Director of the Costa Rican Museum of Art. See Acuña 129–130.

2. Carmen Naranjo, personal interview, 10 August 1992.

3. This was one of eight essays originally published as a series in the weekly *Universidad*, San Pedro, University of Costa Rica, between November 1977 and February 1978 (Acuña 48–50).

4. As of 1990 the estimated population of Costa Rica was just over three million, 49.5 percent of which is female, a population that is equally divided between urban and rural areas. Women are the head of the household in one-third of Costa Rican homes; they have an average of 3.5 children, marry at an early age, have a 93 percent literacy rate and a life expectancy of seventy-four years. More than a quarter of the female population over the age of twelve enters secondary education, and 7 percent goes on to the university (United Nations 5–6).

5. Her efforts have been recognized by a cultural week held in her honor in September 1989, celebrated at the University of Costa Rica's School of Humanities.

WORKS CITED

Acuña, María Eugenia, ed. *Bibliografía comentada de Carmen Naranjo*. Special issue of *Letras* 22 (1990), 1–193.

Gatens, Moira. *Feminism and Philosophy: Perspectives on Difference and Equality*. Bloomington: Indiana University Press, 1991.

González Suárez, Mirta. "Las palabras ocultas." In *Estudios de la mujer: Conocimiento y cambio*, 95–169. Ed. Mirta González Suárez. San José: EDUCA, 1988.

Martínez Santiago, Luz Ivette. *Carmen Naranjo y la narrativa femenina en Costa Rica*. San José: EDUCA, 1987.

Naranjo, Carmen. "Adán y Eva: La primera pareja." *La República* (15 November 1973), 13.

——. *Cinco temas en busca de un pensador*. 1967. San José: Ministerio de Cultura, Juventud y Deportes, 1977.

——. *Cultura*. San José: ICAP, 1978.

——. "El mito de Eva." *Universidad* 25 November–1 December 1977), 5.

——. *Mujer y cultura*. San José: EDUCA, 1989.

——. *Por Israel y por las páginas de la Biblia*. San José: Fotorama de Centro América, 1976.

——. "Los Quijotes modernos: Ensayo de incorporación a la Academia Costarricense de la Lengua." *Alba de América* 8 (1990), 289–304.

——. *Las relaciones públicas y las instituciones de seguridad social*. 2d ed. Aspectos humanos de la administración 132. San José: ICAP, 1977.

Okin, Susan Moller. *Women in Western Political Thought*. Princeton: Princeton University Press, 1992.

"Premio con rango de mujer." *Rumbo* (13–19 February 1987), 8.

Rovinski, Samuel. *Cultural Policy in Costa Rica*. Studies and Documents on Cultural Practices. Paris: UNESCO, 1977.

United Nations Centre for Social Development and Humanitarian Affairs. *Women in Decision-Making: Case-Study on Costa Rica*. New York: United Nations, 1991.

"Vivito y choteando." *Rumbo* (21 April 1992), 14.

Beth E. Jörgensen   MARGO GLANTZ,
TONGUE IN
HAND

L uisa Valenzuela pays a high honor to her
contemporary from Mexico, Margo Glantz, when she singles out the
writer as one of her "favorite witches." In her essay "Mis brujas favoritas," Valenzuela praises all women past and present who, through their
speech and their writing, have given tongue to the forbidden fruit of their
uniquely female knowledge. A writer's writer and a critic's critic, Margo
Glantz participates in the transformation of patriarchal language and culture, which twentieth-century women have undertaken, by unabashedly
appropriating the foundations of Western literature for her own bewitch-
ing purposes in a series of metaliterary and metalinguistic texts.

Born in Mexico in 1930 to Jewish Ukrainian parents, Glantz recognized early her vocation for literature through a passion for reading that,
in her adult life, has produced a significant body of original work. Glantz
subtly combines the creative and the critical in her own brand of literary
essay. A prominent figure in Mexican intellectual life, Margo Glantz has
served as director of literature at the National Institute of Fine Arts
(INBA) and cultural attaché for the Mexican embassy in London, and
she has long taught comparative literature as a professor of graduate
studies at the National Autonomous University of Mexico (UNAM). In
this chapter I will focus on the concepts of reading and writing in two
essays by the author. Viewed by Glantz as primordial activities of the
human impulse toward interpretation and self-creation, reading and
writing in a multicultural context are the central problems confronted in
her work. Like Jorge Luis Borges in her singular dedication to literature
from an early age, Margo Glantz celebrates in her essays the richness of
a life lived in books, while also expressing a certain anxiety about it.

A prolific writer, Glantz has produced more than fifteen books of essays, two novels, countless articles, and numerous translations of works
from French and English into Spanish.[1] Her most significant titles fall
into two groups: literary criticism and book-length creative essays that
treat a single theme from multiple, usually literary, perspectives. As examples of her literary criticism, the following selections demonstrate
the breadth of her decades-long investigation into the Western tradition:
Tennessee Williams y el teatro norteamericano (Tennessee Williams and the
North American Theatre, 1964), *Repeticiones: Ensayos sobre literatura me-*
xicana (Repetitions: Essays on Mexican Literature, 1979), and critical
prologues to a 1986 edition of *María* by the Colombian author Jorge
Isaacs and to a Spanish translation of Gustave Flaubert's *Sentimental Edu-*
cation. The second category, that of thematically structured creative essays, includes *No pronunciarás* (Thou Shalt Not Take the Name, 1980),
which examines the cultural significance of names and naming, a poetically structured essay on whales titled *Doscientas ballenas azules . . . y . . .*
cuatro caballos (Two Hundred Blue Whales . . . and . . . Four Horses,
1981), and *De la amorosa inclinación a enredarse en cabellos* (On the Loving
Inclination to Tangle with Tresses, 1984) on hair in myth, literature, and
popular culture.[2]

Viewed all together, Margo Glantz's writing presents a bewildering
proliferation of topics, sources, and forms. Drawing on Greek mythology, the Bible, popular culture, folk sayings, fairy tales, cinema, nine-
teenth- and twentieth-century French literature, the Hispanic tradition,
North American authors, and the whole gamut of Mexican literature
from the Conquest to "la Onda," Glantz performs a dazzling display of
cultural prowess. Furthermore, the ludic quality of her language, the
high level of erudition, and the exceptionally fragmented style of some
of her compositions defy reading habits based on skimming page after
page of text in linear sequence. On the contrary, Glantz participates in
the modernist challenge to passive reading by requiring that we engage
in a kind of intellectual rumination over her writing. Once the reader has
bitten and swallowed, morsels of initially undigestible text force themselves back up like cud for a long, thorough chew. The influence of
Roland Barthes in Margo Glantz's formation as a reader and a writer can
be seen in the way that her writing demands the "scrupulous browsing"
by an elite reader that Barthes recommends in order to enjoy fully "the
pleasure of the text."

Other obsessions that occupy Margo Glantz's imagination are the
body and the erotic, all manner of transformations and metamorphoses,

and the Old Testament power of prophets and prophesy. For Glantz, censured and transgressive figures such as the Marquis de Sade and Georges Bataille represent the potential for combating what she perceives (and condemns) as the prevailing cultural and political Manichaeism and the homogenizing forces of contemporary society. Perhaps in part as a result of her own ambiguous identity as a child of cosmopolitan, Russian-speaking Jewish intellectuals growing up in predominantly Catholic, Spanish Mexico, Margo Glantz is irresistibly drawn to the territory of borders—borders between discourses, cultures, genders, historical periods—in a Barthesian endeavor to elevate the fluid and the indeterminate over the carefully defined.

Glantz's cultivation of the essay thus equally follows from her history as a reader (she mentions Borges, Barthes, Walter Benjamin, and Bataille as her fundamental models for the genre) and from her desire as a writer to submit the ideas and images gleaned from endless readings to the test of her own disciplined intelligence.[3] For what is an essay but an experiment or a trial that weighs received knowledge in the balance of individual analysis? It is in this sense that Margo Glantz herself uses the word *ensayo* in a comment on literature as an active, transformative "reading" of the world. "Literature can serve as an attempt (essay) to learn to 'unread' a world or as a verbal attempt to order it" (*Repeticiones* 113). Generously cosmopolitan and intensely Mexican, Glantz reads the Western canon and its discontents through the kaleidoscopic lens of her feminine reading I/eye.

The title of one of Margo Glantz's books of literary criticism offers an appropriate metaphor for my own essay on reading, unreading, and ordering the author's language. In *La lengua en la mano* (1983), Glantz carries out a critique of French and Mexican literature of the nineteenth and twentieth centuries, with a particular emphasis on the prevailing representations of the female body and feminine subjectivity. However, the serious playfulness of the phrase "la lengua en la mano," or "tongue in hand," generates associations that extend beyond this one book and across the whole body of Glantz's work. Like the English word *tongue*, the word *lengua* signifies both the organ of eating and speech, and language itself. *Lengua* additionally means interpreter, a figure of mediation between tongues. The image of the "tongue in hand" represents the intimate connection between body and language, eating and speech, by linking the eating, speaking mouth with the hand, bearer of food to the mouth and transcriber of speech into text. Expanding further on the phrase in her "Advertencia" to *La lengua en la mano*, Glantz pays tribute to two uniquely Mexican "figures of speech," Jerónimo de Aguilar and doña Marina, Cortés' interpreters—"lenguas"—and the right hands of conquest. Glantz thus acknowledges that translation is an act of cultural violence as well as communication, and that the threat of domination inevitably accompanies any instance of taking tongue in hand.

Finally, language, the instrument of mediation between the human subject and the world, plays its own treacherous interpretive role in the construction of "reality." Language is the constitutive condition of our human subjectivity, but, because it intervenes between the human being and material reality, language is also an obstacle to any aspirations of perfect, direct access to experience. That is, like the mysterious gifts celebrated by Jorge Luis Borges (whose tongue has a powerful hand in Margo Glantz's writing), language is a blessing and a curse, creating and condemning us at every moment. When critic and translator Glantz reads the work of another, she holds the other's book in her hand, and in rewriting the words of the other she leaves her own secret, traitorous fingerprints on their tongue.

I have chosen two interconnected essays for closer scrutiny: *Doscientas ballenas azules . . . y . . . cuatro caballos* and "Mi escritura tiene . . ." (My Writing Has . . . , 1985). The latter piece, which is a short debate on the relationship between books and life, refers directly back to the 1981 text on whales, as if posing a delayed challenge to the earlier essay's confident reliance on books as primary, even if ambiguous, sources of knowledge. In a scant four pages, the autobiographical "Mi escritura tiene . . ." highlights the enormous influence that literature has held over Glantz's life, puts the authenticity of book-learned lessons into doubt, and then brings the argument back full circle to a realization that literature and not "reality" irremediably delimits the writer's way of being in the world.

In the essay, Margo Glantz conducts an inquiry into the vital ailment (*dolencia*) that she suffers, dispensing symptoms, self-diagnosis, and prescription with high irony. This is a meditation on the apparent pathology of reading when the patient's absorption into the book utterly replaces intimacy with "real" people, animals, and adventures. Echoing remarks made in a 1982 interview with Magdalena García Pinto, Glantz confesses that, apart from her parents, "Whales and their creator, Melville, . . . are the agents of my writing. . . . I don't know much about nature; storybook animals interest me most like the ones that Borges collects" (475). By the same token, books also mediate Margo Glantz's relationships with other people, "whom I almost always approach through a book and not with the skin. That is a misfortune; also a boon" (475).

However, the essay "Mi escritura tiene . . ." seems to announce a radical break with this habit of approaching the world through books, and it seems to signal a reorientation toward a more vital intercourse with the other. Here Margo Glantz testifies to profound changes wrought by two "definitive trips" she took, daring forays into the natural world to witness the annual congregation of migrating monarch butterflies in the forests of Michoacán, and the movements of blue whales off the coast of Baja California. Suddenly praising the real over the read, Glantz downgrades her bookish knowledge to the status of lies and touts a newly forged connection—through the eyes and the skin—with an unmediated version of reality.

But the illusion of immediacy does not hold. A moment's blindness aboard the whale-watching ship and a missed view of a whale that too quickly disappears beneath the surface of the sea force the briefly repentant writer to recognize after all that "my whole adventure has entered through my eyes, my passivity in action is as great as that which rules my readings" (477). Nevertheless, Margo Glantz's readers perceive in her many essays not the mark of intellectual passivity but the fertile creativity born of reading and writing with tongue in hand.

The return to Moby Dick, Jane Eyre, Proust, and Borges in the final paragraph of "Mi escritura tiene . . ." marks a return to Margo Glantz's point of departure. Confirming that the name of the thing precedes (and conditions) her apprehension of the thing itself, Glantz is finally moved to confess that, putting the beauty of butterflies and blue whales aside, she remains wedded to paper whales and the name of the rose. She prescribes a book as a tonic against despair ("me receto un libro"), and she rededicates herself to "that endless anthropophagy through which I digest the fragments and reincorporate them into the eternal circulation of writing" (478). *Doscientas ballenas azules*, written in 1977–1978, is a paradigmatic text for discussing Margo Glantz's contribution to the care and feeding—and the consumption—of the body of Western literature.

Doscientas ballenas azules can be said to address the topic of whales and, more specifically, literary representations of whales. But because Glantz's writing follows the logic of association and not that of rational argument, its "content" stubbornly resists any attempt at an adequate summary.[4] Rather, the essay on whales, highly fragmented and densely intertextual, invites our consideration of Glantz's extraordinary capacity to absorb and transform the written word, to reread the age-old obsession with Leviathan as a sign of our human longing for origins and survival and meaning-making.

Doscientas ballenas azules demonstrates the same overall structure that Glantz utilizes in the essays on names and hair. She extracts a common theme from heterogeneous literary sources and skillfully plays one borrowed text off another within a design that is uniquely her own. In barely forty-five pages of text divided into thirty-four sections, Margo Glantz reads the Bible, Greek and Roman mythology, the writings of Borges and Joseph Conrad, and, most importantly, Herman Melville's *Moby-Dick* to retrace the paper trail left by Leviathan, that consummate navigator, through the Western tradition. This procedure of reading and rewriting the books of the whale recalls Roland Barthes' idea of intertextuality as a "circular memory" that destabilizes meaning and undermines notions of referentiality and authorial originality (35–36).

The instability of identity (individual and collective) and the preservation of difference and individuality within social formations are preoccupations that recur throughout Margo Glantz's essays. Logically, the whale holds a particular fascination for the author, because its ambiguous nature defies our imperfect but persistent attempts to define and categorize the other, whether animal or human. An aquatic mammal, warm-blooded like us and possessed of a "satin intelligence" (*Doscientas* 31), the whale has been fancifully construed in the past as sea dragon and siren, and it was once "scientifically" classified as a fish with lungs. Formerly a land creature who long ago returned to the sea, the whale has completed the evolutionary cycle, and it now exists between air and water, mammal and fish, beast and human. The whale overcomes these very dualisms by uniting disparate characteristics, and thus it serves to caution against dichotomous modes of reasoning. As a figure of successful transformation and adaptation, Leviathan may be a mute prophet of human survival under changing conditions. But threatened from without by extinction and showing an internal propensity for suicide, the whale equally warns us, prophetlike, of our human capacity for murderous self-destruction.

In *Doscientas ballenas azules* and on other occasions, Margo Glantz additionally uses the whale to call into question strict gender distinctions. On the one hand, she exploits the fact that the Spanish noun *ballena* is grammatically feminine to foreground both the nurturing, nursing mother of a single offspring and the virginal whale, free of human contact and control because of her superior marine intelligence. With Mel-

ville clearly in mind, but following her own logic, Glantz also speaks of
the whale as being "poeticized and pursued by man" (García Pinto 114),
clearly strengthening her association of the deep-sea mammal with the
human female. On the other hand, Glantz plays with the fertile polysemy
of the manly term *esperma*, which may take the feminine or the masculine
article in Spanish, and which signifies the male procreative fluid, the
spermaceti of the sperm-whale, and, in American Spanish, the candle
made from whale oil. Once incorrectly thought to come from the whale's
sperm, the spermaceti is a rich, waxy substance found in the head of both
the female and the male of the species. The persistence of the false ety-
mology allows Glantz, writing in Spanish, to play with the untrans-
latable contradiction inherent in attributing *esperma* to *la ballena*.

In *Doscientas ballenas azules*, Margo Glantz celebrates numerous other
paradoxical attributes of the whale's mysterious existence: the way its
visible breath of life betrays it to the hunter's deadly gaze; the fragrant,
highly prized ambergris found buried in the putrid labyrinth of the intes-
tines; and the necessary, life-saving violence of birth, feeding, and death
itself. Her project is to read the varied stories of men's efforts to find
meaning in the beautiful, terrible enigma of the whale, and to enter her
own interpretation into the "eternal circulation of writing" ("Mi escritura" 478).

That Herman Melville's *Moby-Dick* is the primary source of intertextuality in Margo Glantz's essay is only apparently incongruous. The
nineteenth-century narrative of an exclusively masculine world of violent nature and violent attempts by men to subdue nature is also, even
principally, a story of reading, of interpretation and of that peculiar form
of interpretation that is prophesy. "Call me Ishmael," says Melville's
witness-narrator as he opens his account of the whaling ship Pequod's
final voyage. Named after the biblical Abraham's outcast son, Ishmael
is a novice and an outsider among the Pequod's seasoned crew. A low-
ranking sailor, Ishmael is both marginal to Captain Ahab's mad design
on the white whale and also complicit in it through his necessary subordination to the captain's law. But later, as the sole survivor and chronicler
of the ship's destruction, Ishmael's interpretation of events outlives and
betrays Ahab's obsessive dedication to a singular truth. In his own endless speculation throughout the novel on the significance of natural phenomena and human actions, Ishmael the reader and interpreter of signs
is finally unable to fix meaning for himself or for us. Indeed, his survival in a chaotic world, the world created in the violent confrontation
between man and nature, depends on his clinging to a saving contra-

diction—the coffin life-buoy that rises out of the whirlpool of the shipwreck.

"Call me Ishmael, Melville told me, and I obey" (*Doscientas* 31). In *Doscientas ballenas azules* Margo Glantz assumes the place of Melville's Ishmael, becoming the tongue for adventures sought by others. A step further removed from the phenomena that she must interpret, the I-narrator of the essay reads the world not from the deck of a boat but from the shores of a book. The appeal of Ishmael to this Mexican woman reader must lie in their shared relationship of subordination and challenge to the father and the father's law, and in their common recognition of the multiplicity of meaning in human endeavor. In this text and in others, Glantz narrates the tensions created by her confrontation with irreconcilable forces: conquest and resistance in American societies since 1492, technological progress and environmental degradation worldwide, and the conflict between intellectual inquiry and the seductive power of a literature that may have been written, as Barthes puts it, "to the glory of the dreariest, of the most sinister philosophy" (39). Glantz attempts to negotiate the risky territory of hegemonic discourse by claiming the canon and its dissidents as her legitimate inheritance, and by reserving for herself the right to take pleasure—and to take issue—with the other's word.

Finally, Glantz is not only Ishmael but also Cassandra and Jonah, problematic prophets of an out-of-kilter world. Cassandra's curse was to know the future but to see her prophesy ignored by the people. The reluctant redeemer Jonah, on the contrary, won the people's renewed obedience to God, only to lament when a forgiving God undermined the truth of his prophesy of doom. By identifying herself with the prophetic tradition through Cassandra, Jonah, and Ishmael, Glantz makes a double claim for reading and writing. She promotes the role of interpretation over that of revelation in the construction of truth, and she affirms the authority of marginal, even despised, voices in mapping the course of the future. By taking many tongues into her own hands, Margo Glantz exposes exclusionary practices while at the same time reinvesting key works of our culture with new meanings that celebrate the richness of our multiple heritages. Whether dealing directly with problems of gender and subjectivity in *La lengua en la mano*, examining cultural assimilation in *Las genealogías*, or seeming to escape to an exotic world of adventure in *Doscientas ballenas azules*, Margo Glantz's writings on reading provide valuable lessons in the careful, creative interpretation of cultural signs across national, linguistic, and gender boundaries.

NOTES

1. An example of her translation is a rendering of Thomas Kyd's sixteenth-century verse drama *The Spanish Tragedy*. Margo Glantz's most widely read book in Mexico is the 1981 autobiographical novel *Las genealogías*. Like her essays, the novel also confirms the centrality of reading and writing through its constant references to literary works in the context of a personal history narrative.

2. Forthcoming books by Margo Glantz focus on the colonial period in Mexico and include studies on Hernán Cortés, Alvar Núñez Cabeza de Vaca, and Sor Juana Inés de la Cruz.

3. Margo Glantz's interest in the essay also responds to a pedagogical imperative to foster a discourse, literary criticism, that she considers to have been traditionally weak in Mexican letters. In a 1969 interview with Margarita García Flores, reprinted in *Repeticiones*, Glantz speaks at length about her efforts to improve the state of the critical essay through *Punto de Partida*, the journal that she directed at the National Autonomous University of Mexico.

4. Certain elements of Glantz's style bear the trace of her interest in surrealism, a topic for another study. True to her characteristic idiosyncrasy, she favors Bataille and Artaud, the dissidents among the surrealist group.

WORKS CITED

Barthes, Roland. *The Pleasure of the Text*. Trans. Richard Miller. New York: Hill & Wang, 1975.

García Pinto, Magdalena. *Historias íntimas: Conversaciones con diez escritoras latinoamericanas*. Hanover, N.H.: Ediciones del Norte, 1988.

Glantz, Margo. *Doscientas ballenas azules . . . y . . . cuatro caballos*. Mexico City: Universidad Nacional Autónoma de México, 1981.

——. *Las genealogías*. Mexico City: Martín Casillas, 1981.

——. *La lengua en la mano*. Mexico City: Premiá, 1983.

——. "Mi escritura tiene . . ." *Revista Iberoamericana* 51:132–133 (July–December 1985), 475–478.

——. *Repeticiones: Ensayos sobre literatura mexicana*. Xalapa, Mexico: Universidad Veracruzana, 1979.

Valenzuela, Luisa. "Mis brujas favoritas." In *Theory and Practice of Feminist Literary Criticism*, 88–95. Ed. Gabriela Mora and Karen S. VanHooft. Ypsilanti, Mich.: Bilingual Press, 1982.

Elena Gascón Vera # SITIO A EROS

THE LIBERATED EROS

OF ROSARIO FERRÉ

For Justina Ruiz de Conde

In a 1987 essay, Puerto Rican author Rosario Ferré unambiguously states the political and erotic character of her work. Citing Simone de Beauvoir as her forerunner and model, she claims that love is political action that makes the full personal liberation of women possible and brings both sexes together, provided that true social and political change brings an end to love as a passive, dependent experience for women ("On Love and Politics" 8–9).

Ferré's analysis of her own and other great women's writing in her collection of essays, *Sitio a Eros* (Eros Besieged)[1], focuses on the dialectics of the creative woman facing a patriarchal society that frustrates her need for self-realization and creation. Ferré speculates on the existential and erotic decisions of those women artists whom she loves, honors, and admires. All of them have expressed the untold; they all have expressed what remains indetermined between the written word—traditionally dominated by men—and their way of perceiving life. By doing so they have affirmed their peremptory need for love. As she explained in the 1987 article,

> *In* Sitio a Eros *and* Fábulas [de la garza desagrada, *1982*], *I tried to concentrate on this problem* [*love and politics*]. *In both, I wrote about a series of women (historical in* Sitio *and mythical in* Fábulas*) who had to face terrible consequences because they*

> *dared to experience love as an active, not passive,*
> *force.*
> (9)

She took the title of her book from Alexandra Kollontai's essay, *Sitio a Eros alado*, in which the Russian thinker expounds her thesis on a new sexual morality that, along with the great social revolution, would allow a change in the relations between man and woman.[2]

Her intention to transcend the personal in favor of the political, and to relate feminist writing with love, situates Rosario Ferré (b. 1942) within the cultural, social, anthropological, and psychoanalytical revisions of feminism and gender that have taken place during the last two decades, questioning women's lack of power and autonomy. This lack is viewed as the cause of the violence, anger, and nonconformity that produces the political and cultural awakening of woman. Literary and cultural feminist criticism revises texts and canons, attitudes and positions; above all, it legitimizes the plurality of viewpoints. This pluralistic and holistic attitude has gradually modified the perception of woman as Other, as mediator not doer, as an inferior being in a patriarchal society where man is conceived of as a superior being who controls the feminine subject by characterizing it as a sexual, subservient object.

Ferré belongs alongside Simone de Beauvoir, Kate Millet, Adrienne Rich, Robin Morgan, and Dorothy Dinnerstein—feminist writers who have revised the patriarchal theories of Freud and Marcuse and who have searched for a language that not only would represent women's viewpoint but would also be a medium through which women would entirely define themselves.[3] This language is based on two main principles: first, love as a whole dimension that integrates nurturing, caring, sensitivity, tenderness, devotion, generosity, and affective relationships; and second, the dialectics of power comprising freedom of choice, expression, creativity, transformation, and regeneration. Both principles can be understood in psychoanalytic terms as manifestations of the primordial forces that women create in the enjoyment of their own bodies: liberation and affirmation, which patriarchy, from the Fathers of the Church up to Freud, have considered as pathological forces, and which Lacan defines as principles of the indetermination of masculine and feminine beings.[4]

In her essays, Rosario Ferré expresses herself with passion and in a very personal manner. She believes, as other feminists do, in the need and obligation women have to liberate their creative and personal power in order to achieve freedom and autonomy. More specifically, Ferré sees writing as the best way to awaken women's consciousness. In writing, women will find a language and a voice of their own leading them to self-discovery without waiting for happiness to come from a paternalistic ideology that projects it only through men. Ferré believes that women's obligation is to find the source of joy in themselves. As she says in the essay "La autenticidad de la mujer en el arte" (Woman's Authenticity in Art), "The current responsibility of every woman writer is precisely to convince women readers of a fundamental notion: Prince Charming does not exist. He doesn't have any reality outside the imagination, outside our own creative capacities" (*Sitio* 38).

Women have to react against the form of power established in the world by a patriarchal society that conceives of love as a possessive, abusive force that controls women through political and personal domination, and also by controlling economic and physical forces. In this context passion is not liberating because love between man and woman becomes nothing but a dynamic of mutual dependence and exploitation. Ferré believes that passion has to be based on a deep knowledge of the feminine being, and that it is the mission of women writers to spread and to proclaim this news:

> *If they want to become good writers, today's women writers know that, above all else, they will first have to be women, because in art, authenticity is everything. They will have to learn the innermost secrets of their own body and how to talk about it without any euphemisms. They will have to learn how to examine their own eroticism and how to derive from their own sexuality a latent and rarely exploited vitality. They will have to learn to explore their anger and frustration as well as their satisfaction in being a woman. They will have to cleanse themselves and help cleanse their readers of that guilt that secretly torments them. Finally, they will have to write in order to understand themselves better and also to teach their women readers to do the same.*
> ("LA AUTENTICIDAD" *SITIO* 37)

By identifying across time and through her experience as a Western woman, Ferré unites with the women writers she has chosen as subjects for her essays. They all have written from the viewpoint of women in

their multiple roles as daughters, mothers, lovers, and ideological com-
rades of men. But by doing so, they necessarily speak of themselves as
subjects that have been ignored, misunderstood, and disdained by a
dominant male-controlled culture.

In *Sitio a Eros* Ferré talks about Mary Shelley, Anaïs Nin, George
Sand, Sylvia Plath, Julia de Burgos, Lillian Hellman, Virginia Woolf,
Jean Rhys, Flora Tristan, Alexandra Kollontai, and Tina Modotti. They
interest her because the focus of their writing and art was their desire to
emancipate themselves and obtain equality for women either through
their independent lives or by fighting to revindicate women on the basis
of their greater capacity to love. For all of them, love meant commitment
to the poor and the needy, and a continual defense of women's rights as
represented in their autonomy in love relationships. The women with
whom Ferré identifies were vituperated and finally forgotten by the antifeminine forces of their societies: the Puerto Rican bourgeois society for
Julia de Burgos, a messianic and fanatical Lenin for Kollontai, an exuberant and creative Balzac for Sand, and the French government of male culture for Tristan. The patriarchal powers attacked these women in a vile
manner by calling them "virile," "antifeminine," or "counterrevolution-
aries"; they also characterized their need for self-determination, autonomy, and independence as forms of "immorality" and "licentiousness."

In *Sitio a Eros*, Rosario Ferré proclaims the political and subversive
idea that there exists an individual feminine eros that is parallel to,
and independent from, the traditional masculine eros. This means that
women, by becoming aware of their own eros, can obtain a new view of
the world, a new consciousness that their own way of feminine love can
be a better, more vital model than those prevalent in a patriarchal society.
Ferré believes that women writers can be torchbearers in this endeavor
and that in their writing they should let their own subjectivity, their own
passion, overflow:

> *a woman should write in order to reinvent herself, to*
> *dissipate her fear of loss and death, and to confront*
> *daily the effort that living implies. . . . Just like ev-*
> *ery artist, a woman writes as best she can, not as she*
> *wants to, or as she should. Whether she has to do it*
> *in anger and in love, laughing and crying, resentfully*
> *and irrationally, on the very brink of madness and*
> *aesthetic stridence, what matters is that she do it;*
> *she must keep writing. She must devote her body*

and soul to persistence, not to objectivity, not to let-
ting herself be defeated by the enormous obstacles fac-
ing her. She must keep writing even if it only helps
open the way for those women writers who will come
later. . . .
("LA AUTENTICIDAD" *SITIO* 39)

However, Rosario Ferré does not believe that a feminine writing is
different from masculine writing. The difference lies only in the subjects
that concern women. As she says in her essay "La cocina de la escritura"
(The Writing Kitchen), "[W]e are the ones who gestate our children, we
give birth to them, we nurture them, and we concern ourselves with
their survival. This destiny of nature limits us . . . but it also puts us in
contact with the mysterious generative forces of life" (*Sitio* 32). In this
respect, she thinks like feminist theorists such as Adrienne Rich, Mary
Daly, and Robin Morgan. For them, the feminine eros is expressed as a
vital force based on the primordial feelings of motherhood and commitment, analysis and passion. It is an experience that integrates the sensuous and the rational, the spiritual and the political. Like these feminists,
Ferré thinks women affirm synthesis and integration, whereas the values
of patriarchal societies affirm polarization and separation. These women
demand that connections, ambivalence, complexity, and material as well
as philosophical dialectics be valued. They disrupt dualisms such as nature and culture, I and Other, and accept ontological contradictions as
the only real and genuine form of being and becoming.

Ferré finds in the typical female diary the expression of an eroticism
that transcends the physical to encompass a larger totality. As she says in
"El diario como forma femenina" (The Diary as Feminine Form),

The diarist is obsessed with capturing the moment
that passes like a flash before her eyes. Her love of
reality is always pressing, distressingly close. It de-
mands the warmth of the body, the contact with hair,
the rustle of leaves in the wind, the absolute omni-
presence of consciousness. . . . Why have women for
almost two hundred years so assiduously cultivated
this form? Women's diaries abound in every language
but only a tiny percentage of them has been
published. . . . The reason for their abundance might
be due to the very form of the diary, for it accommo-

> *dates itself comfortably to a woman's life. Like her,*
> *it's a restrained form of writing, constantly inter-*
> *rupted, that deals with both the most petty and the*
> *most fundamental details. For lack of time and tran-*
> *quility, its form, like the form of women's lives at*
> *home, never manages to be completed in recognizable*
> *order. Its form is formlessness, the back side of a tap-*
> *estry, the counterface of literature.*
> (*SITIO* 41 – 42)

For Ferré, as for Jill Johnston, Jane Flax, and Rachel Blau du Plessis, women's eros must be centered on typically feminine characteristics, and these are, naturally, the sexual ones. Among them, motherhood is one of the few essentially feminine experiences that men do not have. Rosario Ferré views the value of motherhood as a creative literary force. In an essay on Mary Shelley, "Frankenstein: A Political Version of the Myth of Motherhood," Ferré analyzes the maternal process as a key to the state of bondage and oppression of women. In this respect, Ferré is still close to the first stage of feminism as developed by Nancy Chodorow. In her 1978 book, Chodorow explored the limitations associated with birth and the raising of children for the majority of women. As opposed to a new and more radical feminism, she neither privileges nor exalts the infinite possibilities for happiness, satisfaction, force, and power that come with the creation of another being. Speaking of Victor Frankenstein's mono-logue just before creating a monster, Ferré says,

> *In this monologue Mary succeeds in taking up two of*
> *the most profound themes of feminism: first, she*
> *thinks that man, as far as he tries to usurp the power*
> *to give birth, will hopelessly fail. For that reason*
> *Victor forgets that motherhood is a mysterious process*
> *that both demands humility on the part of the creator*
> *and implies bondage toward the one created. Second,*
> *she deals with that initial rejection implicit in all*
> *motherhood, a theme that makes of Mary a precursor*
> *in the study of feminine psychology. It has only been*
> *recently that, given the consequences for women of*
> *having children, those feelings of rejection are consid-*
> *ered something normal and understandable. If feelings*
> *of guilt and rejection coexist in normal motherhood*

> *with feelings of happiness and satisfaction, nonethe-*
> *less we have to be reminded that Mary's pregnancies*
> *were far from normal. In a symbolic manner, Victor*
> *being chased by Frankenstein on the polar plains ex-*
> *presses Mary's rebellion in the face of the bondage of*
> *motherhood.*
> *(SITIO 56).*

In this respect, Ferré thinks like Chodorow, and she differs in part with other recent feminist theories holding that full acceptance of motherhood will liberate a woman's creative capacity in which are blended the needs for commitment and for autonomy, as well as for interdependence and community. The relation between body and mind is very important for these feminists because its study has led them to understand that the analysis of our deepest instincts does not mean controlling or canceling them;[5] this analysis has also meant a refined understanding of the physical and instinctual grounds of love. Nevertheless, in "La autenticidad de la mujer en el arte," Ferré agrees with them in saying that the liberation of feminine instincts must be carried out by writing. Writing will express the deepest and most intimate zones of the feminine being:

> *In the case of passion, anger, laughter, and arbitrary*
> *subjectivity, I differ radically from Virginia Woolf's*
> *opinion. . . . Just like Anaïs Nin, I think that pas-*
> *sion has great power to transform and transfigure the*
> *human being from a limited, small, frightened crea-*
> *ture into a magnificent figure sometimes capable of*
> *reaching the heights of myth.*
> *(SITIO 39)*

This perspective leads Ferré and the new feminists to exalt the total and holistic integration of everyday life and spiritual life into the ongoing expression of passion. That is to say, women must live within the boundaries of their constant personal and artistic creation. Rosario Ferré is right when she sees the women with whom she deals in her book as vital models entirely devoted to creativity and passion, despite their suffering and their being set apart by their societies, and despite the fact that many of them, like Jean Rhys, destroyed themselves in order to maintain their independence. In her essay "Un cuarteto y su desenlace" (A Quartet and Its Outcome) about the novels of the British Caribbean author, Ferré writes,

> *For Jean Rhys, the reason the world is divided be-*
> *tween two types of women—those who survive and*
> *those who just live; those who see the relation with*
> *men as an economic one and those who see it as an*
> *ideal affinity, both morally and emotionally—lies in*
> *the unequal division of power that characterizes con-*
> *temporary society. The women who throw in the*
> *towel even before starting to fight and who think it is*
> *useless to oppose the other sex become men's allies,*
> *they survive like wives, sisters, and daughters who do*
> *their duty. Those who defy the status quo, those who*
> *demand their independence and the right to live their*
> *own lives, end up alone and forsaken. Of course, the*
> *fight between both types of women is a fight to the*
> *death.*
> (SITIO 89 – 90)

This text agrees with the revisions Nancy Chodorow made to her 1978 book, eleven years later. Says Chodorow, "Now, however, when I speak of feminist theory, I mean something more holistic and pluralistic—encompassing a number of organizational axes—and at the same time not absolute. In my current view, feminist understanding requires a multiplex account . . . of the dynamics of gender, sexuality, sexual inequality, and domination" (*Feminism and Psychoanalytic Theory* 5).

Sitio a Eros participates in the most recent feminist ideas, and Ferré becomes their spokesperson. She also has a didactic interest in wanting to reach out to the cultural grounding of her Hispanic sisters. She wants them to accept their Latina tradition yet also persuade them that their first duty as women is to reach a consciousness of their own power, a power that primarily lies in the force of their maternal and erotic bodies. In other words, she motivates them to use their love and passion.

If contemporary women continuously exercise that power, they will not remain in an eros besieged by the dominant paternalistic society but will reach the eros of women, that is, an eros liberated by their infinite capacity to love and create.

NOTES

This is a slightly revised version of a study published originally in Spanish in Elena Gascón Vera's book, *Un mito nuevo: La mujer como sujeto/objeto literario* (Madrid: Editorial Pliegos, 1992). It has been translated by Joy Renjilian Burgy.

1. First published in 1980, this collection was revised and augmented for a second edition published in 1986. This paper quotes from the second edition.

2. See Clements for information on Kollontai.

3. See Marcuse, *Eros and Civilization*, and Lacan's seminars for the latter's concept of feminine enjoyment. For the feminist theories, see Beauvoir (75), Millet, Rich, Morgan (161), and Dinnerstein (148).

4. For revisions of the Freudian concept of Eros, see Mitchell (*Psychoanalysis and Feminism*), Trask, and Mackinnon. For the Lacanian eros as revised by feminists, see Jardine, Mitchell and Rose, Mitchell (*Women: The Longest Revolution*), and Chodorow.

5. See Ehrenreich, Echols, Rubin, and Lourde.

WORKS CITED

Beauvoir, Simone de. *The Second Sex*. New York: Knopf, 1953.

Chodorow, Nancy. *Feminism and Psychoanalytic Theory*. New Haven: Yale University Press, 1989.

——. *Reproduction of Mothering: Psychoanalysis and the Sociology of Gender*. Berkeley: University of California Press, 1978.

Clements, Barbara Evans. *Bolshevik Feminists. The Life of Alexandra Kollontai*. Bloomington: Indiana University Press, 1978.

Daly, Mary. *Gyn/Ecology: The Metaethics of Radical Feminism*. Boston: Beacon, 1978.

du Plessis, Rachel Blau. "Washing Blood: Introduction." *Feminist Studies* 4 (June 1978), 1–12.

Dinnerstein, Dorothy. *The Mermaid and the Minotaur*. New York: Harper & Row, 1976.

Echols, Alice. "The Taming of the Id: Feminist Sexual Politics, 1968–83." In *Pleasure and Danger: Exploring Female Sexuality*. Ed. Carole Vance. Boston: Routledge & Kegan Paul, 1984.

Ehrenreich, Barbara. *Re-making Love: The Feminization of Sex*. Garden City: Anchor, 1986.

Ferré, Rosario. "On Love and Politics." *Review* 37 (January–June 1987), 8–9. Center for Latin American Relations.

——. *Sitio a Eros*. 2d ed. Mexico City: Joaquín Mortiz, 1986.

Flax, Jane. "The Conflict between Nurturance and Autonomy in the Mother-

Daughter Relationship and within Feminism." *Feminist Studies* 4 (June 1978), 171–189.

Jardine, Alice. *Gynesis: Configurations of Women and Modernity.* Ithaca: Cornell University Press, 1985.

———. "Text, Context: Gynesis." *Diacritics* 12 (Summer 1982), 54–65.

Johnston, Jill. *Lesbian Nation: The Feminist Solution.* New York: Simon & Schuster, 1973.

Lourde, Audre. "Uses of the Erotic: The Erotics as Power." In *Sister Outsider.* New York: Crossling, 1984.

MacKinnon, Catharine A. "Feminism, Marxism, Method, and the State: Agenda for Theory." In *Feminist Theory: A Critique of Ideology,* 1–30. Ed. Nannerl Kehoane, Michelle Rosaldo, and Barbara Gelpi. Chicago: University of Chicago Press, 1982.

Marcuse, Herbert. *Eros and Civilization: A Philosophical Inquiry into Freud.* Boston: Beacon, 1977.

Millet, Kate. *Sexual Politics.* New York: Avon, 1971.

Mitchell, Juliet. *Psychoanalysis and Feminism.* New York: Vintage Books, 1974.

——— *Women: The Longest Revolution. Essays in Feminism, Literature and Psychoanalysis.* London: Virago, 1984.

Mitchell, Juliet, and Jacqueline Rose. *Feminine Sexuality: Jacques Lacan and the Ecole Freudienne.* London: Macmillan, 1982.

Morgan, Robin. *Going Too Far: The Personal Chronicle of a Feminist.* New York: Random House, 1977.

———. *Lady of the Beasts.* New York: Random House, 1976.

Rich, Adrienne. *The Dream of a Common Language: Poems 1974–1977.* New York: Norton, 1978.

———. *Of Woman Born.* New York: Norton, 1976.

Rubin, Gayle. "Thinking Sex: Note for a Radical Theory of the Politics of Sexuality." In *Pleasure and Danger: Exploring Female Sexuality.* Ed. Carole Vance. Boston: Routledge & Kegan Paul, 1984.

Trask, Haunani-Kay. *Eros and Power: The Promise of Feminist Theory.* Philadelphia: University of Philadelphia Press, 1986.

Marjorie Agosín

VISION AND TRANSGRESSION

SOME NOTES ON
THE WRITING OF
JULIETA KIRKWOOD

During the decade of the 1970s under the Latin American authoritarian governments, the women of various economic and social strata acquired a very particular consciousness of their identity as women, citizens, and political beings. Oddly enough, it was at a time when all official communication channels were closed that women, accustomed to private, invisible tasks, found a new way of "making politics," of bringing their presence to bear in public life, in the space of the streets and unofficial, alternative spheres engendered by dictatorial regimes.

Julieta Kirkwood, sociologist, political activist, and faithful defender of human rights, began her essay career during the military dictatorship in Chile when she was a cultural organizer in women's groups formed to foster unity in the face of a dictatorship that, little by little, immobilized the role of intellectual women. She became a visible figure in the 1970s during demonstrations against the Pinochet regime. Her activism centered around a concrete praxis: that of the political life on the streets, the popular protests against a culture of death propagated by the dictatorship. Thus, from a direct, testimonial perspective, Julieta Kirkwood began to formulate her theory of the Chilean woman's way of making politics and history. Over more than a decade of intellectual engagement, she developed what was to become one of the most important studies dedicated to women and politics in Chile.

Ser política en Chile (To Be a Political Woman in Chile) constitutes an interesting and alternative text for many reasons.[1] First of all, this work differs significantly from other historical treaties about women and politics in Chile in that Kirkwood gathers a group of writings prepared primarily for FLACSO (Latin American School of Social Sciences) and written from a radical perspective in which she analyzes the contradictions of women's roles in Chilean political history.[2] She begins with a personal prologue recounting her feminist activism and the vision behind the book:

> *We reconstructed the story of what had been invisible and we proposed to break with the private; we were very brave: heretics by dint of shamelessly, openly turning everything around; . . . we discovered, discovered with passion, laughter, tough fights, difficult reflections, we kept going, we opened the Circle [of Women's Studies], the House [of the Woman, called "La Morada," the Dwelling], we opened books, even the Lila Woman's Bookstore; we were crazily daring, I can see it now.*
> (10 – 11)

Writing sometimes in a very idiosyncratic, lyrical style that captures the exhilarating transgressive mood of the mid-1980s, Kirkwood also makes clear what she hopes her writing will lead to:

> *With my daring I want to encourage the publication of the hundreds of studies, essays, stories, poems that so many of us women for so long have hidden under our beds or in dark bureaus. We need confrontation and the interplay of ideas wide open to millions of bright thoughts and small ideas.*
> (18)

In the six chapter-essays that follow Kirkwood offers a feminist perspective of Chilean political history. Not only is her book an informative overview of women's involvement in Chilean politics from the early 1900s to the 1980s, it is a philosophical inquiry on the relationship between political women and authoritarian governments. Kirkwood reconceptualizes the role of the Chilean woman in her battle for suffrage, develops new theories concerning women's participation in institutionalized politics, and examines the relationship between feminist politics and the dictatorship.

Although the fight for women's right to vote began in Chile in the 1920s with success finally achieved in 1949, women remained unable to secure positions in established political parties. Kirkwood describes the heightening consciousness of Chilean women through the years and their more recent efforts to understand their position in a male-dominated society.[3] In particular, she discusses alternative modes for creating, expressing, and considering the history of Chilean women and their political participation during times of severe political repression when the possibility of political activity was forbidden.

Kirkwood uses a direct and personal language in her book that engages the reader and allows her to experience history first-hand. From the very beginning, Kirkwood establishes a complicity between herself and her reader; history becomes objective and subjective at the same time, allowing for ambiguity in knowledge. In her research on the history of women, Kirkwood reveals that she first investigated official historical records only to discover that the history of Chilean women was far from that expressed by the official story. As she remarks, "As a woman I'm no stranger to history. I'm not just surfacing now; I've always been there, but in a condition of cold history that appears not to move, not to flow, that has always been—necessary—and will always be—routine—to the point that we forget about it until we need it" (14). This quote allows us to understand Kirkwood's unique perspective, which is to write history not simply by annotating the past but by challenging the present as well.

Kirkwood's book clearly reflects her belief that women should convert history into their own story and use it as a tool for political activism. Writing about history, for her, is not a passive task but the creation of another way of being, a new set of rules. In Foucauldian terms, it involves recognizing that every power has a counter-power or, in this case,

> *women's own attempt to achieve their own liberation.*
> *[To write history] . . . is to show their presence,*
> *their visibility. And it is also to point out the* trans-
> formation into subject *of a specific social group*
> *that has not been completely recognized as such by*
> *themselves or by others, and up to now has only been*
> *a passive receptor of well- or poorly formed policies*
> *for its attributed human condition.*
> (66 – 67)

This is the fundamental legacy of Kirkwood's historical studies: her belief that an understanding of the past can be transformed into a strong present-day political activism to change the future. For Kirkwood, women's history provides an arena where the personal and the political come together. She expresses how women move in history, how they create it and how they can reconstruct it. Throughout her book, Kirkwood ponders the relationship of women with their society and its politics. She does not simply write about the established powers, she also creates a dialogue with them. In these conversational, often defiant dialogues, Kirkwood not only discusses history but creates it by her own transgression as one traditionally silenced or marginalized.

For Kirkwood, women's participation or nonparticipation in the official political parties is a very inaccurate measure of their actual political participation. Consequently she studies women's political activity through the organizations they form independently: for example, the short-lived PFCH (Chilean Feminine Party), which came into being shortly before women's suffrage was achieved and died with a political scandal that would probably have only wounded it had its members had more experience in politics. What is most noteworthy from Kirkwood's viewpoint is the fact that this incident in women's history has been treated as a kind of "family secret," giving the impression that women themselves "tried not only to erase the failure and pain of their defeat, . . . but also . . . to deny that it ever occurred" (172). The fact is, women's autonomous political participation as feminists was stifled for decades thereafter and for a variety of reasons.

Even the "global liberation" era of the '60s and '70s did not bring about a reassessment of women's roles in Chilean political history. Kirkwood advances several hypotheses to explain this, but basically the female question was ignored by Chilean women themselves who, if they were involved in the social liberation movement, did not identify women's liberation as a primordial issue (185–186). Their concerns remained subordinated to others because, claims Kirkwood, they lacked the perspective to recognize (reconocer), analyze (conocer), and change (hacer) their circumstances (187).

Kirkwood points out that, from the very beginning, women's history has been limited to the way men see it. It is time for a new theoretical foundation for Chilean history, she says; it must take into account the "unknown and unrecognized history of women in Chile," not the history of extraordinary women but the record of an ongoing, conscious

"feminine demand for the construction of a nonoppressive, nondiscrimi-
natory society" (33).

One of the legacies postulated in Kirkwood's philosophy is the importance of everyday life in politics. By everyday life we refer to the incor-
poration of women's civic participation as an inseparable expression of
their identity. This would apply to different classes of women in society
who all experience the effects of being marginalized from the centers of
power. It is Kirkwood's experience as a political activist, marching down
the streets of Santiago, as well as her link to the rural women's groups,
that solidifies her theoretical basis for associating the authoritarianism of
the Pinochet government with the recent rise of feminism in Chile and a
recognition of the connection between political and domestic authoritarianism. To Kirkwood, the domestic abuse of women is a reflection of
the abuses of power being committed under the violent patriarchal seal.
Those who would seek to reinstitute democracy without reexamining
the whole structure of patriarchal society are separating the public and
the private spheres and thereby prolonging the subordination of women.
During the military dictatorship, and especially during the 1980s, domestic violence in Chile became rampant, even though this did not appear in official records or newspapers. To Kirkwood, the culture of the
dictatorship produced a deep schism and trauma in daily life that mag-
nified the reality of women's existence:

> *we women recognize and observe that our day-to-
> day experience is* authoritarianism. *That women
> live—and have always lived—under authoritarian-
> ism within the family, which is their recognized place
> of work and experience. That there, what is struc-
> tured and institutionalized is precisely the undisputed
> Authority of the head of the family, the father, based
> on discrimination and subordination by gender. . . .*
> (223)

Kirkwood's theories on the relationship between governmental authoritarianism in society at large and patriarchal authoritarianism in the
home as it affects women are especially relevant now, as society is going
through changes, questioning its values and gaining a new consciousness. For the first time in history, Chilean feminism as a movement has

achieved changes for women and a repossession of women's history by women themselves. Kirkwood explains it thus:

> *In developing these ideas, we feminists have found that traditional political practice, however women are involved, is segregationist and subordinating in all sociopolitical sectors, whether the women political actors are shantytown dwellers, peasants, employees, or professionals.*
>
> (43)

This concept is very important for Julieta Kirkwood because it provides a new explanation for the relationship between women and political parties, demystifying the much-believed theory that defined women according to their social class and concluded that their class alone dictated their political participation. Kirkwood feels that the years of the military dictatorship were a time when Chilean women, seeking justice and peace and a right to political expression, forged for themselves a new identity with a new awareness of their reality in both the political and private spheres.

Before Kirkwood's book was published, the history of women's political participation in Chile was meager, and the few treatises, such as Felicitas Klimpel's text, focused on the traditional reading of history from and about the patriarchal model. By 1992, *Ser política en Chile* had gone into its third edition, and it has become an indispensable literary work for all feminist discussions in Chile and other parts of Latin America. There are not many reviews of this book; the recognition it has achieved has been mainly by word of mouth, through encounters between women who recommended its reading. The text is brief and does not present the history of women's participation in Chilean politics in a traditional linear fashion, nor does it exhaust the topic, since many aspects of women's history are not covered. We would define this essay with Kirkwood's words from the book's cover, as "a feminist reading of our history. . . . It is a history to be discussed, to be doubted, to be reflected upon, to give us back our lives . . . which traditionally have been cut out."

We could establish an interesting parallel with what Kirkwood says about the image of lives being "cut out." The military dictatorship annihilated the socialization and the identity of women that had begun with the socialist reforms of Salvador Allende. It is during times of crisis and deep dilemmas that visionary leaders among women take the stage. Among them can be counted Julieta Kirkwood, who understood the possibility of women's existence through alternate means, through informal gatherings around potluck dinners and other seemingly nonsubversive events, where the common bonds shared under the oppressive dictatorship were nurtured and where Kirkwood began to reflect about women's political role in Chile.

One document she consulted on women's suffrage was the 1952 text by Elena Caffarena entitled *Un capítulo en la historia del feminismo* (A Chapter in the History of Feminism). Kirkwood repossessed the voice of women such as Caffarena and then investigated magazines of the period in order to sketch the invisible and alternate history of Chilean women. Interestingly, most footnotes and quotes in Kirkwood's book originate in unpublished documents, flyers, speeches found in libraries. This technique makes her work a research that rescues but also one that values thoughts that had not been valued or fully formed. This is why Kirkwood's thoughts occasionally seem fragmented.

Julieta Kirkwood's book reached the public at a crucial time in Chile's history, when Chilean women began to question the relationship between their identity and their gender. *Ser política en Chile* was published posthumously, and Kirkwood never knew the wide resonance it would have. Her presence and vitality deeply touched those who knew her in her lifetime, and this book was without any doubt her most enduring contribution.

NOTES

1. The work was published originally under this title in 1986 with the subtitle *Las feministas y los partidos* (Feminists and Political Parties). A second edition, published in 1990, carries the subtitle suggested by Kirkwood before her death, *Los nudos de la sabiduría feminista* (The Bonds of Feminist Wisdom). Quotes in this paper are from the second edition.

2. Each chapter in the book was originally a working paper for FLACSO discussion prepared between 1980 and 1983; chapters 3 and 4 were taken from one paper with the same title as the first edition of Kirkwood's book.

3. Further readings regarding the historical development of women's political participation in Chile are included at the end of this paper.

WORKS CITED

Caffarena, Elena. *Un capítulo en la historia del feminismo*. Santiago: Ediciones MEMCH, 1952.

Covarrubias, Paz. *El movimiento feminista chileno en Chile: Mujer y sociedad*. Comp. Paz Covarrubias and R. Frano. Santiago: UNICEF, 1978.

Kirkwood, Julieta. *Ser política en Chile: Las feministas y los partidos*. Santiago, Chile: FLACSO, 1986; 2d ed., *Ser política en Chile: Los nudos de la sabiduría feminista*. Santiago: Cuarto Propio, 1990.

Klimpel, Felicitas. *La mujer chilena: El aporte femenino al progreso de Chile, 1910–1960*. Santiago: Andrés Bello, 1962.

Labarca Hubertson, Amanda. *Feminismo contemporáneo*. Santiago: Zigzag, 1947.

Santa Cruz, Adriana, ed. *Tres ensayos sobre la mujer chilena*. Santiago: Editorial Universitaria, 1978.

Vergara, Marta. *Memorial de una mujer irreverente*. Santiago: Zigzag, 1967.

Rosemary	CRISTINA PERI
Geisdorfer	ROSSI AND
Feal	THE EROTIC
	IMAGINATION

Rosemary

Geisdorfer

Feal

CRISTINA PERI ROSSI AND THE EROTIC IMAGINATION

N ew Year's Eve, 1989. She walks through the door at Daniel's, the small, intimate lesbian bar in Barcelona, after being recognized by the scrutinizing eye of the owner, who guards over her business as if it were "a protective womb that frees [the patrons] from outside hostility" (13). So begins the Preamble to Cristina Peri Rossi's volume of essays entitled *Fantasías eróticas* (Erotic Fantasies, 1991), in which she cultivates the confessional mode, film criticism, commentary on popular culture, literary criticism, and erotic fictions of her own. The "I" of the Preamble, whom we may assign to Peri Rossi in her function as implied author, narrator, and protagonist of the vignette, enters into the sheltered world of a women-only club at the same time that the "I" comes out of metaphoric closets and textual cloaks to proclaim a lesbian identity and subjectivity through the telling of the New Year's Eve adventure.[1] The Preamble initiates a collection of essays that breaks with traditional notions of that genre as one dominated by objectivity, rationality, and suppression of creative writing and of the fictional imagination. To write of erotica under the erasure of the erotic imagination is exactly what Peri Rossi has refused to do. But the "I" of the Preamble does not sustain itself in that dramatized form throughout the essays proper, a shift that in turn brings up questions concerning identities and positionings.

Back to Daniel's, the lesbian bar as "theoretical joint," to borrow from Teresa de Lauretis (iv), where the solitary narrator retreats to a corner, outwardly recognized by none of the women there, knowing no one— "I like to observe without being observed" (13). From this position of voyeur, the narrator takes in the stunning spectacle of a couple—one woman cross-dresses as a man, while the other engages in an exquisite display of homeovestism, their appearances and movements exuding the signs of a calculated simulacrum, a fiction, all "*arte y artificio*" (17).[2] Representation for Peri Rossi is linked to seduction and the erotic imagination: the false man in the couple, in her absolute beauty and perfection, can offer the marvels of "her not-being, her not-having" (18). For Jacques Lacan the *manque-à-être* and the *manque-à-avoir* center on the status of the phallus and thus implicate the psychic signification of the other's desire and of one's own lack, but for the Uruguayan author, this not-being and not-having also invoke an always mobile or fictional sexual identification that produces its corresponding erotic displays. Stuck in the imaginary, cries Lacan; the route to psychosis, shouts Kristeva: but no, we might answer back for Peri Rossi through Judith Butler, out onto the stage of performative gender acts, where sexual identification, a fantasy of a fantasy, is symptomatically encoded through imposture and parody.[3] Lesbian sexual discourse, for Butler, constitutes a privileged site for contesting the Lacanian notion of the phallus, since the "status of 'having' is redelineated, rendered transferable, substitutable, plastic; and the eroticism produced within such an exchange depends on the displacement from traditional masculinist contexts as well as the critical redeployment of its central figures of power" ("Lesbian Phallus" 162).

This dynamic seems to describe Peri Rossi's performance in *Fantasías eróticas*, in that she both displaces eroticism from the stranglehold of masculinity (Freud: there is only one libido, and it is masculine) and recirculates it through the principal signs of power. It has been over twenty-five years since Susan Sontag wrote her pioneering essay, "The Pornographic Imagination," in which she discusses a masculine mode of pornographic production that aims to drive a wedge between "one's existence as a full human being and one's existence as a sexual being" (58) within the context of modern capitalist society. In recent years, we have witnessed a lively interest on the part of women writers and feminist critics in matters erotic: women have produced new modes of "sexual fiction" and have provided serious intellectual commentary on how these texts depart from masculinist origins. This compendium of Peri Rossi's thoughts and imaginings on eroticism signals a key contribution to the growing corpus of female erotica, which has reached a peak in Spain in the series called *La sonrisa vertical* (The Vertical Smile) edited by Spanish film director Luis García Berlanga.[4] From the "pornographic imagination" of Sontag we have arrived at the contemporary "erotic imagination," as Robert Stoller calls it in his analysis of sexuality in the "theatre of risk" (9), which reads much like Peri Rossi's descriptions of the sexual underground and its blatant surfacings in urban culture. Stoller affirms that "the construction of erotic excitement is every bit as subtle, complex, inspired, profound, tidal, fascinating, awesome, problematic, unconscious-soaked, and genius-haunted as the creation of dreams or art" (47). Peri Rossi agrees from the corner at Daniel's as she admires the artful arousal of the erotic imagination staged by a lesbian couple in an act of aesthetics and transgression. And she and Stoller coincide both in their appreciation of aesthetics and in their distinguishing it from the dehumanization and flight from intimacy that take place when the erotic imagination conjures up performed acts of cruelty, humiliation, and degradation. Perhaps Peri Rossi's essays have not departed as much from Sontag's critique of pornography as we might presuppose.

Peri Rossi, the writer, the aesthetician, admits, "I love beauty above all else and I know that it is hardly ever spontaneous, that one must win it and merit it" (16). Thus, it is not surprising that she makes the following analogies: "eroticism is to sexuality what the sentence is to a shout, what theatre is to a gesture, and what fashion is to a loincloth: a cultural activity, the elaborated satisfaction of an instinctual necessity" (41). Note, however, that Peri Rossi makes no suppositions about the essence of that instinct, choosing instead to examine the wide range of erotic variations through literature, art, and classic Hollywood cinema for the first half of her book, following which she plunges (or ascends, as one prefers) into the world of inflatable dolls, prostitution, rape fantasies, fetishism, and sadomasochistic practices. Who are the holders of power selected by Peri Rossi to serve as guides through the high cultural territory of Plato, Ovid, Beethoven, Wagner? Freud and Bataille, for beginners. She takes a fairly classic view of sublimation and fantasy as the necessary responses to impossible desire: where myth goes, there once was id. Curiously, Peri Rossi accomplishes the opposite of her stated objectives in celebrating the erotic imagination, for she insistently reminds the reader that human capacity for pleasure is limited, and any attempt to surpass those limits is a narcissistic defiance that leads to a place beyond pleasure where there is pain and psychosis (77). Of what use is the erotic imagination if we monitor its productions when they threaten to surpass accepted behavioral limits? Is not fantasy and representation precisely the site where the weight of desire may be fully measured, where it may be distinguished from human acts, and where women's subjectivity, pleasure, and power may be exposed and claimed? Perhaps Peri Rossi struggles with this notion of claiming, particularly

since she has shown reluctance to embody lesbian desire in female characters in her fiction; this may indicate an admirable degree of mobility in
terms of identification with the desiring subject and desired object, but it
may also be symptomatic of the wish *not* to push the erotic imagination
into corners. Corners, such as the one in Daniel's, force identifications
and positions, which Peri Rossi boldly confronts in her Preamble to these
essays in a way that she declines to do in her fictional texts. (That the
Preamble may be read as a short story should give us cause to reexamine
the author's identificatory poses.)

It is my view that *Fantasías eróticas* offers more originality and promise
when Peri Rossi leaves behind the icons of high cultural discourse, along
with their explicators, and turns toward specific erotic practices with
their corresponding fantasies and significations. In chapter 5, "The Fantasy of the Passive Object: Inflatable Dolls," the author formulates a logical question: Why would men choose to perform sexually on an inani-
mate object when interpersonal relationships are freer, when women
today are willing to explore their sexuality (or even assert their desires)?
(92). No, it is not a shortage of women that leads contemporary men to
purchase these life-size plastic humanoids: quite the opposite, according
to Peri Rossi, who claims that masculine anxiety stirred up by the unthinkable spectacle of feminine sexual agency and autonomy sends them
member-first into an objectified latex lady: "a completely passive
woman-container, the recipient of fantasies that will never exhibit dis-
appointment, nor dissatisfaction, nor rebellion" (93). One could elect to
analyze this fantasy-made-rubber-flesh as a sex toy comparable to, say, a
vibrator (though a bit less discreet) if one viewed auto-erotic practices as
fundamentally distinct from relations with another human. But if we
accept Stoller's definition of "perversion" as the desire to sin by harming
one's erotic object, or Louise Kaplan's notion that "male perversions
manifest as forbidden sexual acts that impersonate and caricature adult
genital performance" (16), or Otto Kernberg's formulation that "perversions should be defined more narrowly as the obligatory, habitual
restriction of sexual fantasies and activities to one particular sexual component" (65), then Peri Rossi's conclusion on this subject would make
moral and psychological sense: "coitus as power, as domination, as humiliation," that is, a variant of the sadomasochistic sexual relations characteristic of patriarchal societies (94). Contrast this to feminine eroticism,
which Peri Rossi claims is always humanized, because it does not separate
sexuality from the rest of the person nor does it seek to possess; further,
she believes that women would resist the commercialization of standard

mass-marketed erotic fantasies, and would get a good laugh at an inflatable boy doll with a synthetic penis (94–98). Tell this to the founders
of Good Vibrations and to the suppliers of mass-produced fantasies for
women like the Harlequin romances that encourage the female reader to
participate in sexual self-betrayal, according to Tania Modleski (37).

There is, however, much ground on which to agree with Peri Rossi.
Certainly such writers as Andrea Dworkin and Robin Morgan have presented extensive arguments to corroborate this take on masculine sexuality, finding, along with the Uruguayan author, that feminine sexuality,
in particular that of lesbians, in its natural essence embraces a gentler,
more fluid relatedness that rejects objectification and eroticism disen-
gaged from whole selves. In fact, mutuality and relatedness are often
cited as mature psychosexual ideals for men and women, where exclusive
pairings serve as viable and sustainable cover for the wilder polymorphously perverse scenarios that must become integrated into the sex life
of the monogamous heterosexual couple.[5] Recent theories of lesbian sexuality instead posit a strategic rebellion against the shackles of eroticism
devoid of fantasy, including fantasies of dominance, objectification, and
humiliation.[6] As Julia Creet puts it, "the most striking feature of lesbian
s/m writing, and of writing on lesbian s/m, is that it is less a conscious
transgression of the law of the Father ('woman' as lack), than a transgression against the feminist Mother ('woman' as morally superior)" (145).
The lesbian position such as the one Peri Rossi takes up in chapter 5 runs
the risk of reifying an equally oppressive regime of the "Law of the
Mother" that says no-no to forms of sexuality that do not speak in love's
name. (That human sexual malaise is not necessarily eradicated when
eroticism is unchained from the bonds of love is another matter entirely.)
Theorists of lesbian sexuality have been cautious not to conflate rebellion
against the "Law of the Mother" with complicity toward the violence
committed against women in patriarchal societies, but in advocating a
complex accounting of the manifestations of eroticism, fantasy, and desire, they clearly seek a more comprehensive stage for gender performa-
tives of all types. The use of inflatable dolls reveals a rather literal-minded
erotic economy—the ultimate objectification fantasy turned into a real
object—and so perhaps this imaginative paucity is the highest masculine
offense of all when it comes to blow-up Barbies. But when we endeavor
to strip sexuality of its obscure desires, including what Peri Rossi calls
"its obscure desire to possess and humiliate" (98), we may have invented
the most psychologically untrue strip-show of all.

In chapter 7, on "Eros in the Temple," Peri Rossi returns to notions

of "instinct" and "civilization" to arrive at the following: "If eroticism
has any future it is precisely that site of fracture, of recuperation of the
most primitive impulses, now under industrial transformation" (125).
Industrial-age eroticism takes "frank and violent body odors" and recirculates them as Eau de Sauvage, or it picks up cherished articles of cloth-
ing, former relics of ancient cults, and fashions them into peekaboo pant-
ies by Frederick's of Hollywood. It is reassuring to know that Peri Rossi
sees some future for fetish, some role for lights, music, and props, some
place for the postcoital cigarette, but these are about ritual transformation of base instinctual activity into the aesthetics of eroticism, where the
participants are high priests and priestesses whose artful artifice wins admirers and imitators. What we may critique in Peri Rossi's exposition of
this material is the implicit assumption that these scenes of desire represent a higher order of sexual fantasy, a richness of erotic imagination,
when in fact the psychological content of these displays remains quite
veiled to the observer. If Stoller and Kaplan delve into the mental lives
of the practitioners of the perversions that they name and study, it is
through an analysis—a psychoanalysis, to be precise—of that sign system as interpreted through an individual (or a group of individuals, producing a psychosocial analysis). Although this work is not the goal of
Peri Rossi's essays, she nevertheless notes that the imagination as creator
of fantasy must be given priority over the surface manifestations of eroticism, which, after all, may be either a repetitive and compulsive form of
enslavement and dehumanization or an infinitely variable production of
one's most profound humanity.

Now, in the age of late capitalism, Peri Rossi sees erotic imagination
and fantasy as having been insidiously excluded from matrimonial life,
which she calls "the institutional framework of postindustrial societies"
(146–148). Caught in their struggle for higher positions and their search
for love that sticks around, these modern married folks move in a reduced space and in regularized time to the beat of a ringing telephone
and the hum of a television set. The erotic imagination has taken refuge
in two sites, according to the Uruguayan writer: prostitution and alternative sexualities, fundamentally that of gays and lesbians (148). This
notion—that institutionalized heterosexuality seeks to sustain itself by
means of the very forms of sexual abjection that this hegemonic order
has itself defined—coincides with Judith Butler's views on the social construction of identifications through what she terms "gender performativ-
ity." That which is taboo becomes eroticized: the homosexual abjection
(what Butler has called the terror of occupying the position of the femi-

nized fag or the phallicized dyke) is necessary for the production of heterosexuality, and identity operates through a mechanism of disavowal
and repudiation ("Phantasmatic Identification").

Curiously, however, when Peri Rossi points to prostitution as the
playground for cast-out fantasy, she names a site that has been a men-
only pleasure club, unless she believes that female sex workers successfully assert their erotic imaginations through their labors. Culling evidence from Lizzie Borden's film *Working Girls*, Peri Rossi claims that
clients purchase their impossible dreams and their illusions from prostitutes at a more modest economic and psychological cost than investing
in a mutual relationship: "it does less harm and it maintains a strict separation between sexual fantasy and reality" (152). That is exactly the
point. The ability (or liability, if you prefer) to perform a splitting operation between one's sexual self and one's whole self, between one's fantasy
and one's reality, is the key to the erotic imagination: what one does in
society with those desires is a moral choice, and when those needs are
used to oppress others, a moral society reacts accordingly. Peri Rossi
seems to vacillate here: on the one hand she condemns enactments of the
masculine erotic imagination such as those performed in a prostitution
economy because they are in opposition to human intimacy, and on the
other hand she recognizes the necessary roles of "alternative sexualities"
and prostitution as antidotes to the ills of late capitalist coupling, bourgeois boredom, and gender jail.[7] But for women—read *heterosexual
women*, an unpardonable straightjacket for Peri Rossi to throw on after
coming out with lesbian specificity in her Preamble—the most commonly experienced fantasy in this regard culminates in the utterance
made to a beloved man, "I want to be your whore" (159). For the author,
this erotic imagining reveals the contamination these women have suffered from the masculine schizophrenic division between dichotomous
sexualities: legal and illegal, permitted and prohibited, and between dichotomous femininity: good girls and bad girls (160). Almost makes a
girl want to head to a theoretical joint like Daniel's for a long think-
twice about the subjectivities and sexualities of those who embody the
abject others of the hegemonic heterosexual gender order, which, according to Butler, rests on an identity purchased at the expense of the
"outlaws."[8]

In her chapter on "erotic ambiguity" and the "beautiful hermaphro-
dite," Peri Rossi returns to notions of artifice and construction to affirm
the role of fantasy in creating and sustaining sexual identities. Peri Rossi's
statement that transvestism operates in a symbolic mise-en-scène where

impersonation, ambiguity, and artifice signal the primacy of gender incoherence (165–166) is in keeping with more elaborated studies of drag, camp, and transvestism that have emerged in recent queer theory.[9] But Peri Rossi claims that transvestites in particular place illusion over reality, artifice over instinct, whereas a wider critique of gender disorder might look at normative sexualities as equally posturing, equally founded on a phantasmatic identity, equally illusionary and maybe more incoherent than the so-called alternative sexualities. In her discussion of sexual lifestyles in Madrid during the '70s and '80s, Peri Rossi alludes to the tensions between lesbians and transvestites, claiming that lesbians openly rejected the caricature that female impersonators made of the homoerotic object of lesbian desire. Yet, once extracted from the scenarios where gays, lesbians, and transvestites share social space, this variant of the erotic imagination is conceded value as a kind of fantasy in service of what Peri Rossi sees as "full erotic life": "But without going so far as the exaggerated and sometimes ridiculous transvestism of professionals, a full erotic life needs disguises, the stimulus that comes from a change of the marks of exterior identity in order to develop the phantoms of the imagination" (168). Or perhaps the exterior erotic expressions need to change not in order to provide a disguise (of what one *is*) but rather to offer cover (for what one can never fully *be*). Peri Rossi is right on track when she refuses to make a psychological distinction between "feeling" and "being," since, she claims, one believes that one feels and one believes that one is (165), and, she concludes, "*Being* is revealed more in that which it desires to be than in that which it is" (18). Philosophy in the bedroom for a postindustrial age.

In the final chapter of *Fantasías eróticas*, Peri Rossi turns to the role of the senses in erotic life. "Bodies know, bodies taste, in the double meaning of *saber*" (188). But bodies do not know: rather, it is the creative consciousness of the writer that taps into the erotic imagination to render the corporeal and the sensual into words that move us, arouse us, inspire us, or even evoke our repulsion and fear. In her fiction writing Peri Rossi has given proof of her vivid sensorial command of the language of desire, and in her essays, she establishes stylistic continuity with her novels and short stories: "Your body is my body, your breath is mine, your flesh is my flesh, your death is my death" (189). By refusing to relinquish her writerly fantasy in this chapter, and by embracing the confessional mode in the Preamble, the author frames her essays with the marks of a particular psyche engaged in an exploration of erotics that is firmly rooted in inner experience and in language. The essay writer and the creative writer merge in an act of boldness, in an ultimate demonstration of the value of imagination, without which the themes that Peri Rossi explores would be as devoid of originality as the mass-produced and mass-consumed inflatable dolls that she sees as the sign of erotic bankruptcy.

Cristina Peri Rossi offers an innovative approach to the essay in her reworking of the erotic imagination, but she also falls short of a radical critique of the sexual economies she examines. Positioned "on the margin" and "in the middle," as scholarly observer and witty creator, as "seer" and "doer," Peri Rossi suggests new paradigms for the female erotic imagination and sexual desire. She tests the limits of *essay*, understood as nonfiction analytic prose, and as "an attempt," "a try," not in disharmony with the self-contemplating spirit of Michel de Montaigne, whose examinations of his soul might look quite different if he visited some of the sites of gender trouble through which this contemporary Uruguayan writer has guided us, Beatrice incognita. In her introduction to *Inside Out: Lesbian Theories, Gay Theories*, Diana Fuss suggests that "what we need is a theory of sexual borders that will help us to come to terms with, and to organize around, the new cultural and sexual arrangements occasioned by the movements and transmutations of pleasure in the social field" (5). Peri Rossi has made important inroads into this borderland in a collection of essays that stand out for their originality in Hispanic letters and that represent a signal new direction in Peri Rossi's distinguished trajectory as a writer.

NOTES

1. In a chapter entitled "Cristina Peri Rossi and the Question of Lesbian Presence," Amy Kaminsky notes that many of Peri Rossi's stories are not visibly lesbian in content but rather encoded. She concludes that a more direct lesbian presence has become possible for Peri Rossi in the international context—opened up through exile—which tolerates political opposition (in this case, one that encompasses opposition to heterosexist orders).

2. Homeovestism, according to Louise Kaplan, is dressing up to impersonate one's own gender; Kaplan takes the concept from psychoanalyst George Zavitzianos. This act may involve masquerading as the stereotyped notion of a woman, and, in a heterosexual economy, could signify exhibiting oneself as a valuable sexual commodity (251–257). I am extracting homeovestism from Kaplan's clinical context of "female perversions" to appropriate it for a context of lesbian performance. For my purposes here, I wish the term "homeovestism"

to be as loaded as "transvestism," that is, to point to a multiplicity of psycho-sexual-social positions, and thus I dissociate it from the pathological model of the paraphilias (deviant sexual behaviors).

3. In *Gender Trouble*, Butler calls gestures, desires, and enactments "*performative* in the sense that the essence or identity that they otherwise purport to express are *fabrications* manufactured and sustained through corporeal signs and other discursive means" (136). She claims that there is "no gender identity behind the expressions of gender; that identity is performatively constituted by the very 'expressions' that are said to be its results" (25).

4. Some works in this series by women authors include the much-celebrated *Las edades de Lulú* (The Ages of Lulu, 1989) by Spanish writer Almudena Grandes, *La educación sentimental de la señorita Sonia* (The Sentimental Education of Miss Sonia, 1979) by Susana Constante of Argentina, and *La última noche que pasé contigo* (The Last Night I Spent with You, 1991) by Mayra Montero, a resident of Puerto Rico. In the *Biblioteca erótica* collection in which Peri Rossi's *Fantasías eróticas* appears, Mercedes Abad of *La sonrisa vertical* fame has published her *Sólo dime dónde lo hacemos* (Just Tell Me Where We'll Do It, 1991), and Nobel laureate Camilo José Cela has added one of his infamous erotic outbursts, *Cachondeos, escarceos y otros meneos* (Passions, Passes, and Other Moves, 1991). The titles in the *Biblioteca erótica*, along with their warning to underage readers and their titillating cover designs, are indicative of the type of material presented and of the intended audience. Peri Rossi's essays, published in this collection in this particular way (her book has wrap-around breasts spanning the front and back covers) are thus bound to please, and yet the *Biblioteca erótica* binds her to the constraints of quasi-intellectual pop erotica.

5. Kernberg proposes that "normal polymorphously perverse sexuality is an essential component that maintains the intensity of a passionate love relation, and recruits—in its function as the receptacle of unconscious fantasy—the conflictual relations and meanings that evolve in a couple's relationship throughout time" (65). Roy Schafer posits this hope: "to reclaim many disclaimed sexual actions and thereby to help people be whole, responsible, reciprocally related persons" (99), which responds to the hypothetical ideal in psychoanalysis of genitality, that is, "the actual erotic and affectionate interactions" of "total involvement in the immediate personal relationship" (86). Needless to say, Kernberg and Schafer focus on heterosexual genitality as mature ideals: a broader psychoanalytic economy might view "whole person adult sexuality" as independent of a heterosexual or even a monogamous norm.

6. Peri Rossi is wrong when she claims that "there is no lesbian movement that assumes either sadomasochistic paraphernalia or its aesthetics" (107). Certainly publications such as *On Our Backs* and the works of Pat Califia and Gayle Rubin, among others, offer models for a lesbian s/m position and take stock of the movements around the issue.

7. That Peri Rossi should place "alternative sexualities" and "prostitution" in

juxtaposition should raise questions of its own. Peri Rossi is not speaking of these sexual relations per se but rather of their function as spectacle and fetish in post-industrial societies.

8. Linda Williams offers this defense of the female pornographic imagination, which she does not view as contaminated by perverse masculinity: "For obscenity is simply the notion that some things—particularly the dirty confessions of female difference—must remain off the scene of representation. If those 'sexual things' are no longer dirty, if sexual desire and pleasure are no more unseemly in women than in men, then perhaps pornography will serve women's fantasies as much as it has served men's" (276–277).

9. For a fine example of work along these lines, see Tyler.

WORKS CITED

Butler, Judith. *Gender Trouble: Feminism and the Subversion of Identity*. New York: Routledge, 1990.
———. "The Lesbian Phallus and the Morphological Imaginary." *Differences* 4:1 (1992), 133–171.
———. "Phantasmatic Identification and the Question of Sex." Susan B. Anthony Center Lecture Series on Identity and Politics, The University of Rochester. 13 November 1991.
Creet, Julia. "Daughter of the Movement: The Psychodynamics of Lesbian S/M Fantasy." *Differences* 3:2 (1991), 135–159.
de Lauretis, Teresa. "Queer Theory: Lesbian and Gay Sexualities. An Introduction." *Differences* 3:2 (1991), iii–xviii.
Fuss, Diana. "Inside/Out." In *Inside Out: Lesbian Theories, Gay Theories*, 1–10. Ed. Diana Fuss. New York: Routledge, 1991.
Kaminsky, Amy. *Reading the Body Politic: Feminist Criticism and Latin American Women Writers*. Minneapolis: University of Minnesota Press, 1992.
Kaplan, Louise. *Female Perversions: The Temptations of Emma Bovary*. New York: Anchor-Doubleday, 1991.
Kernberg, Otto. "Between Conventionality and Aggression: The Boundaries of Passion." In *Passionate Attachments: Thinking about Love*. Ed. Willard Gaylin and Ethel Person. New York: Free Press, 1988.
Modleski, Tania. *Loving with a Vengeance: Mass-Produced Fantasies for Women*. 1982. New York: Methuen, 1984.
Peri Rossi, Cristina. *Fantasías eróticas*. Colección Biblioteca Erótica. Madrid: Ediciones Temas de Hoy, 1991.
Schafer, Roy. *Retelling a Life: Narration and Dialogue in Psychoanalysis*. New York: Basic Books, 1992.
Sontag, Susan. "The Pornographic Imagination." 1966. In *Styles of Radical Will*. New York: Delta, 1970.

Stoller, Robert. *Observing the Erotic Imagination.* New Haven, Conn.: Yale University Press, 1985.

Tyler, Carole-Anne. "Boys Will Be Girls: The Politics of Gay Drag." In *Inside Out: Lesbian Theories, Gay Theories*, 32–70. Ed. Diana Fuss. New York: Routledge, 1991.

Williams, Linda. *Hard Core: Power, Pleasure, and the "Frenzy of the Visible."* Berkeley: University of California Press, 1989.

Irene Matthews   # WOMAN
WATCHING
WOMEN,
WATCHING

All perceiving is also thinking,
all reasoning is also intuition,
all observation is also invention.
RUDOLF ARNHEIM
ART AND VISUAL PERCEPTION

Since her early professional days as a cub reporter for the *Excélsior* news-paper in Mexico City, Elena Poniatowska has valued the testimonial and documentary usefulness of photographs as a complement to the written word. The Mexican version of *La noche de Tlatelolco* (*Massacre in Mex-ico*, 1971), for example, opens with a thirty-one-page series of photo-graphs of the events leading up to and ensuing from the 1968 massacre of civilians in Mexico City. The text that follows, structured around and through interviews and commentaries from participants and wit-nesses—survivors—is pre-scribed, fundamentally, by that synoptic vi-sual evidence.[1]

In recent years, however, Elena Poniatowska has expanded her testi-monial/illustrative use of photographs into a number of works that ex-amine photographs and photographers themselves as the principal ob-jects of interest. Her most recent monsterwork, a fictional biography of Tina Modotti, follows on the heels of several other extended essays on visual art: *El último guajolote* (The Last Turkey, 1982), which examines "Images of Mexico" under an editorial rubric of "Memory and Forget-fulness"; *Bailes y Balas* (Balls and Bullets, 1991), again an examination of the intertext that joins visual and historical memorials; and, most signifi-

cantly for my focus here, her essay entitled "Algunas fotógrafas de México" ("Some Women Photographers of Mexico"), which served as a
commentary on a North American exhibition of the works of a number
of Mexican woman photographers, and "El hombre del pito dulce"
("The Man with the Sweet Penis"), her introductory essay to the published photographs of Graciela Iturbide on *Juchitán de las mujeres* (1989).
While "Some Women Photographers of Mexico" serves as a sort of con-
textual introduction to the works and the photographers in the exhibition, "The Man with the Sweet Penis" is, rather, an expansive rumination on the sexual and social lives of the women who are the objects of
the camera lens, a rumination that inserts and virtually "disappears" the
photographer into the overwhelming embrace of the edenic context she
is figuring.

My own essay brings to bear yet another gaze on Elena Poniatowska's
gaze at Graciela Iturbide's gaze at the women of Juchitán, who themselves smile or glare back into the lens of her camera as if both colluding
with and challenging its congealing effect upon their busi-ness. My epigraph above suggests that "perception" is essentially intellectual—a linguistic task. I shall examine here how Elena Poniatowska thoroughly re-
renders visual effect in language. But I shall also suggest that, in common
with her tendency to efface the editorial presence in her conventional
testimonial pieces, in looking at looks, Elena Poniatowska avoids "interpretation" and, rather like photography itself—compressing and isolat-
ing its referent inside a simple rectangle—she produces meaning both
from a particular, exclusive, framework, and from the cumulative, metonymical effect of "simple" contiguity.

MEMORY AND
FORGETFULNESS:
LOOKS THAT KILL

Although, as I suggest above, *El último guajolote*
falls into an earlier category in Elena Poniatowska's use of illustrations,
her text in this work prefigures the complex palimpsest of discourses—
anthropological, social, archaeological and personal—that mark her most
recent works.[2] The images of Mexico in *El último guajolote* are taken
from the marketplaces and the streets; the figures are those of beggars,

the regulars in the *pulquerías*, and above all of an underclass of *marchantes*—chicken-sellers, newspaper boys, scribes, piano-movers, people-carriers—the ubiquitous vendors who represent the strengths of the urban populace, gleaning small profit from filling others' bellies or hearts or minds. The last *guajolote*—the last turkey—is a lucky survivor, the one toughened from a December month of walking the asphalt pavements of the city as its brothers and sisters get picked off for Christmas.

Food, or sustenance in one form or another, is a central motif. This version of Mexico's "memories and forgetfulness" opens with a quote by "Jesusa Palancares" from *Hasta no verte Jesús mío* (Until We Meet Again, Sweet Jesus, 1969), Elena Poniatowska's own classic text that partially reconstituted the narrative of a Mexican woman's lived experience over most of the twentieth century. In the epigraph to *El último guajolote*, Jesusa asks her adopted son, Perico, what he would like on his *torta*, and is dumbfounded when instead of one of the cheap and common carbohydrate fillers, he demands *ham!* This domestic barter over a sandwich sets not only the theme but the dialogic tone for the ensuing written and visual commentary in *El último guajolote*. As Elena Poniatowska celebrates the historical and social significance of Mexico's natural, waterborne ecology, as she revitalizes its economic poverty, along with the picturesque nature and the instinct for survival of the Mexicans—the turkeys and the people—who walk, sleep, and live on the streets of the capital, she uses a dual voice that fuses her own desire for identification with the urban vitality of a hardy underclass into a socially critical exposure of the urban neglect that heralds the loss of that lifestyle.

Ultimately, it is the author's urge to participate in the past that frames and "closes" the text, and that responds to her quote from a popular song: "Si se pierde ¿qué se pierde / si se pierde lo perdido?" ("If you get lost, what do you lose / if what you lose is already lost?" *Guajolote* 28). Elena Poniatowska would probably answer: you would lose everything; what really *matters* is what is already lost. Professional writer and—still, familially—an "outsider" to Mexico, Elena Poniatowska carries and profits from a burden of *estrañamiento*, a nostalgic alienation that surrogates Mexican history into a personal past and includes a highly subjective objectivity. In a less personal "take," the photographic subject may be subjected to an objectivity that borders on the terminal. Susan Sontag stresses the fatal attraction of the camera as a "sublimation of the gun"

(14), while Roland Barthes suggests that "Death is the *eidos* of [the] photograph" (15): the lens of the camera, or the eye behind the lens, fixates
its subject in time and space, a "real" time and space that must be forever
unidentical to the flattened form that is the archive of their existence.
Elena Poniatowska wields her pen to revitalize those dead dimensions
through her own subjective reconstitution of the event: she wants her
body to harden and her lungs to fill like the last turkey's as she accompanies him on his stroll through the torrent of street cries in Mexico City.

As Elena Poniatowska personally resuscitates the heartbeat of the two
archival collections that illustrate *El último guajolote*,[3] she becomes the
permeable artery between "what has been" and "what is no longer"
Mexico City.[4] In considering another photographic selection from the
life of the capital in 1921–1931 under the rubric of *Bailes y Balas*, however, Poniatowska this time fixes the record of events into a specific moment in past history: the hundredth anniversary of an independence that
ironically celebrated freedoms as it confirmed intolerances. She reminds
us that the dances and dancing illustrated in *Bailes y Balas* afforded a
"diversion" to the urban populace scourged by religious persecution.
And that illegal church services—another diversion, this time countering
religious persecution by harboring religious fanatics—in turn led to political assassinations, yet another diversion. Elena Poniatowska rarely
"interprets" or "describes" a photograph. Instead, she talks around the
graphic illustrations of funeral processions and firing squads to conjoin
victims and murderers on the same mortal menu through unconfirmable
(but also unarguable) minor details. President Alvaro Obregón is assassinated at dinnertime and dies leaving his "*mole* half eaten" and his
"wines half drunk." In contrast, Obregón's killer, José de León Toral,
prior to his own execution eats a tranquil last meal with the clear "conscience of a good Christian" (*Bailes* 9). Elena Poniatowska adds to the
two scenes of violent death a trace of homely pungency as she records
the chile seasoning "present in the last supper" of both men: a touch of
galley humor less easily digested when we turn to the photograph twelve
pages later where the intense and dapper young assassin lies crumpled in
the dust kicked up by the bullet of his *coup de grâce* (9, 21). Elena Poniatowska continues her unpalatably memorable metonymical sequence in
a similar conjunction of death and domesticity as she relishes the Mexican
Communist Party, "like a green chile, small [. . .] but spicy" (10). She
exemplifies the party's hot young leaders somewhat fatalistically in "Julio
Antonio de Mello [. . .] assassinated by four bullets [. . .] by order of

the Cuban dictator" in 1929; and she exemplifies the party's hot young lovers in Tina Modotti, woman photographer, "who loved [Mello], was walking arm in arm with him as he was killed, and was accused of being an accomplice" (9–10).

WOMAN WATCHING

In contrast to her often personal intervention in *El último guajolote*, when re-viewing the portrayals of her essay "Bailes y Balas," Elena Poniatowska does not attempt to revivify and relive a memorial, but follows an other, testimonial, trace of the photograph—"like a footprint or a death mask" (Sontag 154)—ratifying the posthumous certainty of what is represented. The time frame of "Bailes y Balas" precedes Poniatowska's own time in Mexico City.[5] Like the continual motif of food in the author's Mexican focuses, however, Tina Modotti's constant presence as a photographic and textual symbol for the Mexico City of the '20s and '30s connects Elena Poniatowska to her own "take" on history and identity.

"Some Women Photographers of Mexico," Elena Poniatowska's 1990 essay for the photo exhibition *Compañeras de México*, is, for example, prefaced with a full-page portrait of Tina Modotti by Tina's partner and mentor, Edward Weston. And the essay begins with a lengthy biographical introduction to Tina Modotti, citing and siting Tina's place in the history of women's photography in Mexico. But none of Tina Modotti's own photographs appears in the exhibition of works of *Compañeras de México*. Instead, in Elena Poniatowska's usage, Modotti's image becomes—in Roland Barthes' words—an "irrefutably present yet deferred" referent: a real existence "authenticating" the reconstructive fictionality of Poniatowska's language that slides past the objects on display to contemporize precursors as participants. Elena Poniatowska's essay is written in the present—essayistic—tense: "When Tina Modotti starts taking photographs in Mexico, in 1923, she does it first in the shadow of her teacher, Edward Weston" (43). Photography historically has used a form of intractable shadowing to interpose image against light.[6] Poniatowska's language here recuperates from history the intractable shadows of the photographers themselves—in the present tense, the presence tense, the tense of contingency. In using as a preface to an essay for a women's photographic exhibition a foreign man photographer's portrait of a woman photographer whose photographs do not appear in the exhibition, Elena Poniatowska's focus exposes a double desire: the desire to write willy-nilly *about* her own chosen subject, Tina Modotti,[7] and the desire to associate *with* Tina Modotti through the shared skin of women's enabling photographic light, an impalpable carnal medium (Barthes 81) that connects the gaze and the photographed object empathetically and displaces the inhibiting shadow of the (male) teacher.

This double desire—to establish a carnal yet "professional" connection—continues throughout the essay on "Some Women Photographers of Mexico":

> *Mexico lives in the realm of magical realism. Our*
> *bare feet, our rags, can be changed into royal mantles.*
> *Our* streets, *our* factories, *the crowded masses at* our
> *political demonstrations—everything stimulates Tina.*
> *In Mexico the sky is bluer, the earth blacker. . . .*
> *Tina and Edward quickly make a group of friends.*
> (43; EMPHASIS ADDED)

Here again, it is difficult to separate historical reality—biography—from the individual desire of the writer also to feel the stark and beautiful contrasts offered to the observant and sensitive outsider by the "indigenous" colors of the Mexican landscape, and by the silent and mysterious individual *persona* that makes up the Mexican masses in the streets. Tina Modotti and Edward Weston photographed only in black and white. It is Elena Poniatowska, again, who naturalizes and revivifies the reality of color in her literary "version" of the mechanical lens. And it is she who revives the names of a series of martyred precursors marking out, albeit unsuccessfully, the political, social, and aesthetic way for the society that followed, which the writer recalls with an artistic as well as a political nostalgia: "Tina matured as a militant and produced real art, as real as her militancy" (45).[8]

Tina Modotti "matured," however, at a moment when professional women were anathematized, cursed for being unwomanly; Mexican or foreign, women artists and promoters were classified variously as "madwomen, degenerate, whores, loudmouthed liars, affected, lunatics in pants," in sum, "very odd *gringas*" (45). In addition, Tina's maturation process occurred entirely "in the shadow of" Edward Weston—unconstant in his love and ungenerous in his mentorship. Elena Poniatowska inserts an archetypal—clever yet submissive—woman into her constrictive history but releases her immediately: Edward Weston leaves Mexico and leaves Tina behind; politically as well as romantically imprudent, Tina advisedly exiles herself soon after.[9] So Elena Poniatowska's story of the aesthetic history of Mexico can move on, too.

What follows is a breathless enumeration of names in and allusions to a history of Mexican women in Mexican art under a twin hypothetical rubric: "What did it mean to be a woman in Mexico in the '20s, the '30s? . . . [when] [t]here is no more surprising country in the world than Mexico—What space! What grandeur!" (45, 50). Yet, at the same time as Mexico was opening its spacious, grand doors to talent from around the globe, it was still difficult to be a professional, an independent, woman there. Nevertheless, Tina Modotti and her contemporary, Lola Alvarez Bravo, may truly be categorized as independent, "aberrational" in a macho society: each lived off their work, despite having male lovers.[10]

On the basis of this economic and emotional independence of her artistic heroines, however, Elena Poniatowska recalls and fantasizes over those years of aesthetic and political *apertura* in Mexico, when Mexican art was panoramic in all its senses—when photography learned from muralism and muralism borrowed from photography.[11] She laments: "Muralism finished some years ago in our country. Each painter now has his or her own route. There is no monumentality left except in the construction work that crumbles at the first earthquake" (53). In our current era of shoddy architecture, of consumerism, of an aesthetics as derivative and malnourished as is the dependent economics that encourages the exiling of art, Poniatowska concludes that "it is the women of Mexico who bestow and dignify, who preserve and protect, the same as the photographers—preserving life, nurturing, pampering it" (54). Elena Poniatowska believes that women, and women photographers, have a special sisterhood, particularly in adversity, particularly in the social history of the underclass; theirs is the revolutionary spirit that is the continuum of the life blood of her country: "To take a photograph is to create a bond. . . . The click of their cameras is the beat of their hearts" (55). So many of the women photographers Poniatowska writes about are "foreigners" to Mexico who created their own bonds—a dubious yet deliciously provocative word that implies compulsion, duality, and the submission of personal will to a carnal prerogative—through their visions of their adopted country that also adopted her. In celebrating those women's artistry Elena Poniatowska bonds herself, with certain humility, in a spiritual commune with their prowess. After all, more than a mere geographical or political arena, Mexico—its blue sky, its black earth—"is a state of the soul" (55).

WATCHING WOMEN

My favorite thing is to go where I've never been.
DIANE ARBUS

Unlike Tina Modotti, Graciela Iturbide *is* one of the six photographers selected for the California exhibition. Elena Poniatowska has already collaborated with her in a number of photographic projects, most recently in writing the exuberant essay that accompanies Graciela Iturbide's photo-documentary of *Juchitán de las mujeres.* In this essay, "The Man with the Sweet Penis," Poniatowska uses her metonymical technique of piling on contiguous evidence to form a thick context around the isolated realities of the camera. The context of her words, however, does not merely clarify the opaqueness or the mystery of the thin slices of time and place, the "series of unrelated, freestanding particles" (Sontag 23) that the photographic image frames and offers to the viewer. As she did with Tina Modotti in *Compañeras de México,* Elena Poniatowska once more, almost perversely, addresses not presence in the photographs but absence—in this case the absence of men. The title of the collection of photographs, *Juchitán de las mujeres* (translated as "Juchitán a town of women" in the English-version insert to the book text), is confronted in *flagrante delicto* by Poniatowska's essay title, "The Man with the Sweet Penis." And yet, again contradicting the reader's now confused expectancy, Elena Poniatowska immediately describes Juchitán as truly edenic, a place where sexuality reigns unashamed and unfettered under the name of woman: "Man is a kitten between their legs, a puppy they have to admonish" (2).

This equally "unashamed" biological essentialism is one of Poniatowska's trademarks that punctuates her conversation, her lectures, and her written texts: like a photographer, she emphasizes the intrinsic, and like a camera, she is a "double-edged instrument for producing clichés (the French word that means both trite expression and photographic negative) and for serving up 'fresh' views" (Sontag 173). As photographed by Graciela Iturbide and expounded by Elena Poniatowska, the

women of Juchitán exemplify certain deep assumptions about femaleness
but also challenge the prevailing clichés (visual and rhetorical) that mark
Mexico as a monolithic society built upon *macho* men and submissive,
monotonously pregnant women. But then "Juchitán is not like any other
town," for its women are

> *like walking towers, . . . their hearts like a window,*
> *their nocturnal girth visited by the moon. . . . they*
> *are already the government . . . the people . . . the*
> *guardians of men, distributors of food, their children*
> *riding astride their hips or lying in the hammock of*
> *their breasts, the wind in their skirts, . . . the honey-*
> *comb of their sex overflowing with men.*
> ("THE MAN" 2)

Poniatowska's words here have a certain propriety of excess that transforms solecism into a poetry borne through the magical siesta hour "suspended between blueness and good-night" (3) when time and labor and
intellect are detached and sensuality and imagination revived and forti-
fied. The poetical technique in this essay isolates the visual details of the
photographs and illuminates them lyrically yet within a functional and
startlingly feminist social rubric. Every informed reader already knows
that Mexican mothers are "self-sacrificing [and] drowned in tears" (3).
But the women of Juchitán have "nothing in common" with such weak
will. The *juchitecas* have a very public life, too. They "organize the economy of the whole town," and, contradictorily, "perhaps because the
mother is so important in the community, homosexuality is accepted. . . .
Daughters marry and go away, while . . . [a gay] boy, attached to his
mother, takes care of the family, of the cooking grill . . . and makes
totopos, which is a way of patting the sun flat and heating it over the
grill" (3).

Elena Poniatowska's essay is, in turn, an illumination of sexual mores,
a revelation of social structures, a mouthwatering menu of indigenous
foodstuffs, and an anthropological enumeration for the ignorant. But
such a pedantic analysis makes her words sound didactic and presump-
tuous, when they are not. They are, rather, an event in themselves, a
festival commemorating the *juchiteca*, the yardstick by which the social
and sexual economy of the town must be measured. With the women
of Juchitán, and with their "tiny, fragile, windlike, photographer-pet,

grace-gazelle-Graciela" Iturbide (4), Poniatowska celebrates the power of women, benignly transmogrified through economic control and through the rituals that mark both virginity and sexuality: each future "walking tower" is rendered supine by the enormity of deflowering and ritually redly re-beflowered so that all may know of her twin glories—that she was chaste and that she has been chosen by one man. While an occasional young man may become charmingly and usefully feminized, the women are measured by their femininity under what is, for them, an unremittingly heterosexual standard. Somehow, however, these essentialistic events, archaic signposts in a history of gendered standards that challenge women's chastity with men's virility, and which in other women writers' words are rendered grim and vengeful, in this essay become ironic, playful, innocently melodramatic.[12]

Above all, like el último guajolote—the last turkey—and his friends, the people of Juchitán are street people: "unruly, rebellious, unreliable, and shameless"—appreciated less by Benito Juárez, the politician whose words Elena Poniatowska quotes here (4), than by Graciela Iturbide, the photographer. Graciela "weaves an invisible web around each of her subjects" as she captures "the town's most intimate wrinkles," but she is herself converted into one of Juchitán's artifacts, caught in the web of the juchitecas' daily deeds and Elena Poniatowska's observations:

> Tiny, fragile, she stands before the mole-mountain of lymph, water and fat that is the Juchitec woman, who take her in their arms and lead her by the hand to the river, to wash clothes and bathe. They have her eat iguana stew and whip hot chocolate, guzzle beer in the noonday sun. . . . Graciela, the little anise seed, takes part in all their rituals: sesame seed in all their moles, teardrop of all their weeping, crock for all their stews, sheet on all their beds, flea on all their petates, foam on all their refreshing beverages.
> (4)

Graciela Iturbide is a disappearing artifact—her tininess subsumed into the daily life of Juchitán to record it almost like one of the miniature surgical cameras that photographs from inside the veins and arteries of the body politic, the body social, the body sexual. She vanishes from the record of "The Man with the Sweet Penis" while Elena Poniatowska, herself the size of a sesame seed in relation to the monumental wash of the *juchiteca*, surges toward the end of her essay on a wave of sexual politics. But Poniatowska's isthmian sexual politics are not those of Germaine Greer. Here, heterosensuality reigns unworried by the problematics of gender: "Juchitán is the sorceress of primary passions in a world conceived before original sin" (6). Throughout history, the women of Juchitán have been politicized anarchists, sexual revolutionaries, willing to die for a cause, but also willing to fight dirty: "Even today, the goal of women who fight is to lift their adversary's skirt, so the spectators will see her sex. To have thick pubic hair is a political guarantee; the woman derives her ferocity from its abundance" (7).

Graciela Iturbide's photographs derive their strength and interest from the many (other) forms of abundance in Juchitán: they are often wonderfully intimate but always wonderfully composed. Though reproduced in high contrast, they are dark and shadowed, mysterious, textured, and sensuous. Her subjects are often photographed from below, rendering their size monumental and imposing. Or they are cropped and headless, and the focus of interest is a string of stringy chickens, a pile of iguana tails. Or they are multiple portraits, a bevy of strong female faces smiling complicitly at the camera or framing other, younger faces of their multiple progeny. Or they are a broad male torso cropped at the level of his penis hidden behind a gourd sculpted over with a naked female figurine whose legs splay over the round gourd mouthpiece the man's face bemusedly examines with curled lip. On the facing page a "woman tower" salutes us with a phallic beer bottle raised to her openly grinning lips. Or, as in Graciela Iturbide's cover portrait, her subject is a singular *marchante*'s head, crowned with the live iguanas that are the fruit of her man's hunt.

Elena Poniatowska makes no attempt here (or almost anywhere else in her essay) to interpret or re-reveal these images. As in most of her photo-commentaries, she consciously or unconsciously eschews some perfect affinity with the pictures in favor of a sort of collaborative—visual and textual—analogy.[13] In *Juchitán*, however, the "artistic predilections" she might share with the photographer slide into obsession as she stacks up an incessant prose that dramatizes and sensualizes the local biology and the local geography. "The Man with the Sweet Penis" began with an indeterminate copula: "In Juchitán, Oaxaca, men don't know what to do with themselves except put themselves inside women" (1) and ends in a frenzy of "fierce, desperate fornicators . . .

howling, hammering, erecting, inserting, gestating," animal manifestations of the "luxuriant, dense, savage, lustful, vegetation" of Juchitán,
"which means 'the place of white flowers,' [where] the whiteness is se-
men" (6, 7). There is no escaping Nature as Elena Poniatowska implicates
the very breezes from on high in her assessment of the mythic forces that
operate in Juchitán, "in heat all year round":

> The wind from San Mateo del Mar embraces the
> wind from Ixtpec, and the breeze from Salina Cruz
> climbs to Espinal looking for her mate. Over the
> earth of Juchitán, the winds scatter the maritime
> musk, scents that arouse desire.
>   And hope.
> (7)

In some ways, these last words characterize the most vibrant and the
most critical aspects of Elena Poniatowska's essays. It is tempting to
question Poniatowska's elemental frameworks—food, death, sex—or to
deconstruct her technique of piling on mythic details until they assume
the consistency of fact; or to wonder at her contradictory juxtaposition
of tradition and subterfuge, both of which challenge the matriarchal
paradise that her tone and the photographs of *Juchitán* imply.[14] But in
each of the texts discussed here, Elena Poniatowska looks for the evidences of vitality in a culture she feels is losing its urgency, its sense of
pride, and its sense of self. Like many of the photographs in these texts,
her essays often scrutinize the usual public scenarios—political, masculinist—in a moment of crisis, of being undone. And she replaces those
scenes with other public images, popularized and feminized, often marginal or bizarre, but carrying their own "sesame seed" that opens the
door to the magic in the commonplace and germinates the spirit of the
spectator or reader. Elena Poniatowska's larger framework, embracing
all the others, is *life*. I suggested earlier that Poniatowska's essays on photographs often romanticize an earlier Mexico when living seemed sim-
pler, more honest, more communal, more fun. She does not deliberately
figure herself into that past, but the tone of nostalgia in her writings hauls
the most attractive elements of those earlier periods out of the simply
specular and onto a platform of contemporary desires. As she debunks
politics and renders women and sexuality outrageous, funny, and admirable, Elena Poniatowska, too—although she would be loathe to admit

it—is a principal among those "women of Mexico who bestow and dignify . . . the same as photographers—preserving life, nurturing, pampering it" ("Some Women" 55).

NOTES

1. Contrarily, the English translated version of *Noche* gives precedence to the written words and embeds the photographs in the middle of the text, following Rosario Castellanos' elegiac poem that opens the second segment on "Massacre in Mexico." So in that case, the written testimony prefigures the photographs.

2. *El último guajolote* is published under a series title of *Memoria y olvido: Imágenes de México* (Memory and Forgetfulness: Images of Mexico); "Miradas que matan" (Looks That Kill) is a segment title in *Bailes y Balas* (52).

3. *El último guajolote* is based on photographs from the collections of C. B. Waite and of J. Lupercio. The index shows no original dates for the photographs.

4. Roland Barthes suggests that "the Photograph [in itself] does not necessarily say *what is no longer,* but only and for certain *what has been* (85). Elena Poniatowska's "presence" in *Guajolote* and "absence" from "Bailes y Balas" both somehow confirm the passing of the past, although, as I suggest, she treats each period quite differently.

5. Elena Poniatowska, born in Paris in 1933, is of Polish-Mexican ancestry. She came to Mexico from France with her family in 1942.

6. I am once again borrowing from Roland Barthes, who suggests that the *essence* of photography is its reference to "What-has-been," or "the Intractable." I am switching his referent to the photographer himself or herself, who also "has been" (there) for the photograph to exist (77).

7. The essay on "Algunas fotógrafas de México" was written in 1988–1989, right in the thick of the then apparently interminable genesis of Elena Poniatowska's fictional biography of Tina Modotti, published as *Tinísima* in 1992.

8. Elena Poniatowska mentions in particular the "magnificent people of the Communist Party who were persecuted, like Xavier Guerrero, Juan de la Cabada, Hernán Laborde and his wife Concha Michel, José Revueltas, Diego Rivera" ("Some Women" 45).

9. We learn in much greater detail in *Tinísima* of Tina Modotti's untimely predilections for both the Communist Party and its men.

10. Amy Conger contradicts this idea of independence in "Women Photograph Women," her introductory essay to the catalogue of *Compañeras de México,* when she claims that both Edward Weston and Tina Modotti lived in Mexico off money sent there by Edward's first wife and mother of his four children.

11. Under a series of highly active Ministers of Culture, in the 1920s and 1930s Mexico not only produced a number of world-class artists of its own but

also became an aesthetic center for painters, writers, photographers, and film-makers from many other countries.

12. In Rosario Castellanos' story "The Widower Román," for example, the bride is returned ruinously to her father by her new husband avenging himself on her for his first wife's unfaithfulness (Ahern 155–206).

13. I am paraphrasing some of Jefferson Hunter's remarks in *Image and Word*, where he concludes that "combinations of photography with writing work, when they do work, not by some impossible feat of mixing incompatible artistic modes but by discovering similar artistic predilections" (36).

14. In her editorial commentary on a published selection from *Juchitán de las mujeres* and "The Man with the Sweet Penis," Bernadette Powell also mentions the social contradictions in Juchitán that are suggested but almost erased by Graciela Iturbide's "monumental" camera angles and Elena Poniatowska's prose that never pauses as it shifts between the specific and the iconic in the woman-community on display.

WORKS CITED

Ahern, Maureen, ed. *A Rosario Castellanos Reader*. Austin: University of Texas Press, 1988.

Arbus, Diane. *Diane Arbus: An Aperture Monograph*. New York: Aperture Foundation, 1972.

Arnheim, Rudolf. *Art and Visual Perception: A Psychology of the Creative Eye*. Berkeley: University of California Press, 1974.

Barthes, Roland. *Camera Lucida*. Trans. Richard Howard. New York: Hill & Wang, 1981.

Hunter, Jefferson. *Image and Word*. Cambridge: Harvard University Press, 1987.

Poniatowska, Elena. "Algunas fotógrafas de México" ("Some Women Photographers of Mexico"). Trans. Irene Matthews and others. In *Compañeras de México: Women Photograph Women*. University of California, Riverside: University Art Gallery, 1990.

———. "Bailes y Balas." In *Bailes y Balas: Ciudad de México 1921–1931*. Mexico City: Archivo General de la Nación, 1991.

———. *Hasta no verte Jesús mío*. Mexico City: Era, 1969.

———. "El hombre del pito dulce" ("The Man with the Sweet Penis"). Trans. Cynthia Steele and Adriana Navarro. In *Juchitán de las mujeres*. Mexico City: Ediciones Toledo, 1989.

———. *La Noche de Tlatelolco (Massacre in Mexico)*. Trans. Helen R. Lane. Mexico City: Era, 1971.

————. *Tinísima*. Mexico City: Era, 1992.

————. *El último guajolote*. Mexico City: Martín Casillas, Cultura/SEP, 1982.

Powell, Bernadette. "Editorial" [on *Juchitán de las mujeres*]. San Francisco: Photo Metro, August 1989.

Sontag, Susan. *On Photography*. New York: Farrar, Straus and Giroux, 1973.

List of Contributors

MARJORIE AGOSÍN is a poet and literary critic. Her work has focused on issues dealing with gender and human rights. Among her recent publications are *Circles of Madness: Mothers of the Plaza de Mayo* (1992) and *Las mujeres y la literatura fantástica en el cono sur* (1993). She is associate professor of Spanish at Wellesley College.

MELVIN S. ARRINGTON, JR., is associate professor of modern languages at the University of Mississippi, where he has served on the faculty since 1982. He teaches a wide range of courses in Spanish and Portuguese and participates in the university's Latin American Studies Program. His publications deal primarily with twentieth-century Latin American literature, in particular the Spanish American short story.

MARY G. BERG, a writer and translator who lives in Cambridge, Mass., teaches Spanish and Latin American literature. She has long been interested in women writers and has published articles on Juana Manuela Gorriti, Clorinda Matto de Turner, Marta Brunet, Elisa Mújica, Cristina Peri Rossi, and others. She is currently working on critical biographies of Juana Manuela Gorriti and Clorinda Matto de Turner.

SANDRA M. BOSCHETTO-SANDOVAL is associate professor of Spanish at Michigan Technological University. She is coeditor (with Marcia P. McGowan) of the critical anthology *Claribel Alegría and Central American Literature: Critical Essays* (1993). Her articles on Hispanic literature have appeared in various critical anthologies and journals; her research interests include Latin American women writers, literary and cultural theory, and intercultural communication. She is presently at work on a book-length study of the life and work of Amanda Labarca Hubertson.

ELENA GASCÓN VERA has been teaching in the Department of Spanish at Wellesley College since 1973. She is the author of *Don Pedro, Condestable de Portugal* and *Un mito nuevo: La mujer como objeto/sujeto literario* (1992). She has also coauthored books on Jorge Guillén, María Luisa Bombal, Spanish cinema, and Justina Ruiz de Conde, and has published articles on topics from Spanish medieval literature and feminist studies to Spanish postmodernism.

ROSEMARY GEISDORFER FEAL is associate professor of Spanish at the University of Rochester, where she also teaches courses in women's studies, African and African American studies, and comparative literature. She is the author of *Novel Lives: The Fictional Autobiographies of Guillermo Cabrera Infante and Mario Vargas Llosa* (1986), as well as articles on feminist theory in relation to Afro-Hispanic studies and Latin American women writers. Her forthcoming book treats the relationship among the visual arts, Hispanic literature, and psychoanalytic incursions into modes of representation.

JANET N. GOLD holds a doctorate from the University of Massachusetts at Amherst and teaches Latin American literature at Louisiana State University. She has published numerous articles on Latin American women writers. Her biography of Honduran poet Clementina Suárez is forthcoming from the University Press of Florida.

MARÍA CRISTINA ARAMBEL GUIÑAZÚ is assistant professor of Spanish at Lehman College, CUNY. Her Yale dissertation, "La autobiografía de Victoria Ocampo: Memorias, seducción, collage" (1989), examines the creation of the textual "I" in the writings of Victoria Ocampo. She has published articles on Latin American women writers and at present is working on nineteenth-century literature.

BETH E. JÖRGENSEN, Ph.D. University of Wisconsin at Madison, teaches Spanish American literature at the University of Rochester. Her research interests include Latin American women writers, contemporary fiction, testimonial literature, and feminist theory. Her book, *The Writ-*

ing of Elena Poniatowska: Engaging Dialogues, was published in 1994 from the University of Texas Press.

GWEN KIRKPATRICK is associate professor in the Department of Spanish and Portuguese at the University of California at Berkeley. She is the author of *The Dissonant Legacy of Modernismo* (1989) and coauthor, with the UC–Stanford Seminar on Feminism and Culture in Latin America, of *Women, Culture and Politics in Latin America* (1990).

JILL S. KUHNHEIM is assistant professor in the Department of Spanish and Portuguese at the University of Wisconsin at Madison. Specializing in Spanish American literature, she has published papers on the work of Rosario Castellanos, Gabriela Mistral, Olga Orozco, and Alejandra Pizarnik. She is presently working on a book about Orozco and post-1940s Argentine poetry.

CLAIRE EMILIE MARTIN is associate professor in the Romance, German, Russian Languages and Literatures Department at California State University, Long Beach. She has published articles on Marta Lynch, Isabel Allende, and the Countess of Merlin. Her revised dissertation, "Alejo Carpentier y las crónicas de Indias: Orígenes de una escritura americana," will be published by Ediciones del Norte. She is currently working on a volume on nineteenth-century Spanish American women writers.

FRANCINE ROSE MASIELLO is professor of Spanish American literature and chair of the Department of Comparative Literature at the University of California at Berkeley. Her recent books include *Lenguaje e ideología: Las escuelas argentinas de vanguardia* (1986), *Between Civilization and Barbarism: Women, Nation, and Literary Culture in Modern Argentina* (1992), and, coauthored with members of the UC–Stanford Seminar on Feminism and Culture in Latin America, *Women, Culture and Politics in Latin America* (1990). *El primer feminismo argentino: Textos y tradición del siglo XIX* will be published by Feminaria in 1994.

IRENE MATTHEWS, assistant professor of comparative literature at Northern Arizona University, Flagstaff, wrote her dissertation on "Women Writing and War," a socio-literary examination of women writers of the U.S. Civil War, the Mexican Revolution, and the recent crises in Argentina, Guatemala, and Brazil. She is presently translating a novel by Marilene Felinto of Brazil.

DORIS MEYER is Roman S. and Tatiana Weller professor of Hispanic studies at Connecticut College. She has published various books in the field of Latin American literature, including *Victoria Ocampo: Against the Wind and the Tide* (1979; 2d ed., 1990), *Contemporary Women Authors of Latin America* (1983, 2 vols., coedited with Margarite Fernández Olmos), and *Lives on the Line: The Testimony of Contemporary Latin American Authors* (1988), as well as many articles and translations. Her areas of specialization are contemporary Latin American women's writing and Mexican American journalism in the territorial Southwest.

MARTHA LAFOLLETTE MILLER is professor of Spanish at the University of North Carolina at Charlotte, where she specializes in twentieth-century Spanish poetry. She has published studies on peninsular authors such as Rosalía de Castro, Jorge Guillén, Luis Cernuda, and Leopoldo Alas, as well as on several Latin American authors. Her book on the poetry of Angel González will be published by Fairleigh Dickinson University Press.

ARDIS L. NELSON is professor and chair of the Department of Foreign Languages at East Tennessee State University, where she teaches Spanish American literature. She is the author of *Cabrera Infante in the Menippean Tradition* (1983) and a variety of articles, and coauthor of a bibliography on Central American film.

MARY LOUISE PRATT is Nina C. Crocker Faculty Scholar at Stanford University, where she teaches in the Departments of Spanish and Portuguese and Comparative Literature. She has published extensively in the areas of linguistics and literature, and discourse and ideology. A founding member of the UC–Stanford Seminar on Feminism and Culture in Latin America, she coauthored its book, *Women, Culture and Politics in Latin America* (1990), and coedited a special issue of *Nuevo Texto Crítico* on Latin American women writers (1989). Her most recent book is *Imperial Eyes: Travel Writing and Transculturation* (1992).

RICHARD ROSA is currently writing his doctoral dissertation on the frustrated nationalizing of Eugenio María de Hostos' *La peregrinación de Boyoán* at Harvard University in the Department of Romance Languages and Literatures.

NINA M. SCOTT is professor of Spanish American literature at the University of Massachusetts at Amherst, specializing in women writers, particularly Sor Juana Inés de la Cruz and Gertrudis Gómez de Avellaneda. Coeditor of *Breaking Boundaries: Latina Writing and Critical Readings* (1989) and *Coded Encounters: Writing, Gender, and Ethnicity in Colonial Latin America* (1994), she has also translated Avellaneda's *Sab* and her *Autobiography* (1993) and is now compiling a bilingual anthology of early Spanish American women writers.

DORIS SOMMER is professor of Romance languages and literatures at Harvard University, with extensive publications in the field of Latin American literature. Her recent book is *Foundational Fictions: The National Romances of Latin America* (1991), and she is currently at work on the ethical limits of readerly appropriation.

NANCY SAPORTA STERNBACH is associate professor at Smith College, where she teaches courses on Latino/a and Latin American literature. She is coeditor of *Breaking Boundaries: Latina Writing and Critical Readings* (1989) and has published articles on Latin American women in a variety of professional journals. She is currently working with Lourdes Rojas on a book-length study of Latin American women essayists.